Ozona Country

Books by Allan R. Bosworth

Ozona Country

New Country

The Crows of Edwina Hill (Fiction)

The Lovely World of Richi-san

Ozona Country

by Allan R. Bosworth

Harper & Row, Publishers

New York, Evanston,

and London

For my home town,
and all the friendly and gracious people
who have ever called it home

Contents

Illustrations

Some Acknowledgments

In one way or another, I have to thank nearly everybody in Ozona for help in writing this book, along with a number of outsiders. There is danger of overlooking someone when the list is presented alphabetically, and, if this occurs, I apologize.

My especial thanks go to: Emma Adams, Mr. Will Baggett, Alice West Baker, Lottie Lee Baker, Ernie Boyd, and Mrs. Lela Bunger, of Ozona. Marvin J. Bridges, Executive Director of the Southwestern Animal Health Research Foundation, of Dallas, provided material on the fight to eradicate the screwworm fly. I owe much to Ira and Wilma Carson, Mr. and Mrs. L. B. Cox, Jr., and Maggie Crawford, all of whom are old friends. Monroe Cockrell, of Evanston, Ill., was as usual a rich source of western folklore.

Special credits are due Ernest and Walter Dunlap, the R. A. Harrells, their son, R. A. Harrell, Jr., T. A. Kincaid, Jr., Mrs. Floy Hume, Oscar Kost, and Lowell Littleton, of Ozona. Former Ozonans Claude Denham and W. M. Stoker each wrote a thesis on the history of Crockett County, and I have drawn upon both these papers. Thanks also are due the Rev. J. Troy Hickman, Dr. W. Eugene Hollon of the University of

Oklahoma, and J. W. Holland, San Antonio District Director of the Border Patrol.

I am grateful to Mrs. Ben Lemmons, Sam Martinez, Hurst Meinecke, Gertrude and Mildred North, Arthur and Hillery Phillips, H. M. Phillips, of the *Sheep and Goat Raisers' Magazine*, Leta Powell, Clerk of Crockett County, Claude Russell, the late beloved Houston Smith, the late famed Dr. Walter Prescott Webb, Mrs. Charles Williams, and Evart and Ruth White.

No book I write is ever finished without the guidance and counsel of my literary agent, Marie Rodell, and that of Elizabeth Lawrence, my editor at Harper & Row.

All of the above named have contributed in some way to the content of this volume. Any errors are my own responsibility.

ALLAN R. BOSWORTH

Foreword

U.S. Highway 290 and Texas State Highway 163 intersect at the southwest corner of a pretty pecan-shaded park, near the monument to David Crockett. A sign there says: "OZONA— Biggest Little Town in the World."

Reno said that long before, and so have other towns; it all depends on what is meant by both adjectives. At one time Reno may, indeed, have been the biggest town in terms of its faro tables and divorce courts. But its population has long been in the tens of thousands, and to a Texan that is not a little town.

Ozona, Texas, is listed in *The Texas Almanac* for 1962 as having 3,361 people.

It is the only town in Crockett County, which is bigger than the state of Delaware and twice the size of Rhode Island.

No railroad touches the county, but people get around. In 1962 there was a registration of 2,159 motor vehicles . . . or about three cars per family. And one out of every ninety men, women and children owned a Cadillac.

The Ozona area is cowboy and sheepherder country, only two generations away from the wild, rocky and thorny frontier. Senior citizens remember when there was no fence in the whole vast sweep of grazing land. Their sons remember driving livestock more than eighty miles to a railroad shipping pen.

Their daughters took quiet pride a few years ago when the Dallas *Times-Herald* and an editor of the *Ladies' Home Journal* agreed that Ozona, Texas, was the best-dressed town in the world . . . with Dallas, New York and San Francisco following in that order, and with a nod to Paris and Milan on the Continent.

But nobody was greatly surprised. The *Saturday Evening Post* had already (on Feb. 18, 1950) put Ozona on its cover, with an article called "Millionaires' Town."

I am an old Ozona boy, myself, and something of a Senior Citizen now. I am no millionaire, and I know many Ozona people who are not, either, but they are the salt of the earth. I remember the old days, the hard ways, and West Texas when it was still a little wild.

Ozona is not actually so much of a town as it is a People, and a hospitable and gracious way of life. It has a story that ought to be told before the old days are forgotten.

I have written that story as best I could, with the unanimous support and assistance of all the Ozona people. If there are errors, the fault is mine. If I fail to give proper acknowledgment, I ask forgiveness. If the story is kindly received, all credit goes to those I learned early and easily to love, because they were my kind of folks.

ALLAN R. BOSWORTH

Ozona Country

One More

Wagon

1 Westward

We came, near the end of that day, to the western rim of the last wide divide, and over the ears of the mules was a long curving valley, green as a peach orchard with mesquites, and shouldered by the rimrocked hills. Jay pulled rein on the team, and pointed with his whip handle.

"Yonder she is, Mama," he said. "See the two windmills shining on the top of that hill? That's Ozona—that's the waterworks and ice and light plant. You've got about eight miles to go."

—NEW COUNTRY

ONCE IN EVERY LIFETIME, perhaps, there is a moment to be remembered down all the crawling, changing years. The sights and sounds and smells of it return unbidden, and its taste is ever sharp. Late in the darkness of a wakeful night, it comes back again out of the long ago, to be savored by all the senses and examined in new perspective. Only out of such perspective does one recognize that the moment was both Adventure and Beginning . . .

The Bosworth family was coming to a new place that day. Nobody realized, when the wagon halted at the edge of the divide hill, that this would be a storybook town, or that a chapter was closing on more than twenty years of wagon wanderings all over the wide reaches of Texas and half of New Mexico Territory, with a new chapter to be started here. But to a small and imaginative boy, caught up in cowboy and Indian legend, a line ran somewhere along the lip of the divide. Cross it, and you were in the Old West of song and story . . . cross it, and exciting things were bound to happen.

Only five of us remained in the old Studebaker wagon when we came back to West Texas. Mama and my twenty-two-year-old brother Jay were on the driver's seat; Floyd and Bert and I were back under the tarp. Our three sisters were married. My oldest brother, Dee, was working on a ranch somewhere out here, and he had bought Mama a $200 house in the town of Ozona. It would be the first house Mama had ever owned.

Papa had never owned anything but campfires, and visions of better places beyond the horizon. Mama had left Papa to his fiddlefoot ways, almost four years before, far up on the New Mexican plains; she had turned the wagon back deep into Texas, following her dream of sending the younger children to school. It took time to stop the wheels: we lived on three ranches and in three towns, for short periods. It took time for Dee to save up $200.

The year was 1907, and I was five years old, going on six. I remember that moment on the divide as clearly as if it had been yesterday.

The wheel rumble died with a dry whisper in the gravel; the music of jingling trace chains and the squeak of harness was stilled, and we heard only the lonesome wind. Our little Spanish mules—one a dark bay and the other a bright sorrel—stood astride the rain-washed ruts, their long ears alert. The small cloud of white road dust that had swirled in our wake through several broad Texas counties whipped away on the wind, thin as woodsmoke, and left the wagon stark in the yellow sun of a late September afternoon. The wagon smelled of axle grease and harness oil and linseed waterproofing on the tarp.

Floyd and Bert and I scrambled forward over the household

goods, to look through the pucker of the tarp and to wonder what the town would be like. Eight miles to go meant another campfire: nobody, in those unhurried days, traveled at night. Jay said the houses of Ozona were all hidden behind the hill where the windmills were spinning like bright dimes; we could not see any of them. But for the first time in days of travel we could see where we were going. The windmills offered a point of reference, as lighthouses do for a ship at sea.

All that day we had been rolling across the divide from our last camping place near the town of Eldorado, with no tree anywhere higher than the wagon, with nothing but occasional half-wild range cattle lumbering away from the road, and hundreds of jackrabbits that skipped into the scrub mesquite and then sat erect, their ears almost as big as those on the mules. But now the country was changing abruptly, breaking away from the divide in a series of small, rocky canyons which in turn debouched into the wide green draw. The hills were low and flat-topped, with limestone ledges white as snow under the sun and clumps of blue-green scrub cedar that spiced the air with a scent wonderfully clean. From this elevation we could see at least thirty miles, but except for the windmills and a barbed-wire fence beside the road there was no sign of human habitation. The world seemed made of light and shadow and limitless space; it was a wide saucer of subdued duns and grays and yellows, with more vivid splashes of green, and all of it was covered by a vast blue bowl of high and windy sky.

"It's a big country," Jay said. "Some of the ranches out here are more than a hundred sections. You can drive through a man's pasture gate, and still have thirty or forty miles to go before you get to his house."

"Man alive!" Floyd exclaimed. He was twelve, and Bert was ten. I envied them their advanced ages. It wouldn't be long before they could get jobs as cowboys.

Mama said it was pretty country, compared to some she had seen from the wagon seat, but it still looked mighty lonesome.

She wondered if the ranch where Dee worked was far from town. Jay had made an advance trip out here by saddle horse, and he knew all the answers.

"He's over on the Pecos, about forty or fifty miles northwest of Ozona," Jay said. "He told me he'll be coming to town once every two or three months. Takes him two days, in a wagon."

Then he pulled back on the brake lever, and notched it to keep the wagon from crowding the rumps of the mules on the downgrade. The wind was rising, the way it always does in late afternoon. The wind swept up the hill slopes and spilled over the rim of the divide; it billowed the wagon tarp and slapped it against the arched hickory bows with a sound like Indian drums; it shook the scrub cedars, and keened along the barbed wire. Our wheels slid over a slippery limestone ledge, and the brake shoes began squealing. We lurched down the rough road past the tossing cedars and stands of prickly pear fruited at that season with red and yellow pear apples; we rolled by tall, slender stalked *sotol* that would make fine stick-horses, and by holly-thorned *agarita* bushes and barbed catclaw, and bushel-sized clumps of the coarse, straw-like grass the Mexicans call *sacaguista*. Nearly everything in the land had been named, long before, by the Spaniards and the Mexicans, and some of the names were Indian borrowings. It was hard to realize that the country was new only to us. When you are five years old, a place doesn't exist until you get there.

The wind seemed to be blowing in a different direction when we reached the mesquite flat. There was no timber to break its force. It was both friend and foe, out here. It could spread grass fires faster than a man could run, but it turned the windmills steadily and kept their rods rattling in the pipe day and night to raise life-giving water from deep in the sun-baked earth.

Listen long enough to the incessant West Texas wind . . . listen, when you can, to the penitent weeping of the almost never West Texas rain . . . and between them you can imagine all the stories the land ever knew. For surely the wind and the rain must be telling about the Indians and the buffalo. And how the Spaniards, seeking the fabled lost cities of gold, brought the first horses and the first cows to the country and thus sowed the seeds of riches more fabulous than Cibola ever could have owned. The wind and the rain must remember campfire yarns of the strange U.S. Camel Corps, the buckskin scouts and freighters and stagecoach drivers, and how the cavalry troopers rode hard and the Texas Rangers rode harder. They still whisper the spare, bare-boned and salty recollections of the pioneer cattle and sheep ranchers who already had been in the Ozona country a quarter of a century when our wagon came that way.

In 1907 Navajo elders still knew how to "talk to the ground." In Ozona men could watch tarantulas crossing a dusty cow trail, or listen to coyotes singing on a hilltop after sunrise, and could tell you when it was going to rain. When they killed a snake, they turned its belly to the sky, hanging it across a barbed-wire fence if one was handy, to *make* it rain. They even got down off their horses, at times, to put an ear to the ground and listen for hoofbeats. If a freezing blue norther caught them in a wagon on the divide, they knew how to put a lighted kerosene lantern at their feet and pull a tarp or blanket over it and up to their chins—and some survived because of this knowledge. They were wise in many other ways.

This was because the American frontier came late to the Ozona country, and lingered longer there than in most places. We found these vestiges of the frontier when we came to Crockett County in that year of 1907, along with a great deal of nature magic and all the native poetry and drama of our woodsmoke dreams.

II

Next morning there was a pasture gate or two, and then a fenced lane, with broomweeds and rank-smelling gourd vines on either side of the road. Mexican blue quail and cottontail rabbits ran at our approach; prairie dogs sat up to bark and then dive for their holes. A lane was certain proof that you were coming to a town; nobody was profligate with barbed wire, because everybody hated barbed wire. Other windmills began to show up under the shoulders of the hills, and suddenly we saw the first houses. We swung down into the dry, skeleton-white rock bed of Gurley Draw, and breathed the sharp aroma of wild scrub walnuts distilled by the noonday sun; we came up the western bank of the draw with a cow pasture on one side, and the houses just ahead.

This was Silk Stocking Avenue. Somebody would have had to tell you that: there were no street signs, and not even one to say that the town was Ozona, and all this was in a day fortunate for its lack of billboards. The street ran east and west. Houses on the north side were backed up against Waterworks Hill, most of them behind white or red paling fences. A paling fence was an indication of affluence: it kept out the stray cattle and the wandering Mexican burros, and in its enclosure the property owner could plant a tangle of Bermuda grass, fast-growing and messy mulberry trees, and the showy but evil-scented bird-of-paradise with its red and yellow blossoms—and as time passed he would be sorry for planting any of these. But they required little water, and water was precious.

There were perhaps fifteen houses before we passed Waterworks Hill and came to the town square and the rest of the town extending in an L-shaped fashion to the north. Some of the homes were two stories—another sign of wealth. Floyd and Bert and I were impressed. We had been reared strictly at ground level.

Off to the left, over the roofs of slightly less pretentious dwellings and past a few windmills, was a stretch of green mesquite flat. The baseball diamond lay there, with Gurley Draw running below center field, and beyond all that we could see a separate community standing on rocky and rising ground. Its houses were mainly huts and shacks patched with tin that gleamed in the sunshine and had thatched roofs of *sacaguista,* but there were a few adobes. Floyd viewed this from under the rolled-up wagon tarp, and said it was "Meskin town." He meant "Mexican," but his pronunciation was universal in Texas.

Mama admired the houses on Silk Stocking Avenue, and Jay told her that these were where the ranch owners lived. Mama put away her bottle of snuff. It would take her time to find that about half the women of her age in Ozona also dipped snuff; she always proceeded cautiously in this matter, and never "dipped" in public, anyway. She told Jay he had better stop by the store so she could establish credit—and she said "the" store because we had been in any number of crossroads villages and whistle-stops where there was only one merchant.

Ozona, in 1907, had several stores, being the only town for about forty miles in any direction. It was then sixteen years old, and had a population of nearly a thousand, counting—as its citizens said—the Meskins. The Meskins were very difficult to count, being naturally suspicious of all officialdom; their men-folks were always *vaya con borregos,* or "gone with the sheep," and the kids either ran under the houses or hid in the chaparral.

It was a clean town, wind-swept and sun-washed, with no building yet old enough to be decrepit. A few cowboys rode along the street, and freight wagon outfits went by with a jingle of bells on the hamestraps. Cowboys tied their horses to hitching rails and rattled their spurs across wooden sidewalks to enter Midkiff & Caudle's drugstore on the south side of the square or "Soapy" Smith's drugstore on the west side. They drank ice-cream sodas or grape juice or lemon pop in these places, seemingly unaware that cowboys were supposed to drink stronger brews and raise uninhibited hell; and in all the town there was no other place to go except a pool hall and domino parlor. A spanking-new Methodist church stood just off the square, on Silk Stocking Avenue, and the Methodists not long before had brought a famous evangelist named Abe Mulkey to Ozona to preach the gospel.

We drove around the square. I was insufferably bright in those days, and I read all the signs out loud. The Ozona Hotel. The Kirkpatrick Hotel. The Ozona Hardware: Buggies, Fencing, Implements, Etc. (What was meant by "Implements" was not clear: there was not a plow in all of Crockett County.) G. L. Bunger, Dry Goods & Groceries. A grocery store run by Tom and Dan Casebeer and Pink Wyatt. J. W. Henderson's Butcher Shop & Meat Market. Arthur Williams—Saddle Shop & Coffins. Chris Meinecke, Groceries & Feed. L. B. Cox Mercantile Company. S. W. Westfall, Livery Stable & Wagon Yard.

Near the new Methodist church was a small frame building with a false two-story front, labeled "The Ozona Kicker." This was the office of the weekly newspaper. The two-story courthouse of native stone also was quite new, with a black tin dome on its steeple, and places shaped like clocks on its four sides. It has never had a clock. Just north of the courthouse was a windmill with a graceful metal tower seventy-five feet high— the tallest we had ever seen.

This was the Public Windmill, and on our second turn around the square Jay watered the mules at a trough there. Just then the Elementary School loosed the bedlam of noon recess a block up the street, and most of the kids ran home to eat dinner. As we went on around the square I noticed another sign—Garret's Blacksmith Shop—and smelled the odor of coal smoke in the forge, where they were shaping horseshoes.

Mama had picked out Bunger's store, and Jay wrapped the reins around the brake handle and left the mules to doze while we all went inside. It was a dim and cool place, smelling pleasantly of dried apples and barrels of sorghum molasses and vinegar, freshly ground coffee and strong yellow soap, and the dye in calico and gingham yard goods. Jay bought a dime's worth of jawbreakers, which came in all the hues of the rainbow as well as in black, and no matter what color one began with, all the colors showed up as salivary action wore down successive layers. The taste changed, too, producing a series of minor shocks to the palate and the alimentary canal. Science was wonderful . . .

Mama talked to George Bunger. He had a red mustache and very blue eyes; his manner was thoughtful and kind, and suggested that the interview was of grave importance. Some Meskins came in, and Mr. Bunger waited on them in a detached way, and then came back to listen to Mama. He might have been thinking of the bad accounts on his books and what he currently owed the San Angelo wholesale houses. Mama told him Dee was earning $40 a month on the ranch, and that Jay would get a job. She would need groceries, and some yard goods to make "waists" for Floyd and Bert and me, so we could start school; she would want shoes for Floyd, who had a large streak of pride and insisted he was too big to go to school barefoot. There would be times when she would want a little cash money for schoolbooks and medicine and things she would have to order from Sears & Roebuck; she expected Mr. Bunger to advance this, and put it on the bill. Every two or three months, when Dee came in from the ranch, the account would be settled.

She stated her case honestly and simply, and won it. No credit cards. No Retail Credit Association, Better Business Bureau, or bank references. Nothing but Mama's face and her soft voice, Jay and the three kids hanging around the pants-slicked counter, and George Bunger looking over his steel-rimmed spectacles in his tired and patient way. He said, "That'll be all right, ma'am. You just make out a list of what you want, and it'll be all right."

It was still noon recess, and while Mama was making out her list two boys came in from the elementary school. Neither was more than two or three years older than I was, but they were bigger, and they swaggered in handmade cowboy boots and spurs that turned me green with envy. I could identify them a few days later, when I started to school. The skinny kid with more freckles than anybody ever had was Wesley Berry. The larger, black-haired youngster with a voice like a yearling bull was Armond ("Hop") Hoover.

Wesley went to the candy showcase and pressed his nose against the glass. "Gimme two packages of wax, Mr. Bunger," he said. "Just charge it."

My ears went up like those of the jackrabbits on the divide. *Charge it?* What kind of town was this, where kids dressed like real cowhands and could charge a dime's worth of wax? (We had not yet begun to call it chewing gum.)

Mr. Bunger handed out two packages of Juicy Fruit, an amused light in his eye. He said, "Seems to me you got two packages of wax this morning, Speck. What happened—swallow it?"

"Dadgummed teacher took it away from me," Wesley said. "Oh, I got some stuck under my desk, but it ain't sweet any more." He unwrapped five sticks and crammed them all into his mouth, and then he opened the second package. "Hop, have some of this here wax," he invited.

Hop snorted with gentle disdain. "No, much obliged," he said, in the tone of a man who has put away childish things. Then he reached into his hip pocket, brought out a plug of chewing tobacco, and took a large bite.

What kind of town was this?

My brother Floyd watched Hop Hoover with open admiration. The two had something in common: each had been born *puro hombre,* as the Meskins say—each was all man.

You can be all man at twelve, however, and still not be able to cope with chewing tobacco. Floyd was all the more impressed because just a few weeks ago, on the ranch near Christoval, he had come by a plug of Star Navy and had lured me up on the roof, in the hot sun, to help him try it out. We were both lying pointed downhill on the slope of the roof when it happened, and I have never repeated the experiment since that day . . .

But Hop Hoover seemed to be an old hand at it. He tucked

the quid into his jaw, restored the plug to his pocket, then jingled his spurs outside to spit like a man.

Floyd looked at me. "Man alive!" he said, and I was suddenly very conscious that the jawbreaker in my mouth was kid
stuff, baby stuff. I would have to mend my ways in this town.
Then Wesley Berry said, "Look, Hop!" and crammed the other
five sticks of wax into his mouth. "I can glub mfff frkle whrp!"

"Miss Minta'll take it away from you, shore as hell!" Hop
croaked morosely. They went out the door, and Hop spat
again; they went up past the park and the courthouse, across
the white gravel of the street and through the pitiless sunlight.
We could see Wesley's cheeks bulging from side to side, and
Hop stopping to exterminate a few red ants. To me, they looked
six feet tall.

Mama bought ten pounds of *frijole* beans out of a big sack
standing on the floor. She took a slab of salt pork—pure sow-
bosom with some of the teats on it as proof—from a barrel;
she got canned tomatoes that were good to cook with the beans
and also offered an excellent remedy for sunburn; she bought
sugar and lard and molasses, some Four X Arbuckle coffee
beans to grind in her own mill, a sack of flour, a can of baking
powder for her biscuits, some dried peaches that turned out to
be strongly flavored with resin, and some snuff. Then Mr.
Bunger filled a small paper sack with lemon drops.

"*Pilon*," he said, smiling. "Your son can pay the bill when
he comes to town . . . don't worry about it."

I don't think he even asked what ranch Dee was working on.
But when you bought groceries at Bunger's store—and *always*
when you paid a bill—there was *pilon*. Something for nothing:
a Meskin custom that had become more of a right than a privi-
lege. In childhood, *pilon* was a word out of a dream.

III

That was how we came to Ozona, in September of 1907, when
the town was sixteen years old, and I was going on six. This

gave us something in common: we both were suffering from growing pains, and since neither of us had a blueprint for Planned Development, we were likely to build haphazardly.

Sixteen is a gawky and awkward and irresponsible age for a town that just happened in a mesquite flat, in the middle of nowhere; six, for a boy, is just as bad. At sixteen, Ozona had very little thought of tomorrow, and no idea of wooing any kind of industry. And at six, boys find little girls strangely repulsive, and are disgusted when older brothers begin slicking their hair with vaseline and going—*voluntarily,* mind you—to prayer meeting or Epworth League.

And so the town and I grew up together, after a fashion, and if the old frontier was fading, some of its people, at least, were still around. I did not realize then that if I could remember tents and campfires and wagon travel, there were men around —and I occasionally talked to them—who had fought for the South in the Civil War: men such as B. F. Byrd and Captain C. L. Broome and Uncle Tom Brumley. I talked to them in a child's careless and carefree way: it was long after they had gone before I knew what stories they could have told me.

But to men like them, and men younger than they, Ozona represented a great deal of progress. It was the town Judge Charles E. Davidson and others had created: they put their pride and their faith into it. They were civic boosters. There came a time within my memory when the town had money enough to do anything it may have wanted to do, and still it moved with what to a youngster was an agonizing slowness. The county had been named for David Crockett; its people literally adopted that famous frontiersman's motto of "Be sure you are right, and then go ahead."

But Crockett, once going ahead, was filled with superlatives, and so was Crockett County. Everything it had was the biggest, the finest, and the best. It had built the handsomest stone court-house in all West Texas; it had the biggest bank, with colonial columns running up two stories high. The ranches were the largest—so, even, were the droughts and flash floods, the dust storms and blue norfhers. It had the best water and the most sunshine. To clean up an old frontier brag, Crockett County and Ozona could jump higher, yell louder, and spit farther than any other place in the land.

It wasn't long before it did really have the most civic pride and the biggest booster spirit extant. Wild partisan yells greeted the one-night stand tent show performers who scratched and said, "I just came from San Angelo, and I've got fleas." And at high school baseball games a small but stanch band of rooters sang, to the tune of "America":

> *There are no flies on us,*
> *There are no flies on us . . .*
> *No flies on us.*
> *There may be one or two*
> *Great big green flies on you . . .*
> *There are no flies on us,*
> *No flies on us . . .*

and to a youngster accustomed to seeing flies swarming over the carcass of a cow, this song said that Ozona was alive. It was, indeed. Suddenly it was calling itself "The Biggest Little Town in the World." This was done quietly enough; it pleases me to report that not until the year 1963 did Ozona have a Chamber of Commerce.

I spent fifteen formative years in Ozona before joining the Navy in 1922. Long before then I knew I had fallen in love with the place and its people, with the wide, free spaces and the unfettered way of life. Its values had become mine, and even then I vaguely sensed that the town and I had matured together in that span of time. It was several years later that I began to write—and even then I could not have written Ozona's story. I had not been away long enough. To find a true perspective, one must go away for a far piece and a long time, and then look back and listen.

The story of Ozona is truly a chapter in the story of the Winning of the West. It is charged with a quiet, basic drama, and there are undertones of courage and persistence never portrayed in Hollywood's "shoot-'em-up" Western epics. But the Ozona story is far more authentic, because far more of the West was won by fences and windmills than by gunsmoke and wild "they went thataway" riding. More of it was wrested from the perversities of nature than from the Indians, and there was more real bravery in the long, tedious and relentless struggle with the land, itself, than any of the Western courage depicted on television. Ozona, like most of Texas, was settled by men who came out of the South to make a new beginning. They were quiet men, and reasonable; they were determined and independent; more often than not, they were driven by dreams or goaded by memories. In Crockett County they found room to move in, work to do, and time to think. There was really no place for gunplay heroics in their life, and they were tough in a different way. Their toughness was really strength: nobody needed to carve notches on a gun to prove that strength.

In the Ozona country a man was much alone. He was not pressured to conform to any pattern. He developed his own individuality, fought the elements, became resourceful, and had time to contemplate. He emerged a personality which today is called a "character." And the town was filled with them.

A much-loved man named Houston Smith could have told the Ozona story better than I, because he lived more of it. He taught me history in high school, served as an Army officer in World War I, was admitted to the bar in 1919, and finally succeeded Charles E. Davidson as the county judge. He collected historical material with a passion; he told the story, many times over, in speeches, and in soft-spoken, scholarly conversation in his law office, on the south side of the pecan-shaded square.

But he was a busy man, and he never got around to writing it, although he had planned to do so. Last year, I had a telephone call, in Roanoke, Virginia, from Evart White. Evart publishes the Ozona *Stockman*.

"Allie," Evart said, "we buried old Houston today. I guess it's up to you to write the Ozona story."

Some Indians,

and the

2 Hoover Tribe

The cowards never started, and the weak died on the way.
—OLD TEXAS SAYING

THE LAND SHAPED ITSELF, down the bare-boned ages, out
of the enduring Edwards limestone. Once it had all been an
inland sea, but like everything else in West Texas, this ran dry,
leaving all manner of shelled and crawling creatures prisoned
forever in the hardening rocks. Slow-sculpturing winds and
rains of a million years carved deep valleys and draws, and
left rimrocks and flat mesas standing at the same level while
the earth alternately blew away and washed away at their feet.
Finally, there was vegetation to hold the soil, but in West Texas
there has never been very much of either.

It was a high land, lifting open and wide and free: a country
of cedar-dotted hills, and ten-mile divides as level and green
as billiard tables, breaking unaccountably into wild and rug-
ged canyons. Between the hills were broad flats where in good
years the grass was lush, and white-rock draws always winding
southward to seek the Rio Grande.

The Creator was in a mood both expansive and capricious.
He decreed room here on a magnificent scale, with horizons
running into tomorrow and skies unfathomably deep and blue.

He fashioned a country of infinite distances, lovely to look at in season. But then He gave it more of weather than climate, and whether in divine wisdom or a moment of whimsy, He failed to provide dependable rain.

Ozona country is a land of thirst. When rain comes, it sometimes comes with an incredible violence, and flash floods have helped shape the topography: gentle here, abruptly broken there. But the long periods of thirst, more than anything else, fashioned the landscape, the economy, the growth, and even the physical forms of plant and animal life. Many creatures—including early man and some men not so early—were unable to endure thirst. They either moved on, or perished.

The country was part of a high plateau, with altitudes ranging from 1,500 to 2,500 feet above sea level. It was a dry and healthful place, free of fevers. It was drained by the Pecos River—a salty stream both in its chemical content and in its wealth of Billy-the-Kid type of cowboy legend. The Pecos, rising in the far mountains of northern New Mexico, comes down to mark the western boundary of Crockett County, seventh biggest county in the state of Texas. Along its lower reaches, as it approaches the Rio Grande, the Pecos has carved a wide canyon of fantastic colors and designs which is remarkably like portions of Canyon de Chelly, in Arizona. Archaeologists say that Canyon de Chelly was a refuge for the Anasazi people—the Ancient Ones—as late as A.D. 350. These were Basketmakers, supposedly the ancestors of the highly civilized Pueblo tribes.

But A.D. 350 is a very recent date compared to the evidence of human habitation found in the wind-hollowed caves of the Pecos Canyon. Basketmakers lived in what is now Crockett County at least three thousand years ago, and left their bones along with those of the cave bear, the musk ox and the sloth. They wrote undecipherable mysteries on the rocks, put down their tools and weapons in the deepening dust of Time, and either departed or came to some tragic end. It may be that no

one was left alive to bury the last of them. Certainly something
—thirst, famine, epidemic or war—killed off the Basketmakers
in bunches. They buried whole families together, the children
wrapped in rabbit-skin shrouds tied with a cord made from the
fiber of the *lechuguilla* plant.

The *lechuguilla,* an agave curiously misnamed "little lettuce,"
fared better than the forgotten people it served so long ago in
burial rites. It is extant on the rocky hills, and in living memory has greatly enriched the already picturesque and fervidly
profane speech of Pecos cowboys and sheepherders. The *lechuguilla* cares not whether the year is wet or dry; in all seasons it
produces slightly curved daggers that easily pierce the toughest
of boots or *chaparejos*. No one yet has written a murder mystery in which a *lechuguilla* dagger was the lethal weapon . . .
but give us time.

In the Pecos country there is nothing at all unusual about
such a plant. The whole land is rife with similar examples of
natural selection and adaptation to environment. It is spined
and thorned with Spanish dagger and *sotol,* barbed mesquite
and catclaw, sharp holly-leaved *agarita* or wild currant, tuna-
fruited prickly pear, *tasajillo* with thorned rat-like tails, and
many others. It is no mere accident that the white man came
armed, or that he took a lesson from nature and put thorns on
his barbed-wire fences. Creatures survived in the land only because they were swift and needed little water, or because they
carried their own armor. The armadillo and the formidable-
looking but harmless horned toad (actually a lizard) are prime
examples of the latter. Both are clearly descended from the age
of the giant reptiles whose tracks can be found in the ledge
rocks; their small economies enabled them to live on, while the
dinosaurs did not.

The Basketmakers of the Pecos caves could not have been
a traveled people in any man's lifetime, and one wonders how
they got there. They must have been fleeing aggression, or perhaps there was more of climate and less of weather in their

time. No matter what direction they came from, journeying on foot, the distances between dependable water—judging by water today—would have been appalling. They must have had memories and legends, and tales mumbled by the toothless elders, of fairer places and better times; the Pecos country must have seemed a purgatory by contrast. Their caves were little better than overhangs hollowed by the wind, and the wind was still at them, shrieking dire prophecies along the cliffs. Sometimes the Rain God turned his face away for so many moons that all the grass withered, all the game migrated; sometimes the Rain God heeded their prayers all too well, and made the river rise to flood the lower caves and drown or dispossess their inhabitants.

But if the land remained unfruitful even for years on end, reducing the people to a starvation diet of rabbits and rodents snared in the loops they made by braiding human hair—even if they had to eat snakes and lizards and grasshoppers—there were also alternate times and seasons when the grass billowed waist-high in the winds, and bigger meat—prong-horned antelope, buffalo, mule deer and white-tailed deer—was plentiful. Times, too, of wild plums turning yellow and red in their thorned thickets, catfish in the river, acorns ripening under the live oak trees to be roasted and leached and ground into meal, and the whole miracle of summer suns distilled into wild honey and stored in crevices in the rocks. There would have been lazy springtime days when wildflowers ran riot over divide and hillslope, and soft, well-fed nights under a sky heavy with stars.

Nobody knows what happened to the Basketmakers. A pity, because if they had stayed long enough to father the Pueblo tribes—if they had left more of a record—they would have been the first permanent inhabitants of Crockett County. Nobody can say when they left, but it is certain that for a very long time the region was not inhabited by human beings. The Plains Indians came that way much, much later, following the buffalo—especially after they had acquired horses from the early Spaniards. But they were only camping out; in cowboy lingo, they were only riding the chuck line. They didn't settle down.

The Spanish passed nearby, at least, perhaps as early as Cabeza de Vaca, in 1528, and certainly before the end of that century. They were good explorers so long as they had visions of golden cities somewhere over the world's rim, and the friars yearned earnestly to convert—and enslave—all the Indians. But the Spanish were poor colonizers. There was nothing in this land to tempt them to build one of their mission forts anywhere near the Pecos: there were not enough people. More than two centuries later the Spanish were still only skirting the south and west portions of what is now Crockett County, making overnight camps at three watering places on the dusty San Antonio-Chihuahua Trail.

And so the high, wide, open land—with so much to offer and so much to demand—lay waiting for its people. It waited a long time.

II

The Spanish mission towns of the sixteenth century were America's oldest frontier—nearly a hundred years older than Jamestown. But they were strangely destined to become, after three hundred years, a part of the latest and the last frontier, except for Alaska.

Settlers did not really come into the Pecos and Crockett County region until the 1880's, or almost forty years after the Lone Star Republic consented (with some notable reservations that particularly concerned its land) to join the Union. There were reasons for the delay in settlement: the Indians, the Civil War and Reconstruction, and then the Indians again.

Thirty miles west of the pecan-shaded square in Ozona the ruins of a few crumbling rock chimneys stand like neglected tombstones on a gullied slope covered with a tangle of gray-green chaparral. Owls hoot there at night, and coyotes wail from the rimrocks, and there are ghosts abroad. This was Fort Lancaster, where the hard-butted U.S. Cavalry rode—but not for long. It was the first federal endeavor near the banks of the salty Pecos; it was founded in the 1850's, and then got caught up in the land's magnificent distances and the vicissitudes of war; it died on the vine without having any noteworthy or lasting effect on the development of the country. The fort was never really meant to help open the area to settlers, but merely to protect mail stages on the San Antonio to San Diego run. Some day, no doubt, an entrepreneur of motels and museums will restore it . . . and I wish him well. The foundations are all there, and so are a few forlorn tombstones.

Lancaster was abandoned in 1861, when the garrison joined troops from Fort Davis, farther west, in marching to San Antonio to surrender to the Confederacy. The Confederates later maintained the fort after a fashion, but Southern manpower was needed elsewhere. Under Texas' long and painful Reconstruction, Uncle Sam did not consider Lancaster in the national interest, and it was some twenty years after the war before any white man came by there with the intention of staying longer than overnight. When he did, there were no troops within a hundred miles, and perhaps no Texas Rangers within two hundred—and since the county hadn't been organized, there wasn't even a sheriff. It was no wonder that every man had to carry his own law in holster and saddle scabbard. Or that he had to put on protective armor, of sorts, against the thorns.

The people were long in coming. The continent was too vast, and, admittedly, there were richer and better lands. The American star of empire wended its way westward so long as there were fertile forest acres to be cleared and planted, so long as there was dependable rainfall; it moved on where rivers would float a barge, where the Indians could be killed off or pushed off; it went places where a man and his family could live off the land. When gold was discovered in California, it leapfrogged a continent.

Then it closed the gaps later. It closed them much later down in West Texas, where the land was not at all inviting. What finally closed the gaps was something not nearly so spectacular as the discovery of gold, but much more dependable in the long run. What finally settled the wind-swept western plains was the nation's appetite for beefsteak.

The cattle industry was born in Texas just after the Civil War. It began as an accidental way of life—Texas had the cattle, running wild, and the North and the East wanted them. The railroads grew, and so did cow business. All at once it was big and lucrative, increasingly competitive, always a high gamble; all at once it was a wild, free and romantic way of life.

When it started, land east or west of the Pecos would not have been worth a dime an acre. Only a transient meat hunter could have made a living in the Ozona country, and he would have been scalped before the seasonal migration of the buffalo. The land there was impossible to farm. There was no water to turn mill wheels, no people for factory hands, no consumer's market, and no roads.

The war was fought, and Texas went with the Confederacy. It appears that the Yankees did not heed an admonition plainly stated in the Bible. Isaiah, chapter 43, verse 6, says: "I will say to the north, Give up; and to the south, Keep not back: bring my sons from far, and my daughters from the ends of the earth."

After four years of Robert E. Lee and Stonewall Jackson keeping not back, and the sons of Texas being brought from afar, Texas was in pretty bad shape. But it had some cattle that had multiplied during the war. And West Texas had grass. It was sometimes waist-high, until the Indians set it afire in their lazy, profligate methods of getting meat. Cattle needed grass, and a hungry, growing nation needed meat. Nobody foresaw it, but around 1880 the western part of Texas had a sort of rendezvous with Destiny, at a crossroads of Time, place, circumstances, and progress.

Everything fitted in neatly. The country had no water, but it had wind—always dependable, often excessive. So just then windmills began to be produced—not the cumbersome kind that ground corn for the Jamestown colonists, but simple, light machines that could be hauled in a wagon and were still sturdy enough to withstand a Texas norther.

Around the same time—and this was one of the most fortunate coincidences in all history—J. F. Glidden of Illinois got a patent on barbed wire and was soon selling it by the carload in Texas.

There was never a happier wedding. Windmills and barbed wire went together like pancakes and maple syrup. They complemented each other: each made the other necessary. Together they marched across the wide Edwards Plateau, taming it, taming the Ozona country, and the wide reaches west of the Pecos. A man didn't need a creek or waterhole any more. All he had to have was a drilled well, and a windmill, and the wind working for him day and night.

And fences could wait for a number of years, until the ranges began to be crowded and brands began to mix. The delay was perhaps fortunate. There was a fence-cutters' war, to the east of Crockett County, and not very far away: it raged, bloodily enough, all over Brown and Coleman counties during the eighties, and over parts of Lampasas and Tom Green, and it kept the Texas Rangers busy. But by the time the Crockett County ranges were stocked the fence wars were only a memory, and when the first barbed wire was strung it was respected.

III

Texas has always been fond of "firsts." It has not been many years since newspaper write-ups—especially the obituaries—often referred to "the first white child born in this county," and so on. In Ozona the old-timers still remember Mrs. Laura Hoover as the first white woman to come to that section of Texas.

Her father was a Tennessee plantation owner named Jim

McNutt, who came to Texas before the Civil War. She married young, and was not yet twenty years old in 1881 when her husband—a tall, dark, rangy man of twenty-five named William Perry Hoover—put her on a wagon seat, with their two babies, and headed westward from Kimble County with two hundred head of long-horned cattle. Mr. Hoover and a cowboy drove the cattle, and a boy had been hired to drive the covered wagon that contained all the household furniture they owned, and the food supplies. But the boy turned out to be a greenhorn: when he hitched up, the first day, he put the horses' collars on backwards, and later showed less than skill in handling the reins. After the first day out, he was sent back to civilization, and young Mrs. Hoover took over. She drove the team, held the baby girl in her arms, and watched to see that two-year-old Arthur did not fall out of the wagon.

They were leaving a beautiful part of Texas. Kimble County is in the "Hill Country," a sportsman's paradise, well-watered by the Llano River and other shining streams; they were not going far, as distance is measured today, but in 1881 it must have seemed to Laura Hoover that she was coming to the jumping-off place. They left the rivers behind, and left the post oaks and live oaks of the Hill Country for the flat, windy divides, and there were no roads. Mr. Hoover must have chosen, luckily, a wet year; he would have had to water his herd several times on the eighty-mile drive from the head of the Llano to Beaver Lake, on Devil's River. He stretched a rawhide cooney under the wagon to carry calves too new and too weak to walk, and arrived on Devil's River with the herd intact.

For three months the family camped on Beaver Lake. No fences, and somebody had to ride around the cattle at night to keep them from straying or stampeding when the coyotes howled. And meanwhile William Perry Hoover rode far, day after day, looking for a permanent range.

He had the whole wide country to choose from, and there must have been something solitary and wild in his blood: the site he picked was some forty miles away, under a steep bluff in the canyon of the Pecos, and certainly the wildest and most isolated spot he could have found. Here he built a house—a one-room house of cedar pickets, adobe mud and grass, with one window and one door. Supplies had to be lowered over the face of the bluff by ropes, otherwise the wagon had to be driven an extra twenty miles—ten miles up the Pecos Canyon to a point known as Sheffield Hill, before it could climb out on the divide, and ten miles down the canyon on the return trip. Once or twice a year, the Hoovers made a six-day wagon trip to San Angelo for supplies—more than eighty miles away. The only other sources were at Fort Stockton, eighty miles northwest, and Del Rio, eighty-five miles southeast. The roads were equally bad in any direction, but San Angelo was more of a metropolis.

In the canyon of the Pecos the Hoovers were not living too much differently than those earlier canyon residents, the Basketmakers, except that they had a house instead of a cave, and Laura Hoover could cook on a cast-iron stove fired with mesquite roots. The supplies they bought in San Angelo were all staples: flour and beans, corn meal and bacon, coffee and Irish potatoes and onions, blackstrap molasses and canned tomatoes and corn and peaches. Nothing that would spoil. Mr. Hoover did not have to kill any of his own cattle for fresh meat. He could ride out almost any time and shoot a fat buck deer. He could set a trotline in the Pecos, and catch any number of catfish, and with a shotgun he could always get a mess of Mexican blue quail. The growing family lived well.

But for nine months at a time Laura Hoover saw no other woman. She kept a loaded pistol and used it once to kill a rattlesnake that crawled into the house; she could go up the Pecos Canyon and see wagon trains that occasionally passed on the Chihuahua Trail, and she was busy cooking and sewing for her family. During their trips to San Angelo, the Hoovers left their house unlocked—if, indeed, it could have been locked at all—so that anyone coming that way could use the stove to cook a meal or could take shelter overnight. In a world of increasing suspicions and shrinking boundaries, it is heartening to note that this custom still prevails on the Crockett County ranches.

W. P. Hoover could have found range without pushing so far to the westward, but he was a man who wanted a lot of room . . . and he found it. He built that temporary house— it served for years—with one eye peeled for hostile Indians and the other watching for rattlesnakes. The rattlers were plentiful, as Laura Hoover was to discover; the Indians had been pretty well cleaned out in the past decade, by our shameless slaughter of the buffalo. The Indians were mostly eating their hearts out on Indian Territory reservations, and waiting to get rich from Oklahoma oil lands, but there were a few small, wild, marauding bands still horseback. It was impossible, in those days, to distinguish between Indians and Mexicans: the latter were often full-blooded Indians, with an almost imperceptible veneer of Latin-American civilization washed over them. Down near the mouth of Howard's Draw, in 1882, Indians stole four of W. P. Hoover's horses, and killed two cows. They lingered only long enough to cut the backstraps from the carcasses, and left the rest of the meat for the coyotes and buzzards.

Many a lesser man would have been pardoned for pulling back toward a settlement when that happened. But W. P. Hoover had come to stay. There was a great deal of the tough *lechuguilla* fiber in his makeup, and he did not scare easily.

Remember the year—1882. That year New York City had some two million population. The next biggest American metropolis was Philadelphia, and both the Quaker City and Boston had long buried their Indians, and were centers of civilization and culture. The same could hardly be said for San Francisco, gaudy and bawdy and rich, but in 1882 the town by the Golden Gate could boast 230,000 people. California had been settling up fast for more than thirty years; the American people fixed their eyes on California, and leapfrogged across a lot of country—including West Texas—to get there. In San Francisco a wealthy young upstart named William Randolph Hearst was soon to begin casting covetous eyes at his first newspaper.

The Hoovers had no mail delivery, and saw no newspapers when they were at home. San Antonio, more than 200 miles to the east, was a very old town, but had reached only 20,000 population; El Paso, some three hundred miles westward, had fewer than a thousand residents. Between these two places (as humorous detractors of Texas are fond of saying) was nothing but miles and miles of miles and miles . . .

This was very true, in 1882. Unless the Hoovers happened to make a trip to San Angelo that year earlier than usual, they would not learn for a long time that Billy the Kid had been shot to death, up the same salty Pecos, in New Mexico Territory; they would not receive word of the killing of Jesse James —Jesse Woodson James—in St. Joseph, Missouri, until a long time after poor Jesse was laid in his grave in April of that year.

At the moment W. P. Hoover was more interested in the weather, and the price of cattle on the hoof. His two hundred longhorns were breeding and multiplying, and they were worth a lot more money than they had been when he put the herd together in Kimble County. He had sold no cattle yet. Like a true ranchman, he took pure pleasure in owning them, in watching them, in riding around the herd.

It rained in West Texas in 1882, and the grass came green and high, and W. P. Hoover had money on the hoof. As has always been true in that country, rain was something of a mixed blessing. Some areas got none at all, but W. P. Hoover had rain on the Pecos, and the little village of Ben Ficklin, a few miles south of San Angelo, was washed away on August 24. For many years the Ben Ficklin Flood was as notorious in West Texas as the Johnstown Flood ever had been in the East.

IV

By coming to the Pecos, W. P. Hoover had found, for a while, something that was fast disappearing in Texas and all over the West. He had found free range.

Under Texas land laws, every odd-numbered section of 640 acres belonged to public schools. The alternate, even-numbered sections in what was to be Crockett County (the county was still not organized as such a unit) had been granted to twenty-four separate railroad companies—as an inducement, of course, to touch off a mad race to see who could be the first to lay track through the area. In addition, large blocks of real estate had been set aside for the University of Texas.

For the first four or five years Mr. Hoover did not pay a dime for the grass his cattle consumed. In 1886, however, he paid three cents an acre as a grazing lease . . . and in that year he could have bought the alternate sections of railroad land for a dollar an acre, with forty years to pay, at three percent interest. Other land was sometimes even cheaper. (In June of 1898 James Bryson and W. H. Montgomery of Comanche bought twenty-nine sections of Crockett County land, near Howard's Well, for forty cents an acre. In 1928 land adjoining this tract was reported sold by Bill Odom for $14 an acre.)

There was so much land that not many people could foresee that land values would ever rise. But cattle were different. Texas men had been trailing cattle to the Northern markets for a dozen years, and some had made fortunes. Railroads had cut down the distance of the trail drives, but that worked in the ranchman's favor: he didn't have to drive his herd so far. In 1882 W. P. Hoover's first year on the Pecos, more than a quarter million Texas longhorns went up to the Kansas markets, and all at once they were worth as much as thirty-five dollars a head, if a man got them to the railhead with meat still on their ribs.

Hoover's cattle had been worth eight or ten dollars a head when he brought them from the Llano. On paper, in 1882, he had made a lot of money. But before he could put a herd on the trail the boom suddenly collapsed.

Eastern capitalists, and even syndicates from the British Isles, were rushing into cattle business to make a quick killing, and that is just what many of them did. The ranges in Crockett County, where a few other cattlemen were following W. P. Hoover, were too new and too isolated to be overstocked, but those in many other parts of the country were unbelievably crowded by the end of 1882. Either drought or a hard winter meant calamity. Hoover and the newer Crockett County ranchmen were learning that in that part of the country a cow needed about forty acres of grazing land; up near Fort Worth (according to historian Walter Prescott Webb) an unnamed ranch had 25,000 head on 100,000 acres. The roundup there, in the spring of 1883—a dry year—found only 10,000 of the herd alive.

The big crash came in 1885, when blizzards swept the plains and cattle died by the thousands on the overstocked ranges. Absentee owners—such as the British—and other investors threw what beef they had left on the market at any price they could get.

W. P. Hoover had been sitting tight, building up his herd, selling no cattle at all. He needed very little cash money to run the ranch on the Pecos; he could wait. But, all at once, his cows were back down to $10 a head.

And the cattle business was never the same after the big bust of the middle eighties. The big trail drives were really over: the railroads were reaching out, building down to places like Fort Worth. Most of the wild and carefree "come-a-ti-yi-yippee" went out of raising and punching cattle, and it slowly began to be a real business and not just a way of life. W. P. Hoover and other Crockett County ranchmen tightened their belts and began learning ways to fight droughts and die-ups, and predators. They began to breed up their herds toward the shorthorn and the white-faced Herefords.

Some of them took an even more drastic step. Some were soon to begin raising sheep.

But sheep were a long way off for William Perry Hoover, a cattleman born and bred. He went on raising cattle, and acquiring more land, and rearing a considerable family. There came a time when he and "Mother" Hoover had nine children, and ninety sections of land—or 57,600 acres. And they were millionaires several times over, although neither ever appeared to be aware of any wealth at all.

3 A Town

at

Tailholt Crossing

Out In The West, Where The Air Is Pure, The Climate Agreeable, And The People Friendly—The Best Place On Earth To Call Home.
—MASTHEAD OF THE OZONA STOCKMAN

WILLIAM PERRY HOOVER was the first permanent settler, but in the early and middle eighties he was not the only ranchman who was looking for enough room to swing his rope. And if the Texas county named for David Crockett had anything at all, it had room.

Counties were first "created" and then later "organized." The County of Crockett had been created in 1875 out of the western portion of Bexar County. Bexar must have been a tremendous piece of real estate, since its county seat was and is San Antonio—a city some 220 miles eastward from Ozona. Crockett County itself was huge, and before its organization land was taken from it to form a portion of Val Verde County, to the south, and to make Schleicher County, on the east.

This was even more complicated than it sounds. In 1885 Crockett was attached to Val Verde County for jurisdictional purposes—which meant that the nearest court was 120 horseback or wagon miles away, at Del Rio. It meant, too, that

Crockett County could have become a haven for the lawless, except for the fact that William Perry Hoover and the other early settlers aimed to have order, if not law. It was true that in the latter eighties there was a legally constituted justice of the peace down the Pecos, and west of it, at Langtry, in the person of the fabled Roy Bean. Old Roy held court in his "Jersey Lilly Saloon," fined dead men for carrying pistols, and perpetrated many another piece of buffoonery. He became something of a tourist attraction for the new railroad building between San Antonio and El Paso, but there is no evidence that he ever fooled any of the ranchmen in what he called his "bailiwick."

And ranchmen were drifting into the area, with well drillers in the van. The well drillers were necessary, because in a short time all of the few dependable waterholes had been pre-empted. A man named Joe Moore came from the eastward in 1885, with a steam-powered drilling rig so heavy it had to be pulled by an eight-horse team, and sank the first water well in what is now Crockett County. This was on the Moss ranch, later owned by the Davidson family. The deep-rutted tracks left by the heavy outfit are still visible, and the event is even more permanently etched upon the history of the section. Given water for his stock to drink, and a man could ranch anywhere.

The records are scant, but there are scatterings of names and memories. Fayette Schwalbe was camped under a big live oak tree in 1884, running a herd of cattle along Johnson Draw: the county was organized under the same tree seven years later. S. E. Couch, a native of Canada, arrived in 1887.

The Ozona Historical Society has preserved notes made by Mr. Couch in his own handwriting. "On November 19, 1887, James Mitchell and I camped on Johnson's run near where Ozona is located, on our first trip to Crockett County. On the night of the 20th, we camped at Frank Lantz well then being drilled by Mr. (A. W.) Mauldin.

"Mitchell and I moved our sheep in where Ozona now is, on

January 3, 1888. Couch well at headquarters drilled August 1888."

There is a significant note here. Up to now, the settlers had been cattlemen. Mitchell and Couch brought the first sheep, but for a long time cattle would predominate. J. W. Henderson came down from the Concho country in 1888 with the biggest cow outfit so far—three thousand head wearing the 7N brand, a mark that became famous years before a mile of fence had been built.

"Picnic held at Couch well June 25, 1891, at which time it was decided to organize the county," Mr. Couch's memoirs went on. "First election held July 7, 1891, one voting box at J. W. Henderson ranch casting 11 votes. Ozona and Eureka, 11 miles west, voted on for county seat, Ozona winning. . . .

"People who were here at time county was organized or in the county: Joe Moss, F. M. Drake, J. W. Friend, John Young, Joe Graham, John Perry, Mr. Mauldin, Frank Lantz, Frank Olney, Sam Sowell, Mr. Newton, Porter Kimball, J. W. Henderson, Chas. E. Davidson, Mr. Hoover, James Mitchell, A. H. Couch, S. E. Couch, Mr. Corbett, W. E. West, Jim Baker, Mr. Odom, Mr. Schwalbe, L. B. Cox, and B. F. Byrd."

There were others, and more coming. Except for a few people of Germanic extraction, the Ozona country was settled—like most of the South—by pure Anglo-Saxon, Scottish and Irish stock. A large percentage of them were native Texans, and they remembered Reconstruction days.

Most of them had been "fenced out" of the livestock ranges to the eastward. Crockett County came near to being the last open land, as well as one of the last frontiers.

II

The vote in 1891, to choose between Ozona and Eureka as the county seat, was a rather curious proceeding. Neither was actually a town: Ozona had a windmill and a few tents and wagon camps, and Eureka was nothing more than a ranch headquarters. On the other hand, there was already a town named Emerald on the divide seven miles east of Ozona, and it was two years old.

The election shocked Emerald, which not only expected to be in the running but was confident of winning. But Emerald had been established under dubious premises: first, that the Gulf, Colorado & Santa Fe would extend its railroad tracks southward to the Rio Grande from its new terminus at San Angelo; and, second, that farmers from the North and Middle West could scratch out a living on a section or even a half section of the dollar-an-acre land.

Land in that part of West Texas was never meant for farming. The town of Emerald had been dreamed up by an immigration agent for the Santa Fe who toured Northern states in the wintertime and sold an imponderable quantity: West Texas climate. Prospective settlers came to look, and found sunshine and warmth. It seems probable that no blue northers howled across the Eldorado divides during their inspection trip, and the name Emerald suggests that there had been rain. No country is more green than West Texas—when there has been good rain.

Some of the people bought land. They even planted wheat fields and set out orchard trees. Theirs were the first and virtually the last plows in Crockett County, and theirs were the last quarter-section and half-section and section tracts. Cattlemen were to discover that it took an average of forty acres— more, in some pastures—to support one cow. That discovery pretty well eliminated the small operator, in Crockett County, for all time.

Mattie Noyes Roach of San Angelo remembered how her family came from New Hampshire to Emerald in April, 1889. Given rain in that season, Emerald could have been as green as New Hampshire, but lacking woods and mountains; if the spring was dry, the prospect would have been especially bleak to a New Englander. The place had one house, one tent, a windmill, and a small water tank. The railroad company built a two-room schoolhouse and a store, and what was much more significant, two well drillers erected homes and began putting down water wells on the outlying ranches. Emerald never had a post office or a mail route: mail was sent to the tiny village of Knickerbocker—later a stage stand on the Ozona to San Angelo run—and had to be brought to Emerald by chance travelers.

Emerald never had more than a handful of people, and it survived just long enough to run the gamut of human existence: there was one birth, one death, and one marriage. A prairie fire that burned for a whole week in August, 1890, threatened to wipe out the town. Citizens saw the light of the blaze in the southeast for two nights before it came near enough to menace their homes; they turned out to fight it with backfires, and slap at the running tongues of flame with wet towsacks and saddle blankets dipped in barrels of water hauled in a wagon. There is no evidence that they used another range trick—that of shooting a cow and then dragging the carcass along the fire line with ropes from two saddle horses. But they saved the community, and a section or more of grass for their livestock. For two more nights they watched the glare in the sky after the fire had burned around them.

Eleven months later, just before the election to organize the county, it rained so hard at Emerald that "a six-horse team couldn't pull an empty wagon out of the mud." At the same time a human prairie fire was off and running with a civic zeal that was to burn brightly for more than half a century.

His name was Charles E. Davidson, and he became known as the "Father of Ozona."

III

Charles E. Davidson was a Kentuckian, thirty-five years old, a big man with a massive head, a luxuriant red mustache, and a heavy gold watch chain across his vest. He was the same age as W. P. Hoover, busy building his livestock empire over on the Pecos, but the similarity ended there. Davidson had already had a considerable career, and for the time and place was rather cosmopolitan. He had grown up on an Iowa farm, was educated at Cornell and the University of Iowa, and paid his way through a law degree at Hastings School of Law in San Francisco by teaching at night. After his graduation there he practiced law in California for a short time, then moved to Texas, where he was connected with a land office in Austin.

In 1883 he went to San Angelo, where there was a lucrative business for attorneys specializing in land and titles, and what he learned in helping to survey and map that town was to be important later.

One account says Davidson received title to twenty-five sections of West Texas land as a fee for his very first legal case, in California. Another—and much more probable—says that he obtained a tract of real estate in Crockett County during the seven years he practiced in San Angelo. At any rate, while operating in the latter town, he began acquiring livestock, and a few years later the people of Crockett County were calling him "the cattle king."

There was a great deal more to the man, even at thirty-five, than any mere ambition for wealth. He was an omnivorous reader, and his experience as a teacher schooled him thoroughly in the needs of education. His powers of concentration were remarkable. In later years—after Ozona had such modern conveniences as telephones—he could not hear one ringing on his desk when he was considering some problem. Best of all, he had a kindly philosophy, and always insisted: "Not what you remember, but what you forget, is important."

Very likely Davidson and a Dallas surveyor and landowner named E. M. Powell conspired both to found and to name the town of Ozona. Powell, who owned land at the site, was both entrepreneur and philanthropist. He drilled a well at the spot, and put up a windmill for public use, and then he offered to donate several acres of land to be used for a courthouse, a school, a waterworks and a jail.

At that point the talk of organizing the county passed the spit and whittle stage, and got down to business.

The location was on Johnson Draw, a dry watercourse tributary to Devil's River, supposedly named for Colonel Joseph Johnson who had made a road survey and topographical map of the area between San Antonio and Live Oak Creek in 1849. And there is no way of knowing how common the name was, but old John Young—a cowboy and cattleman who was there before and after the town—called it "TailHolt Crossing on Johnson Draw." (John Young was the principal hero of J. Frank Dobie's *A Vaquero of the Brush Country*.)

There was a name for you, redolent of the frontier soil, and one that might well have been preserved in a state that has (or has had) Muleshoe, Cut 'n Shoot, Study Butte (the *u* is long in both words), Belcherville, Hell Again (later bowdlerized to Elgin), Dime Box, Hide Town, Lick Skillet, Shake Rag, Steal Easy, Possum Trot, Short Pone, and Poverty Slant.

But, alas, the new county seat was not to bear the alliterative and intriguing title of Tail Holt, Texas. Davidson was already riding around the county talking about Ozona, and now a petition was drawn up asking him to be a candidate for the office of county judge. He consented, and with admirable timing made a patriotic speech on July Fourth—three days before the election—under that big live oak tree where Fayette Schwalbe had camped a few years earlier.

In all the county there were only three young and single ladies—Miss Dixie Friend, Miss Ollie Gurley, and Miss Rosa Kirkpatrick. They went around electioneering for Davidson, and ranchmen and cowhands were mightily intrigued. So was Miss Dixie, who had been fascinated by that heavy gold watch chain: she married Charles E. Davidson soon after she had helped him win the election.

No torchlight parades or bands marked the occasion, although a few sixshooters were emptied into the air after the ballots had been counted. Then somebody challenged the election. Young Judge Davidson was way ahead of this move. He was already on his horse, riding 120 miles to the Val Verde courthouse at Del Rio. He returned armed with all the proper documents, and the organization of Crockett County and his office as county judge were secure . . .

Things began happening with dramatic speed. Ozona never had anything like a boom, but in those first few months tents blossomed within water-carrying distance of E. M. Powell's public windmill, and there were wagon camps and campfires in the mesquite flat, and A. W. Mauldin and others were running surveys for town streets. Several houses were put on wheels and moved from Emerald as soon as the roads had dried, the Emerald people philosophically accepting an old American proverb: If you can't lick 'em, join 'em.

There were opportunists, too. Two saloonkeepers in the town of Sonora, nearly forty miles eastward in Sutton County, branched out and opened the first business houses in Ozona. So far, Ozona had only twenty full-time residents, but cowboys began riding in from the ranches, most of them inordinately dry and hankering for a game of stud or draw. The combination saloons and gaming houses did right well for a time, but there was opposition to them from the beginning. As early as 1889 Mrs. J. W. Odom had started a Sunday school in her home for children from the ranches in the immediate area, and as soon as the county had been organized a two-room union Sunday school was built. A Methodist church was established on January 30, 1892, and the Baptist church followed in April of that year. Both began fighting the saloons and the gamblers.

And around February, 1892—six months after the county had been organized—a youngster named Claude B. Hudspeth rode into town leading a pack mule. On the back of the mule was strapped a small hand printing press and a couple of fonts of type.

The town suddenly had a weekly newspaper called "the Ozona *Kicker*." And in the long run Claude Hudspeth could be put down as one of the greatest of all the opportunists. He was reportedly only sixteen when he arrived in Ozona. He went on to become a very useful citizen, serve for a long time as a United States congressman, be a millionaire ranchman, and have Hudspeth County (in the extreme western part of Texas) named for him.

Sixteen is a fine age for a Horatio Alger story, but rather young for a crusading editor, and one suspects that Judge Davidson quickly seized upon the idea of using the new weekly as a sounding board. By February 28, 1892, the *Kicker* was lashing out at conditions in the new town:

Come to Ozona—and be a tough.

High premiums paid on all crime.

Gambling with cards in public allowed, and at all times, including Sundays.

Special rewards paid for scalps of gentlemen and tenderfoots (sic); but will prosecute all murderers of our hoodlums, whiskey bums and scalawags.

Promiscuous hell raised in high places continually; crime is rampant; lawlessness increasing.

Come to the home of the tough and join the enterprise.

Motto—toughness.

Aim—extermination of society.

Desire—to invert the order of this part of the universe, and put hell (shame, shame) uppermost.

Object—to rival San Angelo and have hell on earth.

Before long there were three saloons and gambling houses in the small town. The Devil had Ozona by the tail, with a downhill pull. In the beginning, it appears very unlikely that this concerned W. P. Hoover or J. W. Henderson, or any of the other owners of the outlying ranches. They were not townsmen: they came to Ozona only to buy supplies and were far more interested in finding a good grocery and feed store and hardware firm than in finding a sanctified atmosphere or good moral tone. Few Texas towns of the period were virtuous. San Angelo—cited in the *Kicker*'s editorial blasts—had many more drinking and gaming emporiums than it had any other kind of business establishments; Del Rio was on the border, where wickedness flourished overtime, and even Sonora had its Meskin town with crime rampant.

The ranchmen were a tolerant lot, and inured to tough places. Most of them liked a drink and a game of cards now and then, but they had little time for such frivolities. They were busy staying out with the dry cattle and watching the sky for rain. They had a lot of wormy steers in fly time.

But most of them, too, had young and growing children. They tried schools on the ranches, which were not only expensive but never very successful: cowboys were always marrying the schoolmarms. The only solution was to build a town house in Ozona and leave the wife and kids there eight months of the year, while the rancher kept batch. In this way a rather curious but strong matriarchy developed, and it has a very strong influence even today. The women ran the town houses, sent the kids to school, organized the W.C.T.U. and other groups, and became the civic conscience. The women decided the saloons would have to go, eventually. They were already insisting they didn't want a railroad, with its smoke and noise, its riffraff and "tailenders."

Women were a scarce and honored commodity on all the frontier, but down in Texas the reverence accorded them was also mixed with Southern chivalry, and gallantry knew no bounds. Take, for instance, the cowboy who was getting a cup of coffee at a stage stand. The passengers had only a few minutes for refreshments while teams were being changed, and a lady was obviously distressed because her coffee was too hot to drink. The cowboy got on his feet, removed his Stetson, and bowed.

"Take mine, lady," he said. "It's already saucered and blowed!"

In Texas, what is called "the unwritten law" is still strong enough to clear a man in a murder case. Ozona women had no vote, of course, in those early days. But they pulled their husbands in from the ranches and told them how to mark their ballots. In prideful good humor, the husbands complied.

The women eventually cleaned up the town and shaped it more to their hearts' desire . . . and such was their cleverness, they let the men take all the credit for reform.

In 1890 the census showed only 194 people in all the sprawling county. By 1900 there were more than 1,500 on the rolls.

The First

Ten Years

4 Are the Hardest

It is ordered by the court that the sheriff be instructed to purchase two pairs of handcuffs and two pairs of leg irons, and one single handcuff with clip.

—MINUTES OF THE FIRST CROCKETT COUNTY
COMMISSIONERS' COURT, JULY, 1891

THE FOUNDING FATHERS had anticipated the three saloons and the tough element; they meant to have order, if not very much law. The County Commissioners assembled under the big live oak tree where Fayette Schwalbe had camped earlier. They met for two days while their saddle horses stamped restively and switched flies. A miasma of gnats buzzed in the shade, and there was little oratory. Mockingbirds sang in the top branches of the live oak, and the public windmill made a steady and reassuring sound. The court got a surprising number of things done.

It named a ranchman, John C. Perry, the county sheriff at a salary of $300 a year—a very modest stipend, considering the life expectancy of Western sheriffs of that era—and gave him collateral duties as tax collector and overseer of the waterworks, which consisted of the windmill, one tank, and a horse trough. It voted to spend all of $185 to construct both a courthouse and a jail. Judge Davidson very probably held his peace, and later, when a $621.57 lumber bill came in for the courthouse alone, the authorization was hastily increased. The first courthouse was a two-story frame structure with green venetian shutters; it became the elementary school after the turn of the century, when the stone courthouse was built.

The new town needed a builder, and this was provided right while the Commissioners were meeting under the live oak tree. Sam T. Smith, forty-five, lanky and redheaded, drove his wagon up to the horse trough, and young Judge Davidson went over to talk to him. Smith's family, including a pretty girl of school age named Alma, was in the wagon with a younger boy named Olney. Smith said he was a carpenter by trade. His horses had barely stopped slobbering water back into the trough before Judge Davidson had sold him a bill of goods, and the Commissioners' Court had voted him to membership on the first school board and commissioned him to erect a school building.

Sam Smith first saw to it that his family had a place to live. He built the first house in Ozona, among the fragrant cedar trees just up the hill north of the public windmill. He built many other houses in the next twenty years. In 1925, when he was seventy-nine, Ozona's first house caught fire, and Sam Smith, town builder, died in the blaze.

The people kept coming in while the residents of Emerald folded their tents and moved their few houses from the divide. Everybody was naturally land and cattle hungry, but some people already had cattle, like W. P. Hoover and J. W. Henderson; others already had both land and money, like Charles E. Davidson. There was no spectacular, stop-watch rush such as attended the opening of the Cherokee Strip in Oklahoma Territory and there was nothing of the epic grandeur that marked the Forty-Niners' trek across the Plains and the starvation winter at Donner Pass. But wagons came steadily westward, and herds of livestock raised dust clouds along the divides, leaving fences behind. It was a quieter sort of drama, more intimate and more friendly. Carpenters, blacksmiths, teamsters, cowboys, teachers, sheepherders, clerks, windmill men—anybody could get a job in Ozona.

Kids peered out from under the wagon tarps and speculated on where they were going. They asked the man on the wagon seat. At the end of a hot day, the man on the wagon seat spat tobacco juice into the road and said he reckoned they were going to the jumping-off place. And in the early nineties, when the wagons came down from the divide and around the hill-point, Ozona looked like that—like the jumping-off place. But by the time they got there people had been inescapably conditioned. Nothing else for eighty miles in any direction looked different: a lone windmill, a few raw frame houses with no shade trees, a sprawl of tented canvas, a straggle of wagon camps down the mesquite flat, and everybody coming up to the public windmill for water.

It was here and then that an inevitable way of life developed —one that was to bring at least mild conjecture and criticism of Ozona and Crockett County in much later years.

The people have been called "feudalistic." Instead of armorial bearings, they have cattle brands; instead of turreted Norman keeps, they have ranch houses and splendid "town houses." Instead of serfs, they have the Meskins . . . and so on.

This could well be, and it will be taken up later in detail. The first people came out of the South, after Reconstruction; they inherited the "feudalism" of the Southern plantations. A ranch was not too much different, and the rancher had to have help. The Meskins, who had started the ranch business in the first place, were already natural-born feudal serfs. They had worked for the *grandees* and *hidalgos* in the provinces of Coahuila and Chihuahua, where there was feudalism, indeed; they crossed the Rio Grande and gravitated westward with the spread of the cattle ranches from the Nueces to the Pecos.

And none of them wanted it any other way. The *patron* took care of them, and paid them regularly, and they worked for him loyally and well. The Cattle Brand Book of Crockett County could tell its own story of feudalism and heraldic devices; the history of eighty years has been burned into cowhide, and none of it is bad except where a man—always an American, and not a Meskin—used a running iron.

The Meskins were not that ambitious to get ahead.

Newcomers to Ozona unhitched their teams and took a look at the buildings springing up around the town square, and the mulberry trees greening in the little park. They decided to stay for a while. It was a long haul to any other place, and, besides, there was something in the atmosphere that went beyond the ozone for which the town had been named: there was a promise, electric and vital.

They sought out the old-timers, which meant anybody who had been in the country for ten years or so, like W. P. Hoover, and asked questions. In that ten years the old-timers had developed a drawling insufficiency of words. They had the peculiar comicotragic sense of humor that still has scholars wondering whether Western wit was born of optimism or despair. Their speech was seldom and sparse, and it ran either to extremes of exaggeration or to wonderful nadirs of understatement.

A visitor asked a Crockett County ranchman how long he had been on the Pecos. The rancher—and this could very well have been W. P. Hoover—squinted up at the sky.

"See that sun up yonder?" he asked solemnly. "Well . . . when I first come out here that sun wasn't no bigger than a saucer."

The Bar S, owned by Blackstone & Slaughter, was a very large ranch northwest of Ozona, up toward the Big Lake and Stiles country. Somebody asked a cowboy working for the outfit how many horses they had wearing the Bar S brand. He said he didn't rightly know.

"Would you say you've got forty?" the curious one pursued.

At that, the cowboy stiffened. *"Forty!"* he exclaimed. "Hell, we've got that many *white* ones!"

And many a Crockett County sheepman, fifty years ago, never bothered to tally his flock except on very special occasions. He knew he had, say, thirty black sheep. These were easy to count at any time. If all thirty were present, he could be pretty sure the rest were there.

II

Looking back, it is very obvious that the Ozona country was settled by men of character. Most of them were quietly religious, and all but one or two were of the Protestant faith. This created another gap between them and the Roman Catholic Meskins: there was a time in Texas when the word "Catholic" hinted deep, dark plots, and of all things, had even an unholy sound. Nobody flaunted his beliefs, and there remained an earthiness about even the hellfire-slinging evangelistic services. They tell of a ranchman who finally interrupted a long and fervent prayer for rain by saying, "Parson, it just won't do no good to ask for rain as long as the wind is in the west." And another man broke in on a prayer expressing the hope that people in the East would open their hearts and send a drought-stricken Texas area "barrels of flour, barrels of corn meal, barrels of salt pork and lard and coffee and molasses. Barrels," the preacher went on, "of salt and barrels of pepper—" and then a ranchman rose, cleared his throat, and said, "Hell, parson, that's just too damned much pepper!"

The new community's first decade may have been the Gay Nineties in New York and St. Louis, in New Orleans and other gaslighted places, but in West Texas it was the era of the coal-oil lantern. A woman could put on her best dress, with a bustle and a close-fitting waist and voluminous yards of skirt that had to be held up from the ground—and still have very few places to go. San Angelo was becoming the cowboys' capital, and something of a metropolis, but going to San Angelo meant three or four days on the road, each way, and camping out every night. There were no public accommodations in all the eighty-five miles: it would be several years before stage lines were established. Crockett County did not yet have enough people to support any kind of passenger service, nor enough business houses to bring commercial travelers.

But life wasn't exactly dull in Ozona. Once in a while the churches brought in "camp meeting" evangelists. They scared hell out of cowboys who attended the revivals because there was nothing else to do and because they might "spark" some of the local belles. The cowboys led better lives thereafter—until their horses threw them, or a wormy steer got on the prod, or a windmill quit pumping. For social life the town had frequent Shirtsleeve dances in the courthouse, with one or two fiddles and a melodious Meskin guitar.

"And, my, how those cowboys could dance!" a retired schoolteacher wrote me from Dallas. She should know: the county school board sent her and another young girl packing because they went to the courthouse dances. The community's mores were that strict; a teacher wasn't supposed to have any fun. Methodists allowed dancing, but the Baptists did not, and regularly suspended members of the congregation for "dancing out of the church." Saturday night dances meant that the barbershop was crowded all day. Haircuts were 25 cents, shaves 15 cents, baths 25 cents and shines—with or without spurs—10 cents. Cowboys on the dance floor often wore spurs, but took care to press a silk handkerchief against their partner's back so as not to stain her gown with perspiration. After the works in the barbershop, they smelled of pomade and bay rum and cologne. They danced to "La Paloma," to "After the Ball" and "Sally Good'un," and a little later to "A Hot Time in the Old Town Tonight" . . . "Put Your Little Foot Right There" . . . "Everybody's Doing It. Doing What? Turkey Trot." Then came "Rainbow," and finally a very wicked tune called "Dardanella."

They went down into the mesquite flat and measured off a

quarter of a mile, and raced their cowponies, which were short-coupled and very fast for that distance: in doing this, they helped originate quarter horse races and the quarter horse breed. Kids from town had great sport sneaking along the line of spectators' buggies and hacks and quirting the teams so that they ran away. And in the early nineties Black Jack Ketchum, the outlaw, went all around that part of the country cleaning up on a horse he and a partner owned. The partner posed as a trapper; the horse helped pull his wagon, and looked anything but fast, and there was a lack of communications—the pair had always moved on before word came to beware them. At that time Black Jack was more or less honestly employed as a cowboy west of the Pecos. In 1901, and after a few train robberies, they hanged him up in Clayton, New Mexico. He had already lost an arm shattered by a shotgun blast, but he helped them adjust the noose around his neck and urged them to get on with it because he wanted to "have dinner in hell." When they sprung the trap, Black Jack Ketchum's head was jerked from his body and had to be sewed on again before they buried him.

Outlaws like Black Jack Ketchum came to Ozona, but were smart enough to realize that if they robbed the bank there they would have a long way to go, and some very quick-shooting citizens on their trail. It was a long time before any kind of crime reared its ugly head. The first grand jury returned seventeen indictments when District Court convened in Ozona on March 21, 1892, with the town less than a year old, but there were no shooting cases. Charles Green got five years for stealing a horse. Ben McMahan was charged with permitting his house to be used for gaming purposes—an indication that the *Kicker*'s editorial campaign was bearing fruit—and one ranchman was had up for failing to dip sheep before he moved them, a serious offense in the days before Texas finally eliminated scabies and the cattle tick. There were also hints of rustling, called "moving livestock from its accustomed range."

The seventeenth and last case on the docket is worthy of notice. It alleged pistol carrying by a young man who had come to the area with J. W. Henderson's herd of cattle and was fast branching out on his own. His name was William E. West.

It does not seem to be of record whether young Bill West paid a fine or got the charge dismissed. At any rate, he was currently engaged in taming some very wild range south of Ozona, and nobody was going to tell him he couldn't go armed. In 1894 they had him up again, charged with "carrying a pistol, *formerly known as a sixshooter.*"

The italics are mine, to emphasize something significant to the historian and the sociologist. As any reader of the old wild West magazines knows, "sixshooter," "six-gun," "hog-leg," "smoke-pole" and "shootin'-iron" all bore a connotation of wildness and lawlessness. "Pistol" was a tamer, more conservative word.

Ozona was becoming more and more conservative. Bill West, who stood six feet two, was becoming a very substantial citizen, with or without a gun. He registered his A Wineglass brand and made it famous, and on St. Valentine's Day, 1897, he married pretty Alma Smith—the first graduate of Ozona High School, and the daughter of carpenter Sam Smith. The *Kicker* devoted more than a column to the wedding.

III

Some local wit composed a limerick. It was too clean to rank with the classics collected and published by Norman Douglas, but at least it had some of the irreverence required of all good limericks:

> *This is the County of David Crockett,*
> *Who carried a pistol in every pocket;*
> *He drank so much booze*
> *That it rotted his shoes . . .*
> *But his name's in the District Court docket.*

In sober fact, while there may have been considerable pistol toting, there was little enough shooting except on the part of

Ozona citizens who vied with each other to be the first to an-
nounce New Year's Day and the Fourth of July—by stepping
out into the yard at the streak of dawn and emptying a sixshooter into the air. And Sam Smith's small boy, Olney, was
so enamored of owning a gun that he allegedly stole one from
a neighbor. The weapon was restored, the punishment was
private. But from that day onward the name Olney was forgotten, and he grew up with the name "Sixshooter" Smith.

A considerable part of Ozona's citizens had already begun
leading double lives. These were the ranch owners, who had to
maintain homes in town if they were going to send their children to school, and also had to maintain ranch headquarters
as far as forty or fifty miles away. Life still actually centered
on the ranches, and it was lonely indeed. Anybody who happened by was welcome to eat supper and spend the night: he
could add a little to the conversation. Talk was about all there
was. In West Texas few ranches ever had "bunkhouses" such
as have been described in stories about the big outfits in Montana and Wyoming: the weather was never very severe, and
every cowboy came with his own tarp and bedroll and saddle.
They spread the bedrolls on the gallery or in the yard, or beside
the chuck wagon. They might have a game of dominoes by
lantern light, but mostly they went to bed with the chickens—
and hoped they wouldn't have to get up during the night to
fight a stampede.

There were still no fences. Cowboys rode, every day, around
the limits of the range, turning back stock that might be straying, keeping the brands from mixing. Spring and fall roundups
were often joint affairs, conducted by two or more ranches.
Daily work was tedious: every cowboy carried a bottle of worm
medicine slung from the horn of his saddle, and roped and
doctored wormy cattle. They rode daily by the waterholes, in
dry weather, and nearly always found one or more "pore" cows
that had bogged down in the crusted, sun-cracked mud, at the
edges. Sometimes it took an hour or more to extricate one such

unfortunate, and there was an art to the work that went beyond using a rope. Cows get up hindquarters first, as opposed to horses. If a bogged cow suddenly decided to exert a little effort on her own behalf, the cowboys had to be there, dismounted, to seize her by the tail and pull mightily.

It was hot, discouraging work, but it was not as bad as building fences, when the barbed wire came in, and maybe it wasn't as bad as having to pull the rods out of a 400-foot well, using the windmill tower for a derrick and a horse to walk back and forth all day while each individual rod was uncoupled until the last one—the one with the valve—was brought up. Sometimes this chore was done while hundreds of thirsty cattle milled around the tank or trough, bawling for the water that wasn't there.

The cowboy's work wasn't all riding and roping, but at least he did get into the saddle, with the wind in his face, and feel more of a man. This is something very ancient in our heritage: it goes back to knighthood and the tournaments and jousting lists, to the Crusades and beyond. The horseman takes on additional stature; he is superior to the man who walks.

The cowboy, therefore, felt superior to the lowly sheepherder, who was most often a Meskin to begin with and who, God knows, had many troubles of his own. Before the days of "wolfproof" or woven-net wire fences—before the predators had been trapped out of the pastures—a sheepherder literally had to stay out with his flock. Coyotes and lobo wolves got him up at night; eagles and buzzards preyed on lambs in the daytime—buzzards are supposed to be scavengers, but in West Texas they learned that they could pick the eyes out of young lambs and then pull them down. Rattlesnakes bit sheep on the mouth, so that they could not forage because of the swelling; they died and left dogie, or "Sancho," lambs that had to be hand-raised. A herder was fortunate if he could skin a dead lamb and tie the hide on a Sancho, so that the dead lamb's mother would adopt the orphan.

There was dipping and shearing—both hot, hard, seasonal work—and never an end to it. Sheep always come up with surprise problems. They are not only the most witless of creatures, governed only by the herd instinct—a solitary sheep is always a sick one—but they all have a built-in death wish and will literally huddle and die in the face of danger.

Where was the storied romance in being a cowboy? Where the poetry of the shepherd, piping over the lea? There actually was none, and many a West Texas lad—myself included—found this out the hard way. If your family owned the land, an apprenticeship at cowpunching or sheepherding was eminently worthwhile; if you were working for wages, other professions had distinct advantages. During the nineties, of course, when there was still land to be had, a man could take his wages in cattle or sheep, and after a few years have his own brand. But those few years required sacrifice and hard work, and there was none of the romance of the TV westerns. In fact, any cowboy who rode his horse as they ride in Hollywood would have been very promptly fired.

In the years after the turn of the century, and probably after Owen Wister's classic, *The Virginian,* had been published, a young man from Boston came to Ozona. He wanted, he said, to be a cowboy. He yearned so strongly to be a cowboy that he was willing to pay a rancher the going wages—$40 a month for a top hand—to teach him.

I remember the young man. He was tall, and strangely dark: all the Ozona people ran to blue eyes and red or brown hair. And of course the Boston accent was as bad as trying to understand a Meskin. But he fell into the hands of Bruce Drake, who conducted a cattle commission business in a fenced-off portion of the pool hall, and his education speedily began. A little group of fun-loving citizens took the young man some eight miles out on the divide, on Elam Dudley's ranch, that first night. They were going to have a snipe hunt, they said. They explained that the snipe was a bird something like a quail, and that it could be driven into a tow sack. They left the Bostonian literally holding the sack, and quietly returned to town.

He came in about sunup, weary but still passionately determined to be a cowboy. They had a badger fight, in which he pulled the "badger" out of a sack so the dogs could tangle with it. The badger turned out to be a chamber pot. They inveigled him into a game of poker, had the game raided, and saw to it that he spent the night in jail.

Maybe he was writing a book. He loved all this—it was local color. If nothing else, he was a good sport.

They took him out on the Weaver ranch, only a few miles from town, and told him to cook a pot of beans while they went out into the horse trap and brought in the horses. He asked how many beans, and they told him, "Oh, enough for a tin cup of beans apiece." After they had gone, he measured six or seven cups of *frijole* beans, dry, and set them cooking in a molasses bucket with a stick-tight lid. He did not perforate the lid.

The others returned with the horses just in time to hear a small explosion of steam, and to find half-cooked beans plastered to the rafters and the walls.

In Texas it has always been important to know "Are you laughing with me, or at me?" The Bostonian decided they were laughing with him, and there was no fight. He went back to the home of the bean and the cod soon after that, and never did become a cowboy. Probably he had been disillusioned.

But that story and others made the real cowboys roll and howl with mirth. It brought chuckles from the women who spent months at a time on the ranches and never saw a new face or heard another woman's voice.

Stories were even better if they were about somebody in Ozona—somebody everyone knew. Like Nate Baker.

Nate Baker was one of three brothers—Pete and "Hen" and Nate. He lived in a dirt-floored shack in a little canyon north of town, with his wife and an undetermined number of progeny. He had yellow hair and a reddish beard, and wore patched clothes, but was always scrupulously clean. His soft, twangy nasal drawl suggested Cockney, but I am sure it came from the Elizabethans who settled in the Carolina-Tennessee mountains. His talk combined all the gifts of exaggeration and understatement with a rich, chili-pepper flavoring of border Meskin.

"Say, Floyd," he would ask my brother, "have you seen my old *caballo* horse going down the *camino* road with a *riata* rope around his *pescuezo* neck? He's blind in one eye and can't see out of the other, and he's branded a Busted Spider on the gittin'-up side."

If this was the same horse Claude Russell remembers that Nate rode on an NH roundup, it was more spirited than Nate's description indicated. He sprang to his saddle one morning and dug in his spurs—forgetting that the horse was still tied to a stake pin, for grazing. At the end of the long rope, the horse stopped abruptly, but the rider did not.

Nate's small son, Troy, slowly walked up to where his father lay moaning on the sun-baked ground of the NH divide.

"Paw," Troy warned solemnly, "doin' things like that is plumb dangerous."

They had a saying that, in Texas, everything bites you, throws you, hooks you or falls on you. And Nate's brother Hen was producing a legend or two himself.

Out on another roundup, Hen had a falling out with a fellow cowboy.

"Tomorrow mornin' at sunup," he said, "I'm jist goin' to crawl that man's frame and beat the hell out of him!"

Nobody saw Hen until noon the next day. When they did, he was pretty badly battered, and they asked him what had happened.

"Well, you know I told you last night that at sunup this mornin' I was goin' to beat the hell out of that feller," he said. "Well, you know what happened? It took me until eleven o'clock."

And the Skies

Are Not Cloudy

5 All Day

If it rains in Texas, in September, it don't make a damn who's in the White House.

—OLD TEXAS SAYING

SEPTEMBER RAIN means greened-up pastures, and juicy calf ribs in the spring. But Ozona ranchmen were not long in discovering that many a September is hot and dry, that the annual precipitation in Crockett County averages just a fraction over sixteen inches, and that it is a long way to water in any direction—especially down. The first comers were quick to acquire the few dependable waterholes, such as Howard's Well and Escondido—both historic overnight camping places on the old San Antonio-Chihuahua Trail. The whole land is tilted southwestward, and water runs off it with flash-flood speed. What stayed behind, in Gurley or Johnson Draws, was soon "too thick to swallow and too thin to chew," and cowboys forced to drink out of cowtracks in the mud quickly developed the habit of straining the water through their teeth. They could have understood the wariness of the late Gene Fowler, who all his life would never drink to the bottom of any glass because, when he was a boy in the Rockies, "there was always some sort of a bug surprise at the bottom."

Well drillers and windmills saved the day, and the nineties in the Ozona country might well be called the Windmill Era. It seems rather strange and a little sad that no literature has ever really given the well driller and the windmill man their due. I do not know of a man of either breed who ever got rich, although they helped others to riches. The drillers were a peripatetic sort, always moving westward with the frontier; they might be compared with Johnny Appleseed, on an earlier and more fruitful border. Some of the windmill men stayed, or grew up to practice their trade . . . usually one or two to an entire county. But the time came when a single large ranch had a half dozen or more windmills and could afford to hire its own full-time windmill man. Cowboys were sometimes forced to learn a new skill.

A ranch hand might curse the windmill for its rhythmic creaking and rattling at night, but it was not long before this became a sort of lullaby, and if the noise suddenly stopped due to a breakdown he would sit upright in his bed tarp, knowing that about sunup he would have to be up on the platform, perhaps in a freezing wind, trying to fix the dadblamed thing. Until later models came out with a self-oiling device, windmills had to be greased at appallingly short intervals, and you could always tell a windmill man from afar by the spatter of oil that inevitably dripped on his hat and jumper when he went back down the ladder after finishing a greasing job. Still, there was pride in being an all-around ranch hand. A popular boast came into being, and legend puts it in the mouth of that grand old Texan, John Nance ("Cactus Jack") Garner, who is reputed to have lost his temper with labor leader John L. Lewis and said: "I'm a drinker, a fighter, a wild horse rider, AND a pretty good windmill man . . . and if you'll step out behind the Capitol, I'll beat hell out of you!"

The well Joe Moore drilled in 1885, on land that later became Judge Charles E. Davidson's ranch, seems to have been the first; the E. M. Powell well on the Ozona townsite probably was the second, but from then on through the turn of the century and for long afterward well drillers were exceedingly active. Some used steam drills; others had rigs powered by horses walking in a circle, with water that had to be hauled a long way being poured into the hole at intervals to soften the earth and hasten the progress. Some wells struck "blue mud"—a sure sign, in those days, of a "dry hole"—and the rig would be moved to a new location. The depth might be a hundred feet, two hundred, or four hundred, before the long bailing bucket with a valve in its bottom brought up water. When this sloshed out on the trampled grass, the liquid sound was music, the sight was answer to a prayer.

Having struck water, the ranch owner would then either take his own wagons to the Findlater Hardware Company or another dealer in San Angelo, or would order his windmill and pipe brought down by a freighter. Almost invariably, the tail fans bore the brand names of Eclipse, Sampson, or Aermotor. The Eclipse had a huge, slatted wooden wheel and tail fin, and required a considerable breeze. It would, in the memory of ranchman Ernest Dunlap, "bring up water with every turn of that big wheel—and then not run again until next March." But whatever brand it was, the new windmill worked its magic deep in the earth, day and night, to bring a thin stream of bright water fluting from the lead pipe and splashing into some sort of storage reservoir—a dirt tank scraped out of the ground, a circular stone and cement tank, or a taller one made of galvanized iron. The perhaps apocryphal cowboy who swore he could drink water faster than the new mill could pump it was talking through his Stetson: given time, with the incessant wind, and the tank would be brimming over.

There was no assurance of getting *good* water. Old-timers insisted that the Pecos River was so alkaline a kildee only had to fly across it to get the diarrhea, and the subterranean water was often even more strongly mineral—usually sulphurous. Ranchmen theorized that sulphur water most often came from wells drilled in the mesquite flats. Besides, a windmill on a divide or hillpoint got more breeze. But many of these pumped sulphur water too—some of it smelling uncomfortably like rotten eggs. Nobody ever bothered to bottle this for medicinal use, although not far away on the South Concho River near Christoval, a health resort was springing up around a series of sulphur springs, and small boys who swam in ranch tanks found that sulphur water very quickly healed skinned shins and stubbed toes.

The George Harrell ranch south of Ozona had only sulphur water for a long time. It made wretched coffee, shriveled the *frijole* beans, and formed black sediment in the pipes and troughs. Then Mr. Harrell's only son, R. A. (Alvin), went off to the University of Texas and came back with a degree.

Mr. Harrell, a progressive man, was eager for his son to take over and put his learning to work along scientific lines. There were advancements in livestock breeding, in range management, and in drenching sheep for stomach worms. He asked Alvin what was the first thing he intended to do.

After one is around sulphur water for a time one becomes accustomed to both the taste and the smell. But Alvin was newly home from Austin. He sniffed downwind from the well, and said, "I'm going to do something about this water!"

Mr. Harrell stepped back and waited for geological surveys and other scientific tests. There was none. Instead, Alvin went to Ozona and arranged for Tom Smith to "witch" for water with a pronged willow switch.

Tom Smith—an unlikely name for a necromancer—had been blacksmith and constable in Ozona from the earliest days. A very powerful man physically, he never carried a gun, and he set something of a record by never making an arrest. (This, much later, got him featured in Robert L. Ripley's *Believe It or Not*.) He simply heaved troublemakers out of public places and sent them home.

Now he walked across the mesquite flat at the Harrell ranch

with the willow fork held before him at chest level, something like a man walking in his sleep. George Harrell followed, shaking his head dubiously.

They went a long way through the tangled chaparral. About a mile from the ranch house, the willow dipped sharply in Tom's grasp. He scratched a mark on the hard ground with his boot heel, and said, "Drill right here."

They drilled, and struck abundant water, cold and sweet, which still supplies the ranch house and the stock in that pasture.

Mr. Harrell told the story for a long time. It plainly showed, he said, the advantages of a college education.

II

More people were coming in, more ranchmen were building town houses so their children could go to school. Organized county and unincorporated town were actually a single unit under the Commissioners' form of government, though each had individual problems. In the fall of 1892, when they were rising two years old, the town needed more water, the county needed roads, and both needed money.

That year Crockett County's taxable wealth was set at very nearly $2 million. But taxes were low: 25 cents on each $100 valuation, and 25 cents poll tax for each man. The County had been trying to rid the ranches of predators by paying bounties of $5 for each panther scalp, $2 for coyotes, and $1 for wildcats. Scalps came to the courthouse in such numbers that the building began to look like a hide factory, and the Commissioners had to retrench. They reduced the bounties by half, but added a $2.50 reward for lobo wolves.

Then they authorized the construction of three roads—east to Sonora, south to the several houses in a place called Juno, and northeast to the village of Knickerbocker. The Knickerbocker road was the most important. It would help Ozona people get to San Angelo.

Windmills necessarily played a part in the routing of the roads. Freight wagon outfits had been carrying barrels of water for their teams when the season was dry, but a man riding a saddle horse or driving a buggy could not do this. No ranchman objected to a traveler's watering a team at his windmill, but up toward Knickerbocker and San Angelo there were fences and pasture gates. Any traveler who left a pasture gate open was committing a cardinal sin.

Ozona's town water problems were slowly being solved. A. W. Mauldin, the surveyor and driller, set up a privately owned water system supplied by a windmill in his back yard, and ran pipe lines to the houses of citizens who could afford the monthly service charge. There are no records left to show how much this cost, but pipe was expensive and had to be freighted a long way. The trickle out of the faucet was precious. Many an Ozona kid had his Saturday night bath in a washtub, in water heated on the wood-burning kitchen stove . . . and used successively by older brothers and sisters before it came his turn.

The town, consciously or not, was following Davy Crockett's motto: "Be sure you are right, and then go ahead." Later in the decade it built a rock tank on the hill, large enough to hold 100,000 gallons of water, and several business houses on the square ran their own pipes to it. A real public utility, which would supply homes with water, electricity, and even ice, had to wait until after the turn of the century.

III

In the memory of certain old-timers—the writer included—no deep-throated roar of truck or automobile exhaust will ever be able to match the excitement of arrival or departure that attended the San Angelo stage in its horse-drawn days. There was an atmosphere of adventure about the whole enterprise, and the lure of far places; drummers (the word for traveling salesmen) rode the three-seated hack regularly, and sometimes fancy ladies, but it was told, disappointingly, that the fancy ladies from San Angelo's East Concho Street conducted themselves with the utmost decorum en route and did not even smoke a cigarette. It was a day, of course, when ladies dipped snuff, but any female who smoked was one of easy virtue.

The stage left Ozona at daylight, with the team fresh and flatulent; the driver was always an active young man who could turn the reins over to a passenger, jump down, open a gate, close it and mount again with a spinning front-wheel hub for his foothold. One of the early drivers carried an Army bugle. Ozona citizens, waiting after dark for the post office to open up again when the mail came, could hear the bugle all the way from Four Mile Hill.

Ozona was seven years old when the daily service was inaugurated by a man named Hightower in 1898. This meant that people in Ozona could subscribe to a daily newspaper— the San Angelo *Standard*—and get Spanish-American War news only twenty-four hours old. When it rained in West Texas, the *Standard* printed a large red rooster on its front page; when it rained *hard*, the rooster was turned upside down.

Stage drivers earned $30 a month. It helped when "Mammy" Kirkpatrick, a short, buxom and volatile lady who ran the Kirkpatrick Hotel, offered them free meals in Ozona. All they had to do in return was to direct travelers to her establishment.

By keeping the horses in a fast trot, the drivers covered the eighty-five miles to San Angelo in about eleven hours, changing teams four times—at High Lonesome, Shoeing Stand, Sherwood and Knickerbocker. There were windmills at each place. The names are not much more than a memory now, but Sherwood had enough live oaks along the South Concho River to convince a small boy from treeless Ozona that it had been named for Sherwood Forest. At Knickerbocker a fig tree grew green and luxuriant on the dirt tank dam—perhaps the only fig tree in many miles. High Lonesome was all that its name implied, a bleak and solitary place on the high divide. Shoeing

Stand was a service station created by the stage line, which required forty horses to keep its rolling stock moving. Twenty were being used each day—ten south and ten north—and twenty were in reserve at Shoeing Stand, where they rested from their labors on alternate days, and were shod and groomed. The line had three hacks—one in reserve, two on the road—which had been especially built and equipped with something new to West Texas—Timken roller bearings.

It cost Ozonans $5 to go to San Angelo, or $9 for a round trip. The American mania for speed was just as strong then as it is today, and every stage driver was out to hang up a record. He needed a number of factors: a good team, a dry road, a cool day without too much wind, and someone riding with him on the seat who could take the reins while he opened those pasture gates. A. A. Perry cut the time down to eight hours, one day, whipping up the horses for a whiskey drummer who very probably had been sampling his own wares, because he gave Perry a $20 tip. Frank Matchen was another fast driver; Ralph Watson was more conservative, and wound up later owning the line.

It remained for Walter Dunlap, now a prosperous rancher on the Pecos, to set the all-time speed record. He remembers the best teams; Sam and Prince, Jug and Tom, Broom and Henry, Crazy Jim and Goodeye, Pearl and Nellie, Morgan and Alexander, or Coyote and Van. One day he drew good teams all the way through.

"Crazy Jim and Goodeye were the best horses a man ever drove," Mr. Dunlap says. "The minute you let them go, they broke into a run and didn't slow down until you came to the next station. I had to open thirty-one gates between Ozona and San Angelo. There was a cowboy on the seat with me that day, and when we approached a gate I gave him the reins and then jumped off and ran ahead. He drove the stage through, and I boarded on the fly. We made the run in seven hours and fifteen minutes. But I remember times when the draws were up after a rain, and the trip took as much as fifteen hours."

But that was in 1905 or 1906, when Mr. Dunlap made his record run, and of course it couldn't hold a candle to what was happening in some other parts of the United States, where people in veils, dusters and goggles were really going speed crazy over automobiles. Ozona had never seen an automobile. It was not yet ready for one.

"We called the passengers 'patients,' " Mr. Dunlap went on. "I guess the long trip was hard on them, but at least it was safe. I remember a few thunderstorms that scared the horses, and then the best thing to do was to just let them run out across the divide until they were winded, and you could walk them back to the road. Must have scared the patients a little, when we did that. We used to see herds of antelope—maybe a hundred at a time—and sometimes I'd take a shot at a coyote with my six-shooter."

TV dramas notwithstanding, the Ozona stage was never robbed. Well, yes, there was a time when a certain driver had no passengers aboard but was carrying money. Not too brightly, he hit upon a scheme: he hid the money box near the road, shot some holes in the hack, and drove wildly into Ozona shouting that he had been robbed. The Ozona sheriff was not really impressed. They went back out to the scene of the alleged holdup, and the driver's story didn't hold together; they found the money, and he confessed it was all a hoax.

The wind blew free over the divides, and we were a profligate people in a profligate time: nobody suspected that there would come a day when the antelope were fewer and no coyote would show up to be shot at. Least of all was any idea that Crazy Jim, Goodeye, and Old Paint were on their way out.

Horse High,

Hog Tight

6 and Bull Strong

My apple trees will never get across
And eat the cones under his pines, I tell him.
He only says, "Good fences make good neighbors."
—ROBERT FROST

I F CROCKETT COUNTY RANCHMEN were too late to have
the romance—and hardships—of driving herds all the way up
the storied trails to Kansas or Wyoming or Montana, they still
had the experience in miniature: a trail drive to San Angelo,
where the first Santa Fe locomotive came puffing into town in
September, 1888, took ten or twelve days, and duplicated the
long haul to Dodge City in almost every way. It offered stam-
pedes, dry stretches, and everything but blanket Indians.

And the Old West lingered a lot longer over the rimrocks of
the Ozona country than it did in some other parts of the land.
There was, for example, the matter of barbed wire.

W. P. Hoover and most of the other early settlers had come
to the area to get away from barbed wire, and so did the people
who flocked into Crockett County in the well-drilling era, from
1883 until the middle of the next decade. They were open range
people, to a man, and still they needed no prophetic vision to
see that it would only be a matter of time before they would

have to start digging postholes. As early as 1882 the fabulous XIT ranch in the Panhandle was already beginning to build fence around its three million acres, and word drifted down to West Texas that it was buying fence staples in carload lots. The XIT was one of the "absentee ownership" outfits, controlled by a syndicate that had received the three million acres in return for building the new state capitol at Austin. It ran 160,000 cattle. It covered ten counties, and spawned a legend—untrue —that the XIT brand stood for "Ten in Texas."

Of course the XIT legends eventually filtered down to Ozona and made the local enterprises seem small. But in so far as a history of the livestock industry was concerned, the XIT turned out to be only a large flash in the pan. By 1901, when Crockett County ranchmen were really just getting started, the XIT was already disposing of its land. In the next decade it sold all of its livestock, and the wheat farmers began moving in. *Fin d'siècle.*

The fence and the plow killed the XIT. All along the cattle trails to Kansas, and beyond, trail drivers were running into fences, and plowed fields, and sod-roofed dugouts. The trails were dying, and railroads reached farther into the land.

There was a small stretch of barbed wire shining in the sun of the Pecos in the early eighties, but this, again, belonged to an outside owner. Some ten years before, the International & Great Northern Railroad had sold a piece of Pecos Canyon land to the Western Union Beef Company, which had headquarters at Fort Stockton. This outfit ran the 7D brand, and established a horse camp on Liveoak Creek. Their first fence in Crockett County was a horse trap, enclosing only a few sections.

Meanwhile, cattle strayed, drifted and mixed despite the line riders, and roundups had to be community affairs. They usually began early in April, as soon as the cattle had shed enough of their winter hair to make a brand recognizable at a respectable distance. There was small profit, and a lot of hard, dangerous work, in having to chase and rope and throw some walleyed longhorn cow for a closer examination as to whose iron she wore.

April was when the bloom was on the sage, and that was fine for song and story, but everybody was glad when the roundups were over. The country northward toward San Angelo had been stocked earlier, and it was terribly open and flat. Before fences came there were seasonal problems. Every winter had its northers, and some brought blizzards, with sleet or snow-laden wind howling down from the Panhandle. Cows turned their rumps to the blast and drifted south; they wound up in the Ozona country, where they found some shelter from the rim-rocked hills—and by that time the blizzard was usually over.

Now all that remained was to get them home again, before they ate all the Crockett County grass and maybe had brands slapped on any slick-eared heifers that had so far escaped the hot iron. And so Concho County cowboys had to saddle and ride south, instead of spending a cozy evening in McCloskey's famous Arc Light Saloon in San Angelo.

They came down into the Ozona country, whole crews of them, ready to cut and shoot if need be. But traditional hospitality demanded that local riders turn out and lend a hand before the invaders got all the grass.

So there were occasional roundups in the wintertime, too. People from the Concho or Midland or Sterling City fanned out all the way to Devil's River—cowboys, chuck wagons and remudas of spare horses. Local ranchmen agreed on a general overseer when the cattle had been gathered, and each ranch outfit drew numbers for the time it would be allowed to cut the gather for its own brands. An unbranded calf was always allowed to follow its mother—this was one of the most clear-cut laws of the range country. But when the unbranded calf was weaned it became a maverick.

Fortunes were made—and some in Crockett County were at least abetted—by the niceties of timing in this matter. One day there was an unweaned, unbranded calf. Next day the same animal was a maverick . . . and come-a-ti-yi-yippee-i-ya!

There was an old saying around Ozona, applied to a man who seemed to have done well. "He had a fast horse," they said, "and a long rope."

And after several of those hard winter roundups, even the most bitter enemy of barbed wire was forced to concede that maybe fences would be a good idea.

II

Still, it was not until 1898 that any sizable pasture in Crockett County was put under wire, and then the windmills had been around for more than ten years. Elam Dudley and J. B. Riley—whose land adjoined—decided to fence their lands east of Ozona in that year, which also saw the first stage line to San Angelo. Dudley, later a banker, had bought one section of what was probably railroad land at a dollar per acre. He filed on three more sections, and then leased the alternate sections—two from the state and six from the same E. M. Powell of Dallas who had given Ozona the tract for its courthouse and jail. This gave Mr. Dudley twelve sections, and later he acquired eight more. A ranch of nearly 13,000 acres was a modest holding in Crockett County at that time, but Mr. Dudley had some rather revolutionary ideas.

He wanted to replace his longhorns with purebred cattle. This was a chancy thing, because purebreds were highly susceptible to the cattle tick, while the old longhorns simply shook them off—to infest any pasture they passed through. The purebreds would have to be isolated in fenced, tick-free pastures. This meant a great deal of trouble, and most ranchmen were not yet ready to take such pains. But Elam Dudley had faith in what he wanted to do, and also was most fortunate in having a son-in-law, B. B. ("Ben") Ingham, who was vitally interested.

Ben Ingham's house in town soon became a laboratory for the study of the cattle tick. He had them everywhere, in boxes and cages; he studied their life cycle while he fed them on beef. There came a time when he was appointed tick inspector for the county. The title was no joke: the job, for a long time, was one of great responsibility.

Meanwhile, Elam Dudley fenced his pasture with four strands of barbed wire, strung tautly between cedar posts set about thirty feet apart, with staves attached to the wire but not placed in the ground, in between.

Fence was still a controversial thing. Elam Dudley hated barbed wire as much as anybody else, but he knew it had to come. There had been blood on the wire not far away, in Brown and Coleman and McCulloch counties, during the fence-cutting wars. In 1883 the editor of the Austin *Daily Statesman* commented that "Legislation with a little hemp in it" was needed. The San Angelo *Standard* of October 7, 1886, said: "Leather manufacturers are raising Cain about hides that come from sections where barbed wire fences are used. The defects cannot be discovered until after the hides are tanned."

Everybody in Crockett County—W. P. Hoover and J. W. Henderson, Bill West and Charles E. Davidson, J. W. Friend and S. E. Couch—had come, originally, to get away from fences. But now they had their land and had begun feeling possessive about it, and now the fence posts were marching inexorably across the divides and the mesquite flats and the rimrocked hills. And if you owned a windmill, why not put a fence around the pasture?

A fenced ranch could be operated with fewer cowboys or fewer sheepherders. The actual labor of fence construction seldom fell to the ranch owner himself; he bought the wire, and saw to it that the cedar posts were hauled from the cedar brakes on Howard Draw or the Pecos; the work was done by the same breed of men who drilled wells and put up windmills and repaired them, and built tanks—the people on the fringe of things, who never got rich. And in the long run most of the postholes dug in rocky ground were dug by Meskins.

There was another kind of man on the fringe of ranch opera-
tions, feeding on those bounties the county paid for the scalps of
predators. Professional trappers increased in number as ranch
owners paid them additional money either in salaries or in
bounties, on top of what the county allowed. In his first twenty
years on the Pecos, W. P. Hoover found himself always short of
saddle horses. He bought some good brood mares to raise his
own supply, but it was almost impossible to bring a colt to ma-
turity: they were being killed, in heartbreaking numbers by
panthers. And lobo wolves, equally capable of slaughtering
colts, calves and grown sheep, were increasing in number, supposedly coming down from the northern plains as those areas
were settled.

Barbed-wire fences, of course, were no deterrent to either
lobos or panthers. But a fenced pasture provided a fixed area
in which a trapper could work, until—as Jedediah Smith and
Kit Carson would have said—the canyon had been "trapped
out." The early-day Ozona trappers surely inherited the mantle
of the old mountain men, but they wore it in lesser ways among
the lesser hills, and had to stoop to such unromantic chores as
poisoning prairie dogs and ground squirrels and shooting jackrabbits. They found no beaver streams, tackled no grizzlies,
and made love to no Indian squaws when they came into town
with their plews, and most of them smelled strongly of polecat.
Skunk hides, shipped to Funsten Brothers at St. Louis, were a
profitable sideline—and he who skins a skunk lives with its
ghost for days.

"Uncle Nick" Wigzell was one of the most colorful and the
best remembered of the trappers. He came from England as a
lad, and went up the Trail to Kansas a few times while still in
his teens—shaping his legs for life to fit a saddle and curve
around the barrel of a cowpony. He was a small man, blue-eyed
and truculently forthright of speech. One summer day an Ozona
woman, considerably overweight and very sensitive about it,
met him on the street. "Isn't it hot today, Uncle Nick?" she

asked in friendly fashion. "No," said Uncle Nick, "it ain't hot on nobody but fat women like you."

Uncle Nick "trapped out" a lot of pastures, camping out for months at a time with his wagon. He manufactured his own wolf bait from a recipe that included urine—preferably from a bitch in heat—chopped up liver and "lights," garlic and asafetida, tightly corked in a bottle and buried for several weeks; he washed his traps with kerosene to remove any human scent. One evening when he was setting a double spring Number Four for wolves, on a ranch forty miles from Ozona, he reached behind him for a handful of leaves and dirt to sprinkle over the sheet of newspaper that covered the steel jaws—and thrust his hand against a large rattlesnake. The snake promptly bit him.

It was sundown, and there was nobody within miles. Uncle Nick broke every law that has ever been written for victims of snakebite. He lost his temper. He got very mad at the rattlesnake, and chased it over a half acre of ground until it was finally cornered in a pile of rocks. He dug into the rocks, killed the rattler, and cut off the rattles—fourteen and a button—as a souvenir. Then he went back to camp and tied a string around his wrist, because his hand was beginning to swell and throb.

After that, he had to go look for his horses. They had already been fed their evening morrals of oats and were not easily caught. Uncle Nick didn't get them hitched to the wagon until well after dark, and by then his whole right arm felt as if it was being burned by a red-hot poker. He climbed to the wagon seat and pointed the team toward the Ozona road; he sought solace in a jug of whiskey he had carried just in case of snakebite, and never remembered opening any gates.

The Wigzell wagon roared into Ozona some time next morning, and halted before the office of Dr. A. W. Clayton. Uncle Nick said, "Doc, I been snake-hole bit, and wasp-nest stung. Fix me up!"

Dr. Clayton said, "By George, Nick, it's a wonder you are still alive," and did what he could.

Uncle Nick Wigzell lived to be a very old man, nearly sightless but still mentally sharp. He chewed tobacco until his teeth were gone, and then took snuff. Even when he was almost blind, nobody could sell Uncle Nick "two-dot" Garret snuff—he insisted on feeling the bottom of the brown bottle, and finding three dots. The three-dot variety, he said, was stronger.

Nobody ever told him, either, that the snuff was all exactly the same, and that different bottle molds turned out containers that might have two or three dots on the bottom. He was set in his ways.

I saw him last in 1946. I was standing on the sidewalk talking to the postmaster, N. W. Graham, when Uncle Nick came along. Mr. Graham stopped him and said, "Uncle Nick, do you know who this is?"

Uncle Nick squinted at me across a gap of twenty-five years. "Well," he said after a minute, "he's one of the Bosworth boys."

Less Wild—
but Much More
7 Woolly

Wherever the foot of the sheep touches, the land turns to gold.
—SPANISH PROVERB

Men have been killed because sheep's upper lips are cleft.
—''FORTUNE'' MAGAZINE, NOVEMBER, 1935

THE GOLDEN TOUCH had begun to be quite plainly felt in Crockett County by 1890, but the manslaughter resulting from the ability of sheep to crop the grass shorter than cattle never was—that violence was left to other sections of the American West. Nobody got killed over sheep in the Ozona country, although there had been some hostility from cattlemen when the first flocks blatted their way into the unfenced ranges.

Cowboys up around San Angelo, where John Arden first brought sheep in 1877, were fond of riding their horses hell-for-leather through the herd, scattering sheep sky-west and crooked, but whether this was done under orders from the cattlemen or out of sheer exuberance at being alive, young, and mounted is not known. C. C. Doty drove 7,000 head of sheep into the eastern section of Crockett County in 1880, and had a little trouble with both cowboys and the last of the Indians. The Indians were probably only meat hunters; they stole his sheep by the light of the moon, just as they cut the backstraps from W. P. Hoover's cows. Three cattlemen rode up to Doty's camp, frowned at the sheep browsing as far as the eye could see, and told him to light a shuck within three days or suffer the consequences. Doty was still there, calmly tending his flock and making plans to drill a well, when the riders returned. He told them he liked the country and thought he would stay. Nothing else happened, except that in the reorganization of the area the Doty range became a part of Schleicher County.

S. E. Couch, Robert Massie and J. M. Shannon were pioneering with sheep west and northwest of Ozona. Couch and Shannon had difficulties. too. They decided to move a combined herd of sheep across the Pecos, and were warned by cowboys who rode for the big Western Union Beef Company not to cross the river. Shannon said, "We're going to cross it, all right," and he and Mr. Couch built a bridge.

The site was considerably upstream from where the Pecos enters its narrow, rock-walled canyon, and it was never a wide river. But the banks were steep and treacherous, and cowboys and cattle reportedly had been sucked down into its quicksands. Besides, sheep abhor getting wet.

The Western Union Beef Company riders went to the river at night, and hacked at the timbered bridge until it collapsed and floated downstream. But there was no other violence. Both Shannon and Couch had a great deal of patience. They got more lumber, threw up a new bridge, and moved their sheep across it before sundown.

Cattlemen and predators, however, were not the worst enemies of the pioneer sheepmen. Just when things were off to a thriving start for the woolgrowers, the weather and Grover Cleveland jointly conspired to deal the sheep industry an almost fatal blow. The years of 1892 and 1893 were so dry that West Texas sheep owners already faced the threat of bankruptcy. On top of the drought, President Cleveland abolished the tariff on wool. Duty-free wool came in a flood from New Zealand and Australia, and the price dropped from 18 cents a pound to 6½ cents, and then to 5 cents—and sheep were suddenly worth only a dollar a head.

Speculators were wiped out. Conversely, however, men like Couch and Shannon and Massie bought the dollar sheep, tightened their belts, and hung on. It finally rained, and McKinley —three years later—restored the protective wool tariff. Times were good again.

In the long run, the most lasting effect of the Cleveland policy was principally political. It made Republicans out of a good many Texas ranchmen—this in a state where the name had been synonymous with the hated "carpetbaggers" and Governor Jim Davis' black police during Reconstruction years.

II

Both cattle and sheep ranchers were doing substantial things like building town houses in Ozona, helping finance the construction of churches and schools, and planting mulberry trees in the town square, and then supplying antelope to run in the little fenced park. But nobody was putting on airs in the matter of speech or dress. No stranger in town would have been able to point to W. P. Hoover or Johnny Henderson and say for certain that they were cattlemen, or identify J. M. Shannon with sheep. Sheep dip and cattle dip looked the same when spattered on a workday Stetson, and windmill oil was ubiquitous. Everybody rode horses or drove wagons; nearly everybody took pride in wearing a good pair of shop-made boots.

For that matter, a stranger probably would have had a hard time distinguishing between the outward appearance of Johnny Henderson, owner of the 7N brand, and Nate Baker, who owned nothing but a wagon and team, and an engaging but rueful sense of humor.

They met one day on the street, and gave each other "hidy." Then they squatted on their bootheels on a shady stretch of wooden sidewalk and began to whittle.

"Nate," Johnny said, "you've been astealin' my wood."

Nate looked aggrieved. Johnny Henderson had acquired more and more land; he now was operating nearly a hundred thousand acres, and had put most of it under wire.

"Why, hell, Johnny!" Nate said. "You ain't got any call to say a thing like that!"

"Ain't any use denyin' it, Nate. Seen your wagon tracks. Seen your wagon loaded with cedar from over on Howard's Draw, out of my canyons. Know you been sellin' my wood around town."

"Now, Johnny—"

Johnny Henderson pointed his knife blade at Nate, but not with hostile intent. He said mildly, "I reckon you've got to steal wood somewhere, and I know you ain't the only man who's been astealin' it off my place. Now, I'll tell you what I'm agoin' to do, Nate—I'm agoin' to *give* you a canyon, over on Howard, where you can steal all the wood you want!"

Nate Baker brightened. "Honest, Johnny?" he asked.

"Yep, I sure am. I'm agivin' you that canyon on one condition. You can steal all the wood you want there, but you keep everybody else out. If I catch anybody else astealin' that wood, I'll have to take the canyon away from you."

They shook hands to conclude one of the most remarkable deals in the history of the West. Nate went his way rejoicing, and hitched his team. For several months he stole Johnny Henderson's wood with impunity, and sold it for $10 or $12 a load in Ozona, where firewood was exceedingly scarce.

Then he met the 7N owner again on the town square.

"Nate," Johnny said, shaking his head, "I reckon I'm agoin' to have to take that canyon away from you. You know what I said. Well, other people have been in there, astealin' wood."

"Now, Johnny, I been keepin' a mighty close watch on that canyon, and—"

"Not close enough, Nate. Seen their wagon tracks. Found where they cut my fence. They been in there, all right."

Nate sighed, knowing he had fallen from grace. He said,

"Well, hell-fire, Johnny—I never knowed that anybody but me was stealin' your wood! Why . . . if I'd seen anybody else stealin' your wood, I'd of upped with my thirty-thirty, and there wouldn't of been nothin' left of them but just some toenails and chittlin's!"

A stranger in Ozona would have noticed J. M. Shannon at once—and would have put him down as a $40 a month sheepherder and not the owner of one of the biggest sheep outfits in Texas.

"Old Shan"—they called him that more affectionately than in any disrespect—was a Louisianan who had wandered to Australia and New Zealand, where a man could hardly help learning about sheep. He sailed to Scotland from New Zealand, and met and married Miss Margaret Campbell in 1881, when he was thirty-three, and then brought her to Texas. He learned all about barbed-wire fence by helping enclose the gigantic XIT ranch. Then he herded sheep, became a champion shearer—there was money in shearing—bought sheep of his own, and found the cheap range he was looking for in Crockett County.

He hit the Ozona country at exactly the right time, and his success was spectacular—but not more so than Old Shan himself. A few good years, with lamb crops running more than eighty percent, and wool regaining its price, and he was rich. But he never dressed the part.

He sold his wool clips in San Angelo, which had become the ranch center of all West Texas, and his financial rating was well known there. One day while in that town he was standing on the corner of the famous Arc Light Saloon, wearing his customary patched overalls, run-down boots, and a flop-brimmed Stetson. A cowboy rode up, both dashing and thirsty. He dismounted and tossed Shannon his reins.

"Give you two bits to hold my horse for me, old-timer," he said.

The cowboy was cutting the alkali dust from his throat with

a second or third drink when a San Angelo banker happened along.

"Why, Mr. Shannon!" he exclaimed. "What are you doing?"

"Well," Old Shan said in his high-pitched voice, "I wasn't doing nothing. Just standing here, and a young feller rode up and said he'd give me two bits to hold his horse. Figured I might as well make two bits."

"Mr. Shannon," the banker said, shaking his head, "you're worth a million dollars, and you ought to dress like a millionaire!"

"Well, goodness, sonny!" said Old Shan. "Nearly everybody knows me down here, so I don't have to dress up."

They met some six months later at a livestock growers' convention in St. Louis, and Shannon's clothes were still not greatly improved. Again the banker reproved him.

"Goodness, sonny," Shannon said. "Nobody knows who I am up here, so I don't have to dress up."

Getting

a Little Learning

8 Is a Dangerous Thing

Professor Ellis Sparkman (long-time professor of Spanish at Baylor) recalls that it was the mean boys of Ozona who caused him to quit teaching in the public schools and go into college teaching. One April Fool's morning Mr. Sparkman went into his classroom to find a yearling calf which had been tied in the room all night. On another occasion the mischievous boys somehow managed to get a cow into the belfry of the school. . . . Mr. Sparkman wore himself out spanking young culprits.
—STOKER THESIS

At a date much too late for disciplinary action I could have told Professor Sparkman that it was my brother Floyd, Russell Dyer, Ernest Dunlap, and very probably Forest ("Bunk") Dudley and Vernon ("Pappy") Cox who got the cow into the belfry of the old two-story frame high school building. It did not require too much pulling and prodding to make her climb the stairs: she had climbed them on at least two previous occasions, and came to accept the ordeal with gusty and philosophical sighs. Professor Sparkman erred in not recording the brand she wore.

I was very small when this happened, but I was filled with admiration for such works, and was an avid reader of a book called *Peck's Bad Boy*, which came near being a best seller at the time. Getting the cow up the stairs fell far short of the engineering ability displayed in hoisting a buggy to the steep second-story roof. This was accomplished at least once at the same school by some mute, inglorious Goethals. Tying a dead polecat to the bell rope, on the other hand, was mere child's play—I could have done that, myself, if Mama had allowed me to run at large after dark.

And what else was there to do?

When the Bosworth family came to Ozona in 1907, it was still a marvel to be talked about when one listened to a graphophone that played scratchy records through an ornate morning-glory horn. The pool hall and domino parlor admitted no minors. Nobody yet had seen an automobile. The nearest thing to motion pictures was an infrequent and smoky magic lantern show at the courthouse: 25 cents for adults, 15 cents for children.

We sat through one of these. Colored slides went through the machine, and were combined—but not exactly synchronized—with Graphophone records playing the sad verses of Eugene Field:

> *Ay, faithful to Little Boy Blue they stand,*
> *   Each in the same old place,*
> *Awaiting the touch of a little hand,*
> *   The smile of a little face;*
> *And they wonder, as waiting the long years through*
> *   In the dust of that little chair,*
> *What has become of our Little Boy Blue,*
> *   Since he kissed them and put them there.*

The colored slides showed very plainly what happened to Little Boy Blue. He died. Mama enjoyed this show a great deal and bawled through the whole performance, and so did most of the other ladies present. It impressed me a lot, too. I felt that I would certainly let Mama down if I died, because I had no little lead soldiers or toy dogs such as had been pictured so vividly on the screen. In fact, I had no toys at all, except a Daisy air rifle and a homemade nigger-shooter. These were utilitarian, and were not likely to be left in the dust of a little chair.

But things were looking up. Home briefly from his ranch job, Dee promised me a whole dollar if I would go for a month without eating between meals.

Peanut butter either had not been invented or had not found its way westward. What I ate between meals were split biscuits spread with sugar and then sprinkled with water. I starved for three weeks, and nearly had it made. Then one day when I was playing with Sixshooter Smith's small son, Mrs. Smith came out of the house and gave us some ham and biscuits. We built a campfire and fried the ham—the first I had ever eaten—and I forgot all about my fast. Being too honest, I reported the lapse to Mama, and she said, "Well, you'll just have to start all over again."

Finally, I got the dollar. Mama said, "Well, now that you're starting to school, you need some shirtwaists. We'll take ninety cents to buy the material, and you can have a dime to buy something to play with. Go down to Soapy Smith's drugstore and ask them what they've got, for a dime, that little boys can play with."

This was one of the most terrifying and frustrating experiences in my whole life. The dime was hot in my hand. I needed guidance. I needed a shopping service, and there was none. What I wanted was a little iron dog that would be covered with funereal rust after I was gone.

I went to Soapy Smith's emporium on a hot afternoon and parroted Mama's words to a balding, perspiring clerk. It was not the toy season, and being limited to a dime, he had to climb several dusty shelves to find anything at all. He seized upon a gilt castiron miniature of the famous Flatiron Building in New York. I had no sales resistance, and I bought it.

When I got home I found that it really was a savings bank to receive other dimes. There was no way to play with it at all.

Not too long after this I read Benjamin Franklin's story of the penny whistle with a great deal of sympathy. Except that we made our whistles out of a stick of green wild walnut, and they cost nothing at all.

II

Christmastime in Ozona always saw a community Christmas tree in the courthouse—the biggest cedar they could find on the ranches—and somebody with a real "Ho! Ho!" voice, like Sam Cox, dressed as Santa Claus. Extreme care was taken to see that every child in town got some kind of present, even if it was only a sack of candy. Care also was exercised to see that one of the poorest little girls in town received the biggest and most beautiful doll available. The Bedell children qualified in every way. They were poor, they were towheaded and immensely freckled. They got two dolls, one Christmas, through some back-stage machinations on the part of Santa Claus, and everybody was happy. Because one of the little Bedell girls was named Pansy Sunshine and the other was formally called Dewdrop-on-the-Rose.

Kids like that need dolls, and a lot of them.

It was the intermediate group, later to be called teen-agers, that suffered. I had a good enough time, roaming the hills, hunting rabbits, learning to swim in the draw or in ranch tanks, trapping polecats, shooting everything I could with my trusty air rifle, and riding every Meskin burro I could catch—as training, of course, toward riding a real cowhorse as a cowboy.

But people Floyd's age suffered. There was no Boy Scout movement. There was nothing. Maybe once a month somebody had a party where they played games like Drop the Handkerchief. If they played Post Office in the teen-age circles, I never heard of it. Baseball occupied every afternoon, the year round. Floyd pitched for the town team when he was about sixteen, and Vernon Cox was the catcher. Baseball became their whole life, and they slipped out of the second-story windows at school one day during a study period, and were found playing catch in the school yard.

The third and fourth grades were even more lively. Hop Hoover was being whipped several times a day. He chewed tobacco, and spat with commendable dexterity into his inkwell

David Crockett: "Be sure you are right, then go ahead."

Bill West's family surrey.

OZONA IN THE PAST

Bill West and
Arthur Broome
at a chuck wagon.

Looking west, south of square. About 1915.

B. B. Ingham's old-time ranch house.

Bill West and Wayne, ready to ride the range.

Johnson Draw. The rains have been good.

A THIRSTY LAND

A hardy lamb crop on a West ranch.

Windmills, reservoirs, water troughs supply water where the wind blows free.

Sheep on the Jarrett ranch.

Shearing.

Tramping down wool.

Thoroughbred colts.

A GREAT LIVESTOCK COUNTRY

Aristocrats of the Range.

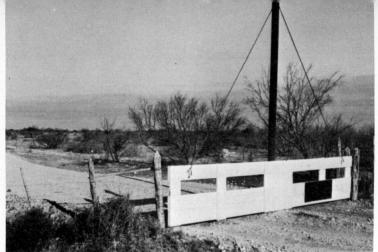

Mrs. Clay Adams

FENCED RANGES BROUGHT THE BUMP GATE

Painting by Clay Adams

R. A. Harrell, Jr., photo

NAME OF OWNER	PLACE OF RESIDENCE	MARKS	BRANDS	LOCATION OF BRAND	Date Registered Month	Day	Year	Date Re-recorded Month	Day	Year	REMARKS

Trained horses ready for the steer-roping contests.

THE RODEO—FUN AND SKILL

In the early Thirties the Ozona rodeo really packed them in.

Action!

No event is more hilarious than wild cow milking.

Armando Reina photo

WHEN IT RAINS IT POURS—The Disastrous Flood of 1954.

J. Troy Hickman photo

Charles E. Davidson, Jr.

R. A. Harrell

Ira Carson

Mrs. W. E. West

SOME OF OZONA'S
TOWN HOUSES

J. W. Henderson, Jr.

Mrs. Clay Adams

Roy Henderson

Mrs. Joe Davidson

Looking east to "Silk Stocking Street."

A MODERN TOWN OUT OF THE FRONTIER PAST

Ozona's only industrial plant manufactures stock feed.

"Biggest Little Town in the World."

when the teacher wasn't looking. It was only when Hop's penmanship exercises began to take on a rusty look, like something from the Dead Sea Scrolls, that he was brought to book. After that the teacher watched for any telltale bulge in his jaw. One day, prowling catlike down the aisle, she suddenly whirled on Hop, pried his mouth open, and found nothing.

"Whatcha tryin' to do?" Hop rumbled. "See how old I am?"

Ozona, in its second decade, had nothing much to offer the very young. Every kid yearned to grow up and go to the Shirtsleeve Balls at the courthouse or take part in the roundups—they hadn't yet begun to call them "rodeos." For the gay blades of around twenty, there were a number of social events: pound parties, basket parties, and moonlight picnics. The Ozona *Courier*—there were two weekly newspapers now—reported on one such event. "The entire evening," it said, "went as merry as a marriage bell."

The town had built its new courthouse of native stone, in 1902. Judge Davidson rammed this project through in his farsighted manner; it cost $30,000, and he called in an architect named Oscar Ruffini, from San Antonio. He fought with Ruffini, they say, for four days and nights, before finally convincing the architect that what he wanted could be built for that price. Native stone was cheap. They blasted out a quarry just behind what was to be the Bosworth house in Ozona, and built the courthouse on schedule. One of Judge Davidson's requirements was that the building be available for social events, and it was.

An edition of the *Kicker* carried a paid advertisement headed "Card of Thanks" which told its own lighthearted story of the times:

To those young ladies whose basket was overlooked and left in town Saturday night, we render our most heartfelt thanks. The chicken was good, the salad was fine and that pineapple and chocolate cake simply superb, to say nothing of the stuffed eggs, sandwiches daintily tied up in ribbon, and the other good things too

numerous to mention. If we have offended, we humbly ask forgive-
ness, but the temptation was greater than we could bear, and then
"Stolen sweets are always best." Again we thank you. Signed:
Monroe Baggett, Will Baggett, Early Baggett, Roger Dudley, Frank
Tanner, and other thieves.

Gay blades, indeed, the Baggett and Dudley boys, and they
became highly successful ranchmen. There is a Bright Baggett
in Ozona, and in those days it was said that Mr. E. B. Baggett,
Sr., roused his sons by calling out: "Eloe, wake up Bright and
Early!"

III

Christmas was really nothing compared to the Fourth of July.
Before the mulberry trees planted in the park were big enough
to provide shade, the town always erected brush arbors for the
Independence Day celebration, and about dawn several citizens
always stepped into their yards and emptied sixshooters into the
air by way of opening the fireworks and the festivities. Ranchmen who had to travel a whole day to come in for the event had
no thought of limiting the observance to the Fourth alone: it
was sometimes a three-day affair, and everything was free.
Ranchers donated beef steers for barbecue, merchants provided
"light bread" and a whole barrel of pickles; men on the com-
mittee cooked vast quantities of Texas style *frijole* beans, there
were gallons of scalding black coffee "strong enough to float a
horseshoe," and a barrel of ice-cold lemonade. After the saloons had been voted out, there was surprisingly little liquor in
evidence.

The *Kicker's* account of the celebration in 1901 was typical:

In the vast crowd, the faces of our county ranchmen and their
families were largely in evidence. Hon. Chas. E. Davidson arose
and read the Declaration of Independence, then introduced Mr.
Joe J. Sheppard, the silver-tongued orator from Arkansas . . . (who)
went on down, showing the wonderful development our glorious
republic had made since such glorious independence was gained.

Mr. Sheppard made an able effort and his speech was frequently interrupted by loud applause. It was a good oration, make no mistake.

Nobody minded the *Kicker's* purple prose or its belaboring the point. It was about this time that Crockett County and Ozona people began to have conscious pride in what they had done and were doing. They realized, all at once, that they had tamed a piece of frontier and were actually helping to mold the glorious republic Sheppard had extolled. And by the next year they were in the mood to build a new courthouse and begin civic expansion.

But on that Fourth of July the good food and good oratory were merely the start. The noonday meal was "dinner"—lunch was a snack you put in a bag—and the afternoon was the "evening." And these terms are still used in West Texas.

At 3:30 in the evening the knights of the ring and lance saddled their prancing bronchos, and the grown tournament riding took place. There were 15 riders; Doss Russell, the old veteran, taking first money, catching every ring, nine in number, at three runs. . . . The grand Shirtsleeve Ball closed the day's festivities.

The *Kicker* was still on its purple kick. The "knights" who took the field were a far cry from the Round Table, and there was no greensward splendid with swords. Sweating riders in brown ducking jackets, leather leggins and brush-scarred boots rode full gallop down the line and tried to spear small wire or metal hoops, suspended by thread, on a lance that resembled a fishing pole. It was tricky business. Such contests died out within the next three or four years. They had no practical aspects. Bronc riding, steer bulldogging, cattle roping—these were part of the cowboy's daily work, and competition in them had meaning.

On Thursday evening, July 5, the cattle roping was held. The *Kicker* soared to new journalistic heights, and mixed a few metaphors:

Bruce Drake was the first man to bat. A little brindle two year old was turned out on Boosie, which trotted off down the slope very unconcerned and looked back as much as to say "come on, if you think you can do business with me." Boosie went down after him on "Whiteman," taking down his rope very leisurely when someone from behind shouted, "Boosie, it's a long-ear, it's a maverick!" Then Boosie downed his lasso with lightning rapidity and had it on Brownie in a jiffy. Brownie went one way and Boosie took an opposite course—Brownie, Boosie and Whiteman all went to the ground together. Boosie got out from under Whiteman and went to the steer, but the latter was up like a flash—Boosie mounted his steed and again Brownie's feet turned to the dark blue sky, but this time the rope broke and no time was made.

The *Kicker* devoted a full three columns to this "roundup" and detailed the exploits of Wesley Westfall, Hugh Brown, "the young puncher from the head of Howard," Doc Everett, "the long hungry puncher from the lower Pecos," Addison Day "on old Dundasher," Sixshooter Smith, Ned and Harry Friend, and many others who were on a busman's holiday. This was their daily work, but they loved an audience.

Not very long afterward, it being the era of "Buffalo Bill" Cody, a much poorer man's version of a Wild West show pitched its tents in Ozona for a two-night stand—and made the unhappy discovery that it had come a little too far west. The townspeople and the cowboys who attended were kind enough —they only laughed heartily and jeered mildly at riding and roping feats most of them could have done better. Then the stellar attraction was trotted out. This was a humpbacked bull of fearsome mien—West Texas had not yet seen the Brahma breed. It was announced that for a fee of $5 anybody was welcome to try riding the bull. A successful ride of two minutes won a prize of $50: "Count it, ladies and gentlemen! Five ten-dollar bills, fifty dollars . . . half a hundred!"

Coots Curry, about nineteen, long and lanky, just happened to be sitting in the front row. Just happened, too, that he had a $5 bill in his pants pocket.

He jumped for this easy money. Everybody knew Coots. The whole audience cheered and applauded and did him a disservice. He got stage fright, and mounted the bull without checking the cinch strap on the saddle.

The horn blew. They turned the bull loose, and after two jumps the saddle turned under the animal's belly and Coots was in the dirt. The ringmaster was saying suavely that it was too bad. The show went on, and Coots went back to his seat and brooded.

He was there again the next night, and in a bit of community togetherness wonderful to contemplate, he had been staked to another $5 bill and was assured that nobody else would accept the challenge. He knew the cues, now, and was at the side of the bull before the ringmaster had finished making the announcement.

This time, however, Coots put his knee against the bull's flank and yanked on the girth like a dowager's maid heaving on a corset lace. The bull, caught in the middle of a laconic sigh, really felt the saddle for the first time.

Coots mounted, used his spurs, and rode the Brahma to what was locally known as a fare-thee-well. He collected his $50, a sum which very probably put the evening's performance in the red.

The owners of the show had planned to take it west of the Pecos, but now the itinerary was changed. It moved on to El-dorado, and put up advance notices in Sonora and Menard; it was slowly and instinctively heading eastward where audiences might be more appreciative. Coots Curry's saddle horse traveled faster than the wagons. He was on a ringside bench at Eldorado—and he was first in the ring.

The ringmaster cried foul, but the sheriff of Schleicher County was present, like a Solomon come to judgment: if the show wanted to go on, he said, Coots would ride. Coots did.

After the Eldorado experience, it was clear to Coots that a whole new career lay before him. He went on to Sonora, bought a new pair of boots, and talked to the sheriff of Sutton County beforehand. The sheriff regarded circus people as city slickers, anyway, and gladly offered protection. By this time it might have been argued that Coots had lost his amateur status, but after the Sonora ride the matter was beside the point. That $50 put the show out of business.

Coots came back to Ozona and resumed his $40 a month cowboy trade. There was always something of a flair to his riding and roping after that.

IV

The town had its two or three days of roundup excitement every summer, but in the minds of small boys that excitement blazed every day on any ranch, and they waited impatiently for the four-month school vacation when the lucky ones would go to the ranches. Bigger boys dropped out of school for two or three weeks around the 1st of April, to lend a hand with the real roundups, and many did not come back until the following September. Then they started in the same grade. After two years, they were usually promoted . . . but it took eight years to finish high school that way, and more than one graduating class consisted of only two or three girls.

Hop Hoover was one who didn't even wait until April. While still in grade school he developed what almost became a habit: he ran away in any season and walked the forty miles to the Hoover ranch, sleeping overnight on the hard divide ground, and negotiating the hike in two days. His father, W. P. Hoover, grimly and patiently brought him back to the halls of learning, after nobody knows what disciplinary action. But Mr. Hoover was well aware that you can lead a horse to water, and so on, and in the long run he gave up.

In our second year at Ozona I was excited, too. Dee had taken a job nearer town, on the Friend Horse Ranch, and there was a house we could live in—the first of several that might have been called summer places, if we had known the term. We owned not one inch of the land, but in my boyish fancy it was mine as far as I could see.

On the ranches I enjoyed a pastime which may have been forgotten in these days of shorthorn or dehorned cattle. Horns from dead cattle could be found in any pasture, long after wild animals had scattered the bones; youngsters playing cowboy could actually rope them while riding stickhorses. Branding irons could be made by bending the end of a piece of wire, and —wonder of wonders—when you brand a cowhorn it gives off an actual bellowing sound, just as a cow does in the branding pen.

I wonder how many youngsters of today have heard that.

When the Bloom

Is on

9 the Sage

He can rope a cow out of a brush patch so thick that a Hollywood cowboy couldn't crawl into it on his hands and knees. He can break
a horse for riding, doctor a wormy sheep, make a balky gasoline engine
pump water for thirsty cattle, tail up a winter poor cow, or punch a string
of postholes across a rocky ridge. He can make out with patched gear, sorry
mounts, and skimpy grub, and still get the job done. He can do it in freezing
weather or under a sun "hot enough to raise blisters on a boot heel." And
all the time, under any circumstances, he works with the thorough understanding that it's livestock that counts, not the cowhand.
— FRED GIPSON,
"COWHAND: THE STORY OF A WORKING COWBOY"

M Y BROTHERS DEE AND JAY were both cowhands like that
when we went to Ozona, and they practiced their trade on several ranches. Hollywood had not been heard of then, so that
comparison would have been invalid. But a few ranches had in-
ternal-combustion engines to be cranked and cussed on those
rare occasions when the wind lay down or a windmill failed
to work. The windmills still turned on Waterworks Hill, but
about four years before we reached Ozona Judge Davidson and
others had organized a $25,000 power and light company, and
the louder sound of a steady chugging began to replace the
creak and rattle of windmills as a signature sound for the town.

[88]

If we sat on the front gallery until 11:25 in the evening we could see lights blink all over Ozona as a signal to householders. Swains then had five minutes to say good night, or to anticipate any serendipities that might come with darkness; mothers had that long in which to put out the cat or light a sickroom lamp. We had no electricity, but when the lights went out around the town square we blew out the kerosene lamps and went to bed.

As I have said, some of our first summers were not spent in town. When Dee got a job working on the J. W. Friend & Sons' Horse Ranch, only about six miles east of Ozona, as soon as school was out and the purple sage was blooming, Mama and the three younger boys joined him there.

Even today I do not know exactly what it was that Dee did on the Horse Ranch, which was part of a broken chain of Friend landholdings. Its range probably had been overstocked a year or two before. When we went there to live for four months there was nothing on about ten sections of land—hill and divide and mesquite flat—but two or three saddle horses, a surly and malevolent bull that looked exactly like the animal on the tags of Bull Durham smoking tobacco, and later a milk cow with a calf two or three days old.

The cow had been supplied from some other Friend ranch, as part of the enticement for Dee to take the job, but it was Mama who did the milking after Floyd had roped and tied off the calf. By and large, Texas cowboys got the milk they needed out of cans put out by Borden's: there may have been a whole generation of cowpunchers who wouldn't have known that very special manual skill, having had no use for it.

At any rate, Mama milked the cow, and said for what seems now like an unconscionable period of time that the milk was no good. She said it was "beezley."

I have tried to run down the derivations of this word, which is not in any dictionary. I do find, however, that old Sam Johnson himself listed "biestings" as milk from a newly calved cow, and that later this was spelled "beestings." Beezley milk is supposed to be good only for dogs and cats—and, of course, new calves standing on their uncertain legs, butting at their mothers' bags, and silently imploring, "Let down! Let down!"

Just when we had the cow with the beezley milk we had a calf that had never known a mother, only it was three weeks before we found this out.

Dee's job seemed mostly having to do with keeping a windmill running for the sole benefit of that angry and frustrated bull, and with keeping fences in repair against damage that came from without. It was perhaps a caretaker's task, guarding the range until the grass came again. But cattle herds had the right of passage, and one night a herd of more than a thousand range cattle bedded down in the pasture adjoining the Horse Ranch, on their way to San Angelo and the railroad. It was a night when a thunderstorm played over the rimrocked hills, and there were spectacular blue and yellow flashes of lightning, and all the sultry tension that precedes a thunderstorm had been built up. The cows were "spooky." They needed only a spark to set them off. The animal heat generated by a herd of cattle encourages static electricity, and there have been times when blue fireballs come weirdly from nowhere, and jump from back to back in the herd, and the soothing songs of cowboys are drowned and lost in the growing murmur of fear. At such times the cattle ran, blindly and unreasoningly, with havoc and hell to pay.

When they ran on the Horse Ranch, they ran with a roar rivaling the thunder, and I stood on the front gallery and watched and heard them go by, splitting into two waves to pass the house. They took out three barbed-wire fences, which gave Dee weeks of repair work, and they left their dead at each barbed-wire barrier for Bert and me to skin at fifty cents a hide.

It was not until three weeks after that night of panic that I learned the story of smaller, individual tragedy. The old Durham bull had been roaming the pasture all this time, lamenting his lack of female companionship. He became especially vocal at sundown, when he lumbered up to the dirt tank to water: he complained, then, that the hand of man and all barbed-wire fences had been set against him. He had always been danger-ous, but now the sounds he made were those of pure annoy-ance. I went out one evening when the windmill was silhouetted against the western sky—after Mama had already milked the cow in the corral and had allowed the calf to feed—and I saw the bull in all his massive grandeur on the tank dam. He swung his horned head as if the gadflies were upon him. And butting against his masculine flanks in a vain search for nourishment was a shadow-thin red calf, not more than three weeks old.

I ran shouting to the house. The bull was on his way back to pasture by then, his shadow still following the only cow scent available. Dee was away somewhere; Floyd and Bert came with me, and Bert, barefoot, stepped over what looked like a cow-chip in the trail, and we had to stop to kill a big, coiled rattle-snake.

But we finally caught up with the dogie calf. He had obvi-ously been born on the night of the stampede, and had been separated from his mother for three weeks. I was very small, but I lifted him with ease and carried him back to the corral. He found one of my fingers, and began sucking on it vigorously, and he was mine alone from that thrilling instant.

And how had he survived? Maybe a little dew on the grass and weeds, and nothing else. He was a *range* calf, heir to the longhorns, and born to fight drought and chaparral, coyotes and lobo wolves, and any cowboy bent on branding him and marking his ears. He was tough.

Mama said too much food, too quickly, would kill him. We gave him a few spoonfuls of buttermilk, just because butter-milk was handy. I stayed up late with him that night and fed him again. I fed him at sunrise. After two days on controlled rations, we let him at a pan of buttermilk where he drank his fill.

I know, now, that many a Four-H boy and girl have raised their prize Four-H calves, and I am proud of them. But there was no Four-H then. If there had been, Bully might well have won a blue ribbon. The buttermilk did it. In spite of his poor start in life, he thrived and grew prodigiously. His voice changed. When I beat upon a tin dishpan as a signal that it was buttermilk time, he came chasing up through the horse trap with his tail high and his back humped, snorting and pitching.

And in the four months that he belonged to me, unbranded and still symbolizing the only herd of cattle I have ever owned, he escaped the ultimate fate of most bull calves. When we went back to Ozona at the end of the long summer, Bully was too promising an animal to be castrated: the Friends agreed he was breeding stock. They offered me $25 for him. Dee would not allow that to be paid. He was saying, in effect, that it was the livestock that counted, not the cowhand. Bully had been nurtured on milk from a cow wearing the Spanish Gourd brand, and was now eating Spanish Gourd grass. He was still a slick-ear, which actually made him a maverick. But, aside from the moral compunctions of claiming him, I realized sadly that I had no brand of my own. It cost $2.50 to register a brand.

So, there was no financial transaction. In September we loaded the wagon to go back to Ozona and school. I stepped outside and hammered the dishpan, and Bully came high-tailing it from the far corner of the horse trap. He nuzzled me and slobbered on my hand. I scratched him between his stubby horns and cried a little, and gave him a last ration of butter-milk. He always clenched the rim of the pan in his mouth and swigged the milk like a toper, and he never spilled a drop.

He followed the wagon down to the gate on the Ozona road and stood there watching and bawling until we were out of sight.

II

Anybody could see how Ozona was growing, not only in mate-rial fashion but in social and cultural ways. In that winter of

1908 a good many housewives were beginning to cook on New Perfection kerosene stoves, instead of using the familiar cast-iron wood stoves bearing the insigne "Buck Stove & Range Company." Wood was too scarce. Mama got a new kerosene stove that saved me a tremendous amount of work in ranging all over the hills and carrying small, dead scrub oak by the armful. She was afraid of the new stove, and Bert and I had to carry it out into the yard on occasion so it could explode without burning down the house. We watched at a safe distance, and were disappointed: there was never an explosion.

On the other hand, Monk Baker's mother—just down past the school from our house—blew out a coal-oil lamp one night, and it began to flicker and flame in the bowl below the wick. She opened the door and threw the lamp into the yard just in time. It was just in time, too, to spatter burning oil all over the family cat when the blast occurred in mid-air. The cat recovered, but thereafter became suspicious of any type of illumination.

For a little while the town had two weekly newspapers. Then Miss Clemmie Dodson of the *Courier* bought out the *Kicker,* and changed the name of the consolidated sheet to the *Optimist.* Progressive ladies of Ozona signed up for Lyceum programs in the courthouse. A Mexican circus came to town, and with my own eyes I saw a sleight-of-hand artist peel an orange and remove a lemon, peel the lemon and find an egg, crack the egg and extract a pecan, break the pecan and produce a sparkling diamond ring that must have been worth a sight of money. To this day, no one has ever explained this horticultural marvel, and when I began reading about Luther Burbank I waited for him to match it.

The town had a bank organized by local ranchmen, a saddle shop, two hotels, two drugstores and two doctors, two general stores and two groceries. It had approximately two hundred students in the three-school educational system. There was one livery stable, two wagon yards where you could spend the night for as little as two bits, and two blacksmith shops. It had the electric light plant throbbing on Waterworks Hill.

It also had two inventors who were doing their best to put the electric light plant, the livery stable and blacksmith shops and wagon yards out of business.

I remember one of these only by the name of "Mr. White," and I do not remember his connections. In an old barn off the southeast corner of the square, he was inventing perpetual motion—and any kid could see that he almost had it. He had mounted a buggy wheel on a horizontal axis and had replaced a two-spoke section of the rim with a rather heavy piece of timber. He chewed tobacco and spat on the dirt floor, and was very friendly: he would let any kid spin the wheel and listen to him talk about perpetual motion. The man who invented perpetual motion, he said, would free millions of wage slaves and solve all the problems of mankind. None of the small boys quite understood this, but they watched the buggy wheel, fascinated. It ran smoothly for a while, then slowed down. The added weight of the timber pulled it over the hump for eight or ten revolutions, and it was plain that Mr. White was on the right track. Then came a turn when the wheel fell back. Mr. White shook his head and said he guessed he had a little more work to do. But we all knew he was close.

Down at Blake Mauldin's blacksmith shop, the other inventor was coming even closer. He was a helper at the blacksmith's trade, spending his spare time and working nights on a buggy and a three-horsepower gasoline engine, and trying to wed the two.

Proprietors of the livery stable, the wagon yards and the two blacksmith shops should have been apprehensive at the young man's efforts. They were not, at all, but guffawed loudly instead. Somebody had dubbed the dark, silent young man "Simple Simon," and I don't think his real name was ever known. Word got around that he was harmless enough, but still not quite right in the head—and maybe some people had said this earlier about young Tom Edison.

Then, one afternoon, Simple Simon cranked the gasoline engine with explosions heard over half the town, and drove the buggy out of the shop. He piloted it noisily along Main Street, and a cheering squad gathered and followed him.

Dim Patrick, who had won a number of sock-footed races at the Fourth of July celebrations, offered to outrun the gas buggy. The race began, but the gasoline engine conked out in the mesquite flat near Johnson Draw, and the rig had to be towed back to the blacksmith shop by a horse. Nobody remembers what happened to it there. Simple Simon left town a few days afterward, and one wonders if Detroit ever sampled his wares.

But then the word went around that Simple Simon was not simple at all. It was just an act, somebody said. He was really a detective, after someone.

The Pinkerton legend was strong, in West Texas, and in those days. A real detective commanded the utmost in respect, and the very word, even unsupported, shone with an aura of romance and mystery. Any man with a little stage presence and enough money to pay tonight's hotel bill could have made out very well, in Texas, by just dropping a hint that he was a detective. And some of them did.

III

The automobile, which was to change Ozona's entire way of life, actually dawned on the community in the fall of 1907. It had been "invented," according to American standards, some fifteen years earlier—Charles E. Duryea is supposed to have tooled the first American-made car down the sedate and elm-shaded streets of Springfield, Massachusetts, on April 19, 1892 —when Ozona was less than a year old. But Springfield was a far piece from the sunburned high divides of the new ranch country, and nobody read about the event, down there—and nobody saw the handwriting on the livery stable door.

It was not until the fall of 1907, after we had come to Ozona, that a drummer named Ben Lemmons (who later sold a whole

freight car load of shoes to Pancho Villa for his barefoot ban-
didos) created a sensation by chugging up to Mammy Kirkpatrick's hotel in a chauffeur-driven Rambler—ancestor of the
Nash. He was trailed by a cheering squad yelling, "Get a horse!
Get *two* horses!" Several cowponies tied at a hitching rail took
alarm, but not nearly enough. The dust of Mr. Lemmons'
passage subsided in the town square; the excitement did not.
Within the next year, things began to happen.

Ralph Watson motorized the San Angelo stage line by paying $1,400 apiece for a span of two-cylinder, chain-driven,
side-winding Buicks, with carbide headlamps. These replaced
the horse-drawn hacks on the daily run and retired such fine
teams as Crazy Jim and Goodeye. But they also failed to make
money, even when the passenger fares were increased, and
there were times in rainy seasons when the line had to resort
to horse-drawn hacks. Mr. Watson, a former driver, tried his
best, and finally went back into the sheep business.

Crockett County was not quite ready for the automobile,
and it came late down there. The old-timers who had not
wanted a railroad were still joking about the T. H. & W., or
Two Horses and a Wagon—just as Ozona people say today that
the best of all ranch breeds is a mixture of Hereford and Oil
Well.

At any rate, Old Paint was not yet ready to give up.

It was not very long after this that Mama and I went to spend
another summer on another ranch—this time with Jay. He
was up on the high prairie country far north and west of Ozona,
and a long way from anywhere, working for the Bar S—the
big Blackstone & Slaughter outfit. We took the mail stage to
San Angelo as far as a new station called Barnhart, where the
railroad was building. Jay met us there with a wagon, and we
drove far into the night, and finally came to a small three-room
frame house that stood in a low valley of thick mesquite and
chaparral.

A small part of the mesquite flat had been cleared and

plowed. Wells had been drilled here, to find that water was plentiful and much nearer the surface. Jay had charge of the Bar S "farm," where alfalfa was grown to help feed livestock on one of the biggest ranches in the whole country. It was a flat place and must have been dreary in the wintertime, but that was a lush, green summer and the brush was full of cottontail rabbits and Mexican blue quail—and huge rattlesnakes.

Jay loaned me his .22 repeating rifle. I had never had anything more than a single shot and was greatly impressed until I saw the hump in the barrel.

"You'll have to shoot it a few times to get used to it," Jay said. "I got mad one day and slammed the barrel over a rock —that's why it's crooked. But you can learn how to shoot it."

I learned. You had to aim about six inches below and to the left of a target at forty feet, and you could hit the bull's-eye. It was all a matter of correcting sights to get the range. I could step out on the gallery any day and hear rattlesnakes singing down in the flat; I could go warily down a dozen cow trails winding through the mesquites, and kill two or three young cottontails and enough quail for our supper. And always, with them, three or four huge, deadly rattlers.

Rattlesnakes move with their commissary. When rabbits, birds and woodrats are plentiful, as they were on the Bar S, the rattlesnakes are everywhere. When woodrats are burned out and an epidemic kills off the cottontails, the snakes are gone.

This division of the Bar S had a windmill with a large, moss-grown dirt tank that was fine for swimming. I nailed a few boards together to make a raft, and then stepped a mast on it and hoisted a square of old tarpaulin. The wind drove me across the tank on this craft, and one of the Bar S cowboys went slack-jawed in wonder.

"Say!" he told Jay. "That kid brother of yours—he's shore smart! He ought to get himself a patent on that there thing! Why, he's an *inventor!*"

I have forgotten the cowboy's name. I heard a number of years later that he went overseas to fight the Germans in 1917, so I suppose that he learned wider horizons and realized that I had not discovered the principle of sail, after all.

That would have been as good as inventing perpetual motion.

The Hills
Were Higher
10 Then

Youth now flees on feathered foot.
—ROBERT LOUIS STEVENSON

By 1910 THE TOWN OF OZONA—like some of its knicker-bockered, barefoot junior citizens—had entered upon a period of adolescence. It was growing up leggy and unshorn, freckled and wild, braying with unseemly laughter after stumbling over its own feet. Anything could have happened during the first decade of the century, and it was well that people like Judge Charles E. Davidson were around to steer a safe course.

It was very strange in a newly opened area, but Crockett County suffered a loss in population. The census in 1900 had counted 1,591 inhabitants, or roughly one person for every two square miles of territory; in 1910, this had dropped to 1,296.

Civic pride was wounded. Somebody—no doubt an anti-Dry—blamed the vote that had thrown out the three saloons. But this was palpably absurd: the loss of three drinking emporiums certainly did not account for the removal of 300 people. The town itself was still growing slowly, with two or three new houses being built in a year, some years. Lima, or "Mexico," over across Gurley Draw and beyond the baseball diamond, was expanding too. Judge Davidson had already begun talking about the need for a new and modern consolidated school to take care of the more than two hundred pupils who attended at least half the year. And in their shock at discovering a population loss, residents of the county paid little attention to other vital statistics revealed by the census.

In 1910 cattle still showed a substantial increase and numbered 79,765 head on the county's ranches, representing a lot of money on the hoof. But it was the sheep count that was indicative of the future. Sheep went up to a total of 109,945. There were 4,000 horses, including jacks and mules—and it is unlikely that there were a hundred mules in the entire area. Apparently nobody counted the Mexican burros, which would have been a difficult task: every boy in Ozona was out catching them and riding them, when he could, with a rope or wire hackamore. There was neither pleasure nor transportation in this sport, but it made the Meskins extremely angry.

And there were 8,793 goats, all Angoras, that would bear watching. They could climb the steepest and most rocky hill, and find sustenance where a jackrabbit would starve. They bred prodigiously, and sheared a good crop of mohair, which was becoming valuable. The meat of a barbecued kid, turned over a slow and smoking mesquite fire and seasoned with chili peppers, was food fit for Olympus—and still is.

The loss in population must have taken place in the county itself rather than in Ozona. A. P. Hoover and S. E. Couch, Johnny Henderson and J. W. Friend and Bill West, the Owenses and Coateses and Baggetts, Harrells and Childresses, Kincaids and Phillipses and Davidsons—to name only a few of the major operators—were buying out the smaller ones who had rushed into the country to acquire a few sections of land or take small leases. To a man, the bigger ranchmen needed more grass. Anybody who had drifted in from the East figuring on doing dry-land farming was speedily disillusioned by dryness to a degree he had never encountered before. Up the

Pecos beyond the Crockett County line, they sold "irrigated" tracts—only to see the water sink into the sand, no matter how much was pumped, long before it could reach the end of a short row.

The economy was being stabilized. That was hard on the man who had enough money to acquire only, say, 2,000 acres of ground—but it would have been even harder upon him if he had tried making a living off the land.

A number of young men had drifted west to be cowboys, but they could become disillusioned, too, and either turn clerks or go to a railroad town and become brakemen. George Davis, who wound up as caretaker for the Ozona waterworks, needed only three months of life as a jolly cowboy to last him, he said, "for three thousand years." After George sold his saddle, completely disenchanted despite all the songs and a growing Western literature, he gave a moving account of his life on the range:

"I was just a youngster and had armed myself with a big sixshooter, and felt that I was ready to take on most anything that might come along. We worked for three months, and it rained nearly every day. My bed and clothes did not dry during the entire time. I caught a fine crop of body lice, and they dealt me fits.

"The boss told me when the herd started for Colorado City to return to the ranch. I had had enough of cowboy life to last me three thousand years. I told him I had quit, that I was going to town. . . . I bought me some new clothes, went out to a lake of water, laid my new clothes down on one side and went across and took off my old ones and plunged in. I landed on the bank where my new clothes were and dressed up and left my cowboy outfit on the opposite side. It may still be there for all I know. I have never returned to that life again."

It was not George Davis, but a successor in the waterworks job named Burchett who later felt called upon to defend the purity of Ozona's water. There were times in the old days when the water did have a slight mineral odor, which may have come from the tanks or the pipes. A character named George Edwards walked all the way up Waterworks Hill and said to Burchett, "I heared you had a dead horse in your tank."

Burchett promptly chased George Edwards all the way to the bottom of the hill, sprang upon him, and trounced him severely.

When this was over, George rose from the dirt road and said, mildly, "Hell, I never knowed you was mad!"

II

What I remember best about circa 1910 was that prior to that time a four-month vacation from school had seemed an unending summer idyll, whether we were on a ranch or not; all at once it was terribly short, and the authorities were conspiring to cut it to three months. And everything I knew was being demeaned and cut down in size and space: automobiles on the San Angelo stage run had whipped the time to six or seven hours, provided mesquite thorns did not puncture too many tires, and there were perhaps a dozen automobiles in Ozona itself, doing an average of fifteen miles an hour on the ranch roads—and that was something, compared to the time of a wagon team. The Kansas City, Mexico & Orient was building track down from San Angelo to Alpine. It would not touch Crockett County—which wanted and got no railroad—but it would come within thirty miles, at a whistle-stop called Barnhart. My brother Floyd was working as the Ozona telephone operator one day when his eyes grew large, and he said, "Say . . . I was just talking to Barnhart, and I heard a locomotive whistle, just as plain!"

The people tossed off the railroad lightly and joked about the T.H. & W., or Two Horses and a Wagon, but the automobiles were coming in, around 1910 and 1912. Bill West, who took wonderful care of his horses and had ridden some pretty bad ones, burned up two new air-cooled Franklins before he concluded that air cooling of that day might not be quite the thing in a high, dry country with so much ozone in the breeze. He bought a third car with a water-cooling system. That one burned up, too, in a short time. Nobody had reminded Mr. West that he would have to replenish the water supply, and probably he longed for simpler days when the West family had the only surrey, with the fringe on top, in town.

Having waited a long time for the automobile, Ozonans expected that when it came the auto would spring full-fledged from the brow of Detroit, and this was not necessarily so. The automobile was not yet thinking for itself. One ranchman's wife got out to open a pasture gate, and her bemused husband, worrying about the dry spell and the price of beef, drove ten dusty miles before he realized he had not taken her back aboard. Walter Dunlap—a champion driver on the old San Angelo horse-drawn stage—had a dozen gates to open and shut before he reached his ranch on the Pecos. His new car was not idling properly: every time he stopped, the engine died and had to be cranked into life again. Walter lost his patience with this, and hit upon the idea of not stopping at all. When he came to a gate, he circled in the mesquites while his dutiful wife jumped out and opened it. He circled on the other side until she had closed it and could make a Pony Express mount.

The only thing was that those automobile tracks in the brush were quite a mystery to other people who used the ranch road.

There were other motorcar adventures. But, meanwhile, there were also other faint stirrings of culture important to a small town and a small boy who happened to be growing up together.

Take, for instance, ice cream. Anybody who thinks ice cream and culture were not synonymous on the American scene had better go back and read about Dolly Madison, at the White House. Ice cream was a long time arriving at Ozona, because of a shortage of ice. When it did come, people blew on each spoonful, just as they did on hot soup.

Soapy Smith's drugstore began making ice cream twice a

week, and always vanilla. I found that if you arrived early on the scene with some strong-armed and willing partner, you could get the job turning the three-gallon freezer on the drugstore's back porch. The task began easily enough, and then Arthur Smith—the clerk who was going to be a doctor—prescribed more ice, and pounded it into the freezer until it took two men and a horse to turn. He insisted that the ice cream be frozen stiff. The other boy and I panted and struggled, sucked on pieces of ice, and swore we'd never take the job again. One of us had to sit on the freezer while the other turned the crank, and finally Arthur Smith had to sit on it with his superior weight. When the crank would not make another turn, we were paid: the ice cream that clung to the dasher was ours, plus any ten-cent drink at the soda fountain under the big whirring electric fan, plus a dime in cash for each of us.

Twenty cents a week was big money to a small boy in Ozona, circa 1911.

During all of the next year we witnessed the construction of Judge Davidson's consolidated school, and though we considered all schools in the same light with prisons, this was a diversion when the weather was too cold to go swimming. It was a two-story and basement building of native stone taken out of a quarry in the hill behind our house, and some detractors were already calling it "Davidson's Folly," because it was costing $100,000. The judge did not swerve from his purpose; he lived to see the day when the town was very little bigger, but needed four schools.

Swarming over the construction after working hours, small fry discovered two underground passages that were part of the ventilating system—wind blowing through the cupola at the top of the building pulled fresh air through the tunnels. It was quickly learned that a small boy could gain access to the building at midnight by lowering himself into the tunnels and crawling to the center of the basement, where the bell rope hung. Underground passages held a great deal of fascination at that time. I read and reread a book called *Julian Mortimer*, which, alas, can no longer be found. It was full of secret, underground passages.

III

Texans had an old saying. If a man had "heard the owl and seen the elephant," he was traveled—even sophisticated. He had maybe gone up the Trail with a herd of longhorn cattle.

I feel sorry for people who have seen elephants all their lives, so that they cannot remember the first one. An elephant deserves always to be regarded as exotic, and not commonplace, and there should not be too many days with elephants in them.

Ozona had never seen an elephant, that time when Ben Gilbert and I got the word that a real circus was coming to town. We played hooky from school and were down in the mesquite flat when the first wagons arrived. This circus was coming from the westward, which was not only strange but probably unprofitable: it hadn't had a showing in the whole 120 miles from Fort Stockton, and that meant at least three days.

Ben and I were speedily hired to work out the price of admission by helping put up the tent. Before the maintop could be hoisted, a sixty-foot piece of three-inch pipe was raised for the center pole, only it didn't stand, despite its guy-wires. Ben suddenly yelled, "Look out, Allie!" and I remember the frozen horror on the face of a circus boss who thought he was going to see me driven into the ground. I was utterly bewildered by the shouting, and simply took two steps and then halted.

The pipe slammed the earth exactly two steps away from where I now stood. Ben sat down weakly, and the circus boss shook for a little. Then Ben looked westward on the Sheffield road, and said, "Well, here come the elephants!"

All American boys ought to see their first elephants like that, and not in a zoo compound. These loomed as large as houses, their trunks swinging as they trudged along the dusty road a half mile distant. They had walked at least forty miles that day, building up an elephantine thirst all the way from Liveoak Creek to Ozona. And there was no S.P.C.A. anywhere around.

I said, "Yep—here they come!" as laconically as if elephants walked into town any old time, and we went on working to get that center pole up so it would stay. Then the circus boss handed us each a five-gallon can, showed us a big tub, and told us to start filling it with water. The nearest hydrant was up by the baseball diamond, a long way off, and I am sure those were the two driest elephants in captivity. The show that night was wonderful, even if the young clown also performed on the trapeze and played a cornet in what passed for the band. For weeks thereafter Ben and I planned to run away to join a circus and become clowns who doubled in brass. We rigged a trapeze under the big live oak below our house and "practiced" faithfully every evening. I got to where I could do twenty-two chin-ups.

Youth was fleeing on feathered foot, all right, but not nearly fast enough. Anybody could see that the bigger boys, like Floyd and Ernest Dunlap and Russell Dyer, were having much more fun. They had frying pans, cans of lard, salt and matches cached in at least a half dozen little canyons in the hills around Ozona—each hiding place being handy to somebody's henhouse. Their midnight feasts on fried chicken were known as "dead suppers," but they were lively affairs. The night they decided to steal some chickens from old "Dad" Hallcomb proved to be the most lively of all.

Russell Dyer, agile and adventurous, was usually the front man in all the gang's undertakings. He was first inside the Hallcomb henhouse, and was groping along the roost for a fat pullet when the chickens set up a terrible squalling.

The back door of the Hallcomb residence slammed as Dad Hallcomb came out to investigate. All the boys except Russell

Dyer got out of the henhouse and over the fence. Russell was too far inside. A huge shipping box for an upright piano stood against the rear wall, and he squirmed into this for conceal-ment. The chickens quieted, and Dad Hallcomb concluded that his approach had frightened away a coon or some other ma-rauder. He had forgotten to shut the henhouse door that eve-ning; now he closed it—and snapped a padlock on a stout chain. Then he went back to bed.

The other members of the gang came back to do what they could, which was nothing. It was a solidly built structure, boarded halfway up the front, and with heavy net wire nailed above that. Nobody had any wire-cutting tools—and, besides, the situation was hilariously funny. Ol' Russ was just going to have to stay there all night.

But the others had no intention of going to bed and missing the show in the morning, when Dad Hallcomb opened the door. They raided an easier hen roost, had their "dead supper," and rolled on the ground in their mirth. Daybreak found them con-cealed behind the Hallcomb fence and in the shrubbery, watching.

Roosters began crowing in the henhouse, and one of them had an unusually raucous voice. As the light grew stronger, the gang saw Russell Dyer being a showman and adventurer to the last. He was perched atop the piano box, between two Rhode Island Red roosters, flapping his elbows against his sides and crowing lustily.

Dad Hallcomb came out, stretching and yawning. He was a big, bald-headed man who had been a blacksmith, and he had a blacksmith's muscle. Ol' Russ was going to catch it now; Dad Hallcomb would probably pick him up by the scruff of the neck with one hand and warm the seat of his britches with the other. The hidden spectators could hardly wait.

Ol' Russ flapped his wings and crowed again. Dad Hallcomb neither smiled nor batted an eye. He went into the barn and got a pan of cracked corn. He was whistling softly to himself as he took the lock off the chain and opened the door. The chickens scurried out around him, and he began throwing out handfuls of feed.

Russell Dyer, the last to leave the perch, hopped down, flapped his wings and crowed just outside the door, then cut a buck and wing around Dad Hallcomb with his right arm sweeping at the ground.

Dad Hallcomb did a marvelous dead-pan job of pretending that he saw nothing unusual at all. He dusted his hands and started back to the house, still whistling. Ol' Russ crowed a last time, then hopped over the fence.

The story got around, and probably grew with the telling. Nobody could ever decide who had had the most fun.

What

Can't Be Cured

11 Must Be Endured

The rattlesnake bites and the scorpion stings,
The mosquito delights with its buzzing wings;
The sandburs prevail and so do the ants,
And those who sit down need soles on their pants.
The summer heat is a hundred and ten—
Too hot for the Devil, too hot for men;
The wild boar roams through the black chaparral—
'Tis a hell of a place is the Texas Hell.
—E. U. COOK, "HELL IN TEXAS," CIRCA 1886

"OZONA OZONE," boasted a Christmas edition of the *Kicker*, "is a panacea for almost all our poor mortal ills."

Maybe it was both the high, dry air and the lime in the drinking water. At any rate, most of the old-timers lived long and active lives, and their children were growing up in health and high condition. People said nobody ever died in West Texas. They just "dried up and blowed away."

My generation never heard of orange juice. We had no spinach, Pablum, or "enriched bread" in our formative years. Kids ate potatoes, stewed dried fruit, canned tomatoes, beefsteak (rolled in flour and then fried to the texture of boot leather), and beans, beans, beans. Not many drank any milk after they had been weaned. A few people in town kept cows,

and swore at them, but on the ranches where there might be
thousands of cattle nobody had the time to devote to a single
cow and her calf. She wasn't a milk cow, anyway; she might
give as much as a gallon of milk in a day, and chances were
even that it would be bitter from horehound or broomweed.
She usually remained half wild and would hook you if she
could, in the fixed belief that you were torturing her offspring
and "knocking it in the head with the churn dasher." She would
put her foot in the bucket, hit you in the face with her tail, and
kick over the lantern.

We didn't have orange juice, but we had pickle juice. Everybody bought pickles by the gallon. It was well known that
pickles killed stomach and intestinal worms and gave tone to
the whole digestive system, as well as lending zest to food.
West Texas people consumed a terrific quantity of pickles, in
those days, and maybe the idea was not at all wrong. A recent
best-selling book, *Folk Medicine,* by Dr. D. C. Jarvis, makes
a great point of the uses of vinegar in a guide to good health.
All I know is, we got pickles, and we liked them.

But there were other panaceas, besides the ozone and the
water. Some of them had been brought west in the saddlebags
and the wagons, and were therefore representative of all the
South and the backwoods country of East Texas. Not many
of these were found in Soapy Smith's drugstore. Kids stood
around hot school stoves in wintertime, exuding a dreadful
odor from the bags of asafetida hung around their necks like
lockets; kids on the ranches were often forced to drink a tea
brewed from—of all things—dried sheep pills. Kids were sent
forth in spring to gather horehound leaves so their mothers
could make a repulsively bitter product falsely called candy.
Any youngster who exhibited nervousness by picking at his
nose was deemed to be infested with worms: he not only got
pickles but was regularly given spoonfuls of sugar liberally
drenched with turpentine. A bronchial cough, or soreness in the
chest, got the red-flannel treatment with a poultice that might
mix kerosene, vinegar, axle grease, turpentine, and red pepper.

And it was well known that the best way to cure night sweats was to put a pan of water under the bed, and warn Little Willie not to mistake it for the chamber pot. It was known, too, that if Willie amused himself around the evening campfire by poking sticks into it and writing in the air by waving the burning ends, he most certainly would wet the bed later. This may have been a piece of psychology to keep Willie from getting burned, but perhaps the power of suggestion was in counterplay: kids who played with the fire very often *did* wet the bed.

Springtime weeds were rife with "red bugs" (chiggers), and the remedy was fully as painful as their bites: the itching lumps were rubbed with a mixture of kerosene and bacon grease, and this sent kids running through the mesquites with all the verve of a dog that had just had turpentine put under his tail. For any kind of sore, a poultice could be made by crushing the leaves of jimson weeds, a lowly plant that thrives in back lots and alleys and gains very little when called *Datura stramonium*. Sulphur and molasses was a favorite spring tonic after the asafetida bags had been removed. There were old-timers who carried brass in their pockets—one had a round, hard object he said was a petrified potato—to ward off rheumatism. Others rubbed their limbs and joints with snake oil.

Patent medicines were on everybody's shelves, and some were advertised on ranch gates. Cardui . . . Black Draught . . . Carter's Little Liver Pills . . . Scott's Emulsion . . . Dr. Pierce's Favorite Prescription and his Golden Medical Discovery . . . Beef, Iron and Wine Tonic . . . Tanlac and Peruna, and other elixirs that sometimes had a wonderfully high alcoholic content. These undoubtedly did some good, along the same lines as one ranchman's prescription for the treatment of influenza: "One quart of whiskey and a dozen lemons. Directions—throw the lemons at a fence post and drink the whiskey."

But there were other things, mystical and wonderful and rich with folklore. Mama was not actually a superstitious woman, but she had the heritage of the plantation South and it frightened her terribly if anyone brought a hoe or an ax into the house—that meant, she said, that there would be a death in the family. It was a rather large family, counting aunts and uncles and cousins, some of whom were getting along in years. Any news of a death within six months, in some far-distant part of Texas, fulfilled Mama's dread prophecy.

Most fiddle players kept rattlesnake rattles in their violins to prevent dampness. It did not occur to me until years later that although rattlesnakes keep to dry ground, their rattles are about as absorbent as the horns of a cow. But I still remember an itinerant fiddler named O'Connor who adhered to this practice. He sat on our front gallery in the moonlight, and played "Listen to the Mockingbird." At one point in the rendition he spun the fiddle a few times, and, sure enough, you could plainly hear the flutter of the mockingbird's wings.

Anybody who shot a deer in those days naturally cut open the stomach in hope of finding a madstone. So far as I know, nobody ever found one, and the nearest madstone was supposed to be owned by a man who lived near Sterling City, beyond San Angelo. Belief in the efficacy of madstones appears to have been purely American. The word has been dropped by some dictionaries, but as late as 1949 this was published:

"Ernest Gravois . . . estimates over 4000 actual cases in which the application of the Mad Stone brought about instant relief and final cure of snake bites, black widow spider bites, bee stings and mad dog bites . . . and ailments resulting from poison infections in the blood stream."

I have always wanted to own a madstone, just as I should like to have Aladdin's lamp. In this case, I do not know where to separate fact from fancy or medical science from folklore and the curative powers of hypnosis or suggestion. I have read about cases of rattlesnake bite in which a young victim, told that whiskey would effect a cure, drank a whole quart of liquor *without becoming drunk*. This I would have to see.

All I know is that as I grew up in Ozona it was sometimes a long way from the ranches to a doctor and that one went to a doctor only in cases of grave emergency. Nathaniel Baker, small and barefoot and one of Nate Baker's younger progeny, indulged in a rather dangerous sport one afternoon at school recess: he grasped the spokes of a wheel on a freight wagon that was going by, braced his feet on the rim, and intended to do cartwheels with the wheel's revolutions. It was an ancient pastime, but Nathaniel slipped, and the heavily loaded wagon ran over both his legs, neatly slicing skin and flesh from both shins. They carried him, screaming, to a doctor. But that was unusual; it took something that spectacular.

When Boots McKinney threw a rock at a bird in his back yard, and the rock slipped in his grasp and neatly knocked me out of the post oak tree where I was sitting, nobody took me to a doctor. Boots had thrown a flat stone, and it cut my upper lip as sharply as a knife, until my gums and teeth showed through. But Mama said it would heal—and it did. A stitch or two might have prevented the scar I still carry.

And then later I went with M. C. Weaver to the Weaver ranch, about eight miles from town, to see if we could start a gasoline engine and pump some water for the cattle in a time of drought.

We walked about four miles to the Weaver pasture, and then after expending a great deal of energy we caught a Weaver horse aptly named Old Dunny, made a hackamore of wire, and rode him double to the divide windmill. M.C. climbed halfway up the tower to uncouple the windmill rods so that we could transfer power to the gasoline engine below, and I busied myself priming and trying to start the engine.

He yelled, "Look out!" suddenly, and I looked up. An eight- or ten-pound wrench designed for uncoupling windmill rods had just been jiggled off the plank where he stood. It struck me squarely on the bulb of the nose, and the blood spurted a yard. M.C. almost fell off the tower, exclaiming, "My God, Allie, I've killed you!" and I groped my way to the horse trough and broke a thin sheet of November ice and ducked my head.

Nobody said anything about going to a doctor. The bleeding finally stopped. We mounted Old Dunny again, and wore our rumps raw riding him, with no saddle, back to the road. When I reached home, my sister Maude had just come in on the evening stage for a visit. She didn't know me, because both my eyes were blackened and swelled almost shut. After they told her who I was, she hugged me and said, "My, Allie, you look so fat!"

II

The girl was exceptionally pretty in a very soft and feminine way. She had that high fresh coloring found fortunately often in the English countryside: brown hair, red lips and blue eyes, and a skylark lilt to her whole being. I have wondered since, many times, how it happened that she came to Ozona and an ultimate tragedy. As I remember it, there was a brother in the area, but no parents. And if there had been a compulsory education law at that time, the girl might well have been in high school. She was probably only sixteen when she took her first job as a cook on one of the ranches.

At that time, any of the bigger outfits had a half dozen young cowboys around, some of them handsome enough and all of them lonely. After a hard day in the saddle they had nothing but cards or dominoes, or a graphophone to play a few records over and over. Old Nate Baker, a family man who had worked on a number of ranches himself, summed things up later. "Hell!" Nate asked, not unkindly. "Just what the hell else was there to do?"

People were kind enough in material ways when the baby came, but any small town of the period would have had the same reaction: this was a scandal. The girl was too proud to endure the looks on the street. She also was so proud that she pointed her finger at no man. Then, after relatives in some other place had taken the baby, she went back to the only thing she knew—cooking for a ranch. She was forty miles from Ozona.

The ranchman's wife was poorly; the girl was cook and scullery maid and nurse to three children of preschool age. It was an old ranch house, stove-heated, and built high enough off the ground to allow a cooling breeze to blow under the floor in summer. There were knotholes in the floor of the living room. Many a Texas house is built off the ground that way. The late George Sessions Perry described such a dwelling perfectly when he wrote about the boy who yelled, "Run under the house, kids, here comes Papa!"

The Papa of the ranch was gone, that day, and so were all the other menfolk. They had saddled at sunup, and were miles away combing the remote canyons and divides to round up strays and doctor wormy cows.

The three-year-old girl of the family was playing on the living room floor. She had stuck her arm through one of the knotholes, and now she began to cry. When her mother asked her what was wrong, she said, "Pig bite me, Mama—pig bite me!"

This was at first dismissed as nonsense. There were no pigs nearer than a pen down by the barn and corral. But the crying continued, and when the mother picked up the baby there was some difficulty in pulling her arm out of the knothole. The hand and wrist were already fearfully swollen and showed a series of small, bluish punctures, always in pairs.

The child had been bitten, not just once, but several times—and, judging from the size and lateral spacings of the fang marks, by three different rattlesnakes.

In the kitchen, where she was washing the breakfast dishes, the girl heard the mother scream and fall in a faint. She came running.

What happened then was a marvel of wits and fortitude hardly to be expected of a teen-ager who had been downgraded as so careless in other regards. From somewhere out of her memory the girl coolly dredged an old folk remedy that had been written off before her time as a mere superstition, and has since been denigrated on many an occasion.

But the wonderful fact is this: it worked.

III

The mother revived only enough to wail and moan and wring her hands in complete hysteria, while the other two children clung to her and cried. The girl had no help. She tied a cord around the baby's arm just below the elbow, to check spreading of the venom, and slashed the punctures with a knife to make them bleed. Then she ran to a chicken coop where several Rhode Island Reds had been penned to be fattened for a Sunday dinner. Thrusting these into a tow sack, she brought them squalling to the house.

Now she got a butcher knife from the kitchen and unhesitatingly ripped open the belly of the first hen. She plunged the child's hand into this bloody cavity while the chicken was still alive and fluttering, and tied it there.

She threw the sack containing the other chickens into the front seat of a Dodge touring car the ranchman owned, and she cranked the engine.

This was the first time she had ever driven a car, but she had seen other people drive. If you tried long enough you found the proper gear.

A Sancho lamb—a pet, hand-raised lamb—bleated from the corral. The girl caught him, tied his legs, and put him into the car.

Then she cranked the party line telephone, calling the ranch twenty miles up the line—the only one between there and Ozona—and praying there would be an answer. A long and two short rings.

A woman's voice answered.

"Snakebite!" the girl said briefly. "Catch up all the chickens you can—catch up a dogie lamb—leave the gates open!"

Somehow she got them all into the car: the snake-bitten child with her on the front seat, the hysterical mother and frightened older children in the back. She drove with one hand and held the baby with the other, through a bedlam of squawks and bleatings and hysterical sobbings. Blood plastered the upholstery and feathers blew on the wind. The first chicken expired within minutes, but its body heat served a little longer, drawing out the venom.

There were pasture gates to open. When she stopped at the first one, the girl pulled another fluttering, squalling sacrifice from the tow sack, and did her work with the butcher knife.

The road was unpaved, uncertain, and rocky where it climbed the divide. The Dodge of that vintage had a gearshift exactly the opposite of other automobiles, but in low gear it would really pull. Fortunately for the girl, the high-pressure tires held without blowout or puncture.

She came through the gate of the middle ranch in a storm of blood and feathers, with all the chickens dead and discarded, and the pet lamb dying. More chickens and another lamb were taken aboard here, and the rancher's wife said she would telephone Ozona and tell the doctor to stand by.

The most expert of drivers could have done no better than fifteen miles an hour on the ranch roads of that day, and in the automobiles of the time. The girl wheeled the car into Ozona, with the radiator boiling, in less than three hours after leaving the ranch. She had thrown out the second supply of chickens several miles back, and now had the baby's hand in the belly of the second lamb. It lay on the blood-slippery seat beside her, still bleating in a weak, piteous quaver, its eyes glazing. The car looked as if it had been driven through a slaughterhouse and a poultry-packing plant in a high wind, and nobody would have recognized the girl.

But she held her head up in the presence of the little group that had gathered, and she looked the doctor in the eye.

"By George!" he said after examining the child. "This is a miracle! Why, she's hardly sick at all!"

Little else remained to be done. Medication to guard against infection, a sedative, and that was all. The doctor gave the mother an even bigger sedative. He patted the girl's hand and bestowed upon her a warm, benevolent wink.

That was all the reward she ever got, beyond the fact that she could have worked for all her life on that ranch.

I remember her, but I do not remember where she went from there. Wherever it was, I wish her well, and think that they might have even put up some sort of monument for her in the town square. She had all the virtues required to establish the town and make the county great.

Lest I be charged with perpetuating folklore with only a single incident for its foundation of proof, let me quote this from my friend Monroe Cockrell:

The houses were far apart in that bleak country (near Trinidad, Colorado) so we drove into a farmyard to ask for directions. Well, a woman, several children, and a couple of men were seemingly running wild all over the place, brandishing sticks and hollering. They paid no attention to us, so we got out of the car and waited. By and by, they caught a chicken, and then all ran for the back steps of the house where a little girl was sitting. One of the men grabbed an axe, split that chicken wide open, and then they tied it, feathers and all, around the leg of the little girl. We found out that she had been bitten by a rattlesnake. A few days later, we stopped there on our way back to town and found that the youngster was doing nicely. Don't tell me that some of these home remedies don't work.

When All
the World Is
12 Young, Lad

When I was but thirteen or so
I went into a golden land,
Chimborazo, Cotopaxi
Took me by the hand.
—W. J. TURNER, ''ROMANCE''

PEERY HOLMSLEY was the one who discovered that practically all the old outlaws had gone the way of the Comanches,
by the year 1912, and that there wasn't even a good feud in
Ozona. He called a council under the Big Tree just below our
house, one day after school, in an attempt to remedy the situation.

Ben Gilbert was there—he and Peery were fourteen—along
with Peery's younger brothers, George and Larry, and the
Joslin boys, Mason and Harry. All of us lived on the west side
of Ozona, away from Silk Stocking Avenue; all but Ben and I
lived across Johnson Draw, as far west as you could go and
still be in town.

Peery looked around to make sure there were no spies in
the broomweeds and prickly pear. He stepped back and sur-
veyed the wire nests we had built in the forks of the bigger
live oak limbs. There was always something of the old Plains

scout about Peery; nobody would have taken him for the son of a doctor who had married one of W. P. Hoover's daughters and was both practicing medicine and serving as the Ozona postmaster at that time.

"I got some information," Peery said darkly, the way Tom Swift used to say things. "The boys on the east side of town are organizing a gang. You know what that means. It means we've got to organize a gang over here."

"Who's organizing a gang?" Ben wanted to know.

"Well, from what I hear, it's Walter Augustine, and Albert Bailey, and Tip Smith, and Massie West—you know, people like that."

Ben Gilbert was the practical type. He wanted to know what this gang on the east side proposed to do. Peery didn't know, but whatever it was, we had to be prepared to fight them. Mason Joslin, who always reminded me of Dick, the tall, serious Rover Boy, agreed at once. Mason was a studious sort and always wore a coat and necktie and shoes to school. His father admired Eugene V. Debs, read *The Appeal to Reason,* and wore some kind of button in his lapel, and some of this had rubbed off on Mason.

"Mason," Peery said, with an uncanny knack for picking his lieutenants, "you work up a countersign and a password, and a secret code. We'll call our gang the B.G.W.—the Brave Gang of the West. We'll show that S.C.G.E. a thing or two!"

"What's S.C.G.E.?" Ben asked.

"The Sorry, Cowardly Gang of the East," Peery said. "Now, the first thing we've got to do is capture a spy, and torture him, and find out just what they're doing."

Lord Baden-Powell, a British general, had founded the Boy Scouts in England in 1908 and had established the American organization in 1910. A Boy Scout troop would have satisfied the instinctive desire to form a clan, a gang, a secret society, but nobody in Ozona, at that time, had heard of the Scout movement, and we were on our own. It so happened that we came pretty near to duplicating the Boy Scout uniform, at that: all of us had brown ducking pants, and we persuaded our mothers to make us brown shirts to match. This was copying nothing—it was Peery's idea of protective coloration. But it did come as near as was possible to the fringed buckskin worn by Buffalo Bill Cody, Kit Carson, and Captain William F. Drennan, who had written a wonderful book called *Twenty Years on the Plains and in the Mountains*.

Miss Glee Stafford, teaching the fifth and sixth grades, had just finished reading *The Adventures of Huckleberry Finn* to us; and then, after we moved into the new school building, we found the book that should have come first, *The Adventures of Tom Sawyer*.

There was a great deal of Tom Sawyer in Peery, with his insistence on doing things right, and of course there was much of Don Quixote too. As for Huck Finn, Ben Gilbert and I had been actively planning to float down the Pecos and the Rio Grande on a raft, living off the country. But Mama put her foot down, and so did Ben's parents. Dee laughed, and said the Pecos was always either high or low, and that we'd get snagged on the salt cedars and shot at by the Mexicans.

So we never got to go. But now the B.G.W. was off and running, and Mason Joslin came up with some fine secret signals, such as scratching one's back to tell another member of the gang "I have important information for you." There was a secret handclasp, and a motto and passwords that I cannot remember. We organized, and swore to secret oaths, and waited for the S.C.G.E. to perform an overt act. And, meanwhile, we had fun.

The whole countryside was open to exploration, as much as if no white man had ever set foot in it before. About six miles southwest of Ozona, near what later became the Bert Couch ranch, we found a rocky, winding canyon that ended in a sheer wall at the edge of the divide. Peery called this "Escondido" after a famous waterhole farther on toward the

Pecos—the word means "hidden," and the description was apt. Carrying single-shot .22 rifles, and sometimes having no more than two or three cartridges to the man, we established B.G.W. headquarters in Escondido, secreted matches and salt and lard in the crevices there, and hiked to the place every weekend. There was a dirt tank on the divide just above the canyon. On a dare, we all swam the tank on a cold February day, and on another dare we ate—raw—the liver of a duck we shot on the water.

Then, on our way back to town, we came quite suddenly upon the carcass of a yearling calf, still warm, that had obviously been killed by a panther. Big cats, such as panthers, rip open the chest cavities of their prey and eat first the "lights" and the heart. This had been done here in a small post oak motte, and it was an ideal place for setting traps. Larry Holmsley and I—being the youngest—were dispatched over the hill to Ozona to bring traps, while the others stood guard and rested from the long hike.

We brought back three big, double-spring, Number Four steel traps. We set them in a semicircle before the carcass, so that any animal approaching it would be almost certain to spring a trigger. Then, as the sun was going down, we started back to town.

A few minutes later, there was a terrible howling. We backtracked and rescued two of our own dogs that had been lured by the fresh beef, and although we reset the traps, nothing came near them.

It was always like that for us. Adventure was just around the turn of the trail, just over the hill, and just up the canyon. But when we got there it was gone. Even the S.C.G.E. failed to cooperate, and it was extremely difficult starting a feud without some active opposition.

Peery said we would have to spy on the S.C.G.E. to learn what they were doing. Since Ben and I were the only B.G.W. members who lived east of Johnson Draw, this duty fell to us. And since Ben was rising fifteen years old and regarded the

B.G.W. as a hunting and shooting club—he never really accepted the gang motif—I was the one who had to do the intelligence work. I concealed myself in the brush on Waterworks Hill and watched the eastern part of town for hours. And I must say I never saw any evidence of secret and unlawful assembly. It looked to me as if the kids over there were doing their chores as reluctantly as anybody else.

I reported this to Peery. He said we would have to capture one of the S.C.G.E. people.

Massie West and Albert Bailey would have been hard to handle. I was exchanging books regularly with Walter Augustine. He collected Tom Swift, and I had some Horatio Alger and G. A. Henty. Besides, Walter was developing as a baseball pitcher, and was pretty athletic.

We hit on Monk Smith, who was a year or so younger than I, and some smaller. Peery planted anonymous letters, and one afternoon after school we lured Monk across the draw and into the hills, using flattery and the desired association with older boys. Then we leaped for him, and he ran. The chase split the B.G.W. in half, but finally a signal went up from a big cedar tree where we had an observation platform. Monk had been captured, and was tied hand and foot.

The clan gathered, and Mason said the next proper thing to do was to give Monk what he called the "third degree," and if he wouldn't talk we would then have to give him the "bastinado," which was beating him on the soles of his feet. Like most of the rest of us, Monk had been going barefoot all summer, and had become very nearly immune to the bastinado. But he said it would be getting dark pretty soon, and he had some chores to do at home or he'd get a licking there. He began to cry.

Mason offered him amnesty if he would tell us all he knew about the S.C.G.E., but Monk only cried the harder, and we finally had to let him go. Then we had to face up to a hard fact: there was no S.C.G.E. and never had been.

Peery tried desperately to hold the organization together,

but without an active opposition this was an impossible task. Ben and I were hunting in the Henderson pasture one day and met F. M. Joslin, the father of the Joslin boys. He squinted at our brown clothes and smiled, and said, "Boy Scouts, eh?"

It was an idea. I had just seen a copy of *The Appeal to Reason* in which Mr. Debs or one of his cohorts had written: "Don't let your son join that hellish organization, the Boy Scouts of America." From that time on I was determined to be a Boy Scout, because I was at the age where any kind of hellish organization had great appeal. But I didn't know the address of the Boy Scouts, and they had to wait.

II

Ben Gilbert and I were watching a big live oak tree, over the hills west of town, that spring. There was a hawk's nest in the higher branches: maybe, we told ourselves, it was the nest of a golden eagle. We lay on the rimrock for hours at a time, spying on the tree, and we knew when the babies had been hatched because we saw the mother hawk bringing a wood rat one minute, and a lizard or ground squirrel, or a snake wriggling in her beak, the next. This round-the-clock feeding should have given us warning, but at school we had just learned about the ancient English sport of falconry, and we were eager to train our own birds to perch on our wrists and rise to the chase when we removed their hoods.

It sounded easy, and so—in all loving-kindness—we perpetrated one of the unintentional cruelties of boyhood. One day Ben stood sentry with his .22 rifle while I shinnied up the tree and inspected the nest. The mother hawk, a fierce yellow-eyed creature with a four-foot wingspread and razor-sharp talons, made several passes at me and struck me twice with her wings. Ben fired, uncomfortably close to me, not trying to hit her, but only to frighten her away. I slid back down the tree and reported that there were two babies, each about the size of my fist, and covered with white down. They already had fearsome beaks.

"We'd better wait two or three weeks," Ben said. "Let's go put chicken wire across the front of our barn, and fix a perch for them. We'll have 'em huntin' rabbits for us in no time at all!"

Every boy in West Texas, at that time, knew how to hunt and trap. Both Ben and I had single-shot .22 rifles—the barrel of mine was wired to the stock—but cartridges cost fifteen cents a box, and we hunted more often with our nigger-shooters. We had an old bullet mold, and found enough scrap lead to melt down and cast into pellets that were used only when the chance was good. Ben had an uncanny eye for aim, either with a gun or a nigger-shooter, while mine was good one day and poor the next. There was only one unwritten and unbroken rule: one never, *never,* killed a mockingbird.

We converted the Gilbert barn into an aviary, and then one afternoon after school I climbed the live oak again. The mother hawk came screaming to whip me with her wings. The babies, sprouting pinfeathers and as ugly as sin, stood up in the nest amid a litter of bones and scraps of hide. They shook their wings, and pecked at me, and said, "Pert! Pert! Pert!"

I reached for one of them. He grabbed my finger in his beak, and wrestled with it, drawing blood, but I lifted him in my hand and laughed with joy. I held something savage and wild, a creature akin to clouds and the wide blue spaces of the sky above me, and it was the nearest I would ever come to soaring out over the rocky hills. "Baby!" I said. "Baby, we'll take care of you!"

The mother hawk paid no attention to Ben's next shot, and ripped at my shoulder with a force that almost knocked me out of the tree. But I had on a brown ducking jumper, tough enough to withstand her talons. I went down the tree with a young hawk in each side pocket, and we made our way home in triumph.

Next day after school Ben and I went out over the hill and killed two wood rats and several lizards. The wood rats weighed almost as much as the hawks, and we thought we had provided well. What we didn't know was that our young pets—we had named them Sam Houston and Davy Crockett—were accustomed to eating much more than their own weight every day. They consumed the provender in a very few minutes, and then screamed "Pert! Pert! Pert!" Next afternoon they disposed of one cottontail, a wood rat, two lizards and a gopher snake—and were still hungry.

On Saturday we hunted all day. They ate everything we brought them, and screamed for more. We began to have an enormous respect for the mother hawk.

The next two or three weeks were a nightmare. The school building was only about a block from Ben's barn, and we could hear the hawks crying out plaintively long before the bell rang for dismissal. Then we had to hunt, and it seemed as if even the lizards were growing scarce and wary. We had already burned the wood rats' nests for a mile around, and now we guiltily sacrificed a neighbor's chicken that had ventured up the canyon. The cottontails had cleared out.

And our consciences began to bother us. I asked Ben if he thought killing one wild thing to feed another wild thing was all right. He said grimly that the mother hawk did it, and he guessed we weren't doing any more than she would have done. He figured, from the way Sam Houston and Davy Crockett were taking on, that we hadn't done as much.

No matter how much food we brought to the barn, the young hawks shrieked that they were starving. They learned to stand on the perch with one foot and reach for tidbits with the other; they showed no inclination to perch on our wrists, but were viciously willing to lacerate them. We played hooky on several desperate afternoons when the larder was low, and we could hear the hawks screaming at noon. And then we began to have sleepless nights, after it was too dark to hunt. Sometimes the hawks were still crying "Pert! Pert! Pert!" until midnight or later, and we lay listening, knowing that we had failed to provide.

Finally we came to the sad conclusion that Sam Houston and Davy Crockett could not even be supported, much less tamed. They were trying their wings now, making short flights within the confines of the barn. Ben was confident that they would go back to the wild with no trouble, and be able to forage for themselves. But to make sure, we decided to take them more than two miles away, beyond the perimeter of the area we had hunted out.

On an evening soft with spring we carried them far over the hills and set them free. They said, "Pert! Pert!" and flew joyfully enough, we thought, into a live oak tree. We watched them for a moment, and then went home.

Next afternoon, sure that all would be well, and still nagged by conscience, we hiked over the hills to see if there was any sign of them. Probably, Ben said, they had moved on. Probably each had taken over his own territory for hunting. After all, they were strong and brave—they would do all right.

We approached the tree where they had been left the evening before. We separated, covering all the ground around it, and suddenly I heard Ben call, with something of anguish in his voice. I looked that way, and saw, just beyond him, our hawks. One was prostrate. The other stood over him, his beak crimson as he pecked and tore at his brother's body. I saw all this, and knew what was happening, and knew, too, the guilt—the *real* guilt—that belonged to Ben and me. I couldn't look any more, and then there was a shot. Ben came over where I was, and he was crying.

Maybe we made up for the hawks, one day. Up in the Henderson pasture north of town and not far off the San Angelo road we heard a thin, rusty sound of a cat's crying.

It was a very faint sound, and muffled; it took some time for us to locate it. When we did, we found a pitiful jumble of a tow sack tangled with a thorned mesquite branch and attempting to move along the bank of Johnson Draw.

We cut the sack open with a pocketknife and extracted a gaunt, big-eyed shadow of a cat, too weak to stand on her own legs. She had been washed that way by the last rain, and since rains are momentous events in the Ozona country, we remembered it. The cat had been in the sack exactly three weeks.

She tried to rub against our legs, and fell down. The very fact that she was alive should have told us that we could carry her back to town and still arrive with a spark of life. But it didn't seem that way to us, at the moment. That cat had to be fed within minutes. We were breathless—we were panic-stricken—with this idea. The cat had to eat.

We carried her down into the live oaks of the draw. She didn't weigh a pound, but now she was cuddling up to me and purring in a way that broke my heart. I found a couple of empty sardine cans that had been discarded by picnickers, and put water in them, and she lapped up the water and what grease had been left. We realized then that she hadn't had a drink of water in three weeks, either.

Ben went out in the live oak motte with his nigger-shooter, it being one of the times when he had no .22 ammunition. I petted the dry, scrawny cat, and held her to make sure she wouldn't go away, and this was a foolish enterprise—she wouldn't have left us for anything. Finally there was a shout from Ben. "Got one!" he said.

He came bringing a bird already stripped of its feathers, but still warm. The cat fell upon this savagely, and after eating it was able to stand on her feet again.

But we carried her a mile back to town. At the edge of Ozona we put her down, and followed her. It was just growing dark. Ben and I were in a towering anger toward anybody who would abandon a cat in a tied sack, and we knew that the cat would go home.

She did. We followed her down the main street, and watched her turn off toward the southeastern corner of the town square. She went to the front gallery of a house there. We knocked on the door.

The family living there was named Smith. The oldest daughter—she taught my Sunday-school class—opened the door.

The cat went inside. Miss Smith expressed great wonderment and delight, but she didn't fool Ben at all. That was one of the times when I was very proud of Ben. He said, "You tied the cat in a sack, didn't you?"

Miss Smith said, "Well, she was going to have kittens, so we put her in a sack—we didn't tie it—and dumped her out on the road north of town. But we didn't mean to—"

"We had to cut the twine that the sack was tied with," Ben said. "That was three weeks ago because the rain washed her to the draw. You figure on keeping her, now?"

Miss Smith said, oh, yes—she was very glad to get the cat back.

Ben never went to Sunday school. He was fifteen, and Miss Smith was perhaps twenty. I looked at the two of them and was pretty sure Ben had a better chance of going to heaven, despite her church activities.

"You know what happened, don't you?" Ben went on. "She ate her kittens. It was the only way she could live. And then she would have died of thirst if it hadn't rained."

Miss Smith said, "Oh, the poor thing!" and repeated that she was glad to get the cat back, and Ben and I got out of there. I could see that something was bothering him, but we were nearly back to our homes before I learned what it was.

"Allie," he said then, "I hate to tell you this. But you know that bird—it was the only one I could get a shot at, and—well, it was a mockingbird!"

That just made everything twice as bad, as if the cruelty had been compounded. I said, "Well, it was an emergency! It was a matter of life or death. That cat wouldn't have lived another hour."

We tried to believe that, but killing a mockingbird preyed on Ben's conscience for days. I went to Sunday school the next Sunday, and Miss Smith was there, her face shining with good works. I don't think Mama ever quite understood, but that was my last Sunday school for a long time. I didn't go again until I felt the turn of the seasons and became interested in a girl who was very active in church doings.

III

The gang instinct was still strong in all of us, and, indeed, it was encouraged by the practices of the grownups. The Masonic Lodge met on the second floor of the bank building, and stories got around about secret rituals, and how somebody being initiated "rode the goat" last night. I watched the place without ever seeing a billygoat being led upstairs, but of course that didn't mean anything: everybody knew a goat could be in permanent residence there, subsisting on nothing but scraps of paper. Dee attended the meetings of both the International Order of Odd Fellows and the Woodmen of the World, but he never told me any of their secrets. All he ever said was that they were having an oyster supper—and that was mysterious enough. I suppose the oysters came in cans, but even so, I had never seen or tasted an oyster. When I asked Dee what they were like, he hemmed and hawed and said, well, when they were out of the shell they were pretty hard to describe, having practically no shape. I realized later that this is about as good a description of an oyster as you can find.

It must have been during the summer of 1913 that movies came to Ozona to stay.

There had been a traveling motion-picture show a year or two before, showing in a sort of canvas stockade that had walls eight feet high, and bleacher seats, but no roof. This outfit presented *The Great Train Robbery* and perhaps an early western; everybody who saw the first night's performance swore you could hear the splash when a cowboy jumped his horse off the riverbank. The second night, Floyd and Bert bought tickets and seated themselves on the highest tier. Then, as the show started, they reached down over the canvas wall and pulled Ben and me up beside them. We all agreed that a magic lantern show was nothing after that.

It seems strange that movies were so long in coming to town. The *Kicker,* in 1907—the year we moved to Ozona—printed a long and newsy letter written by the Methodist preacher of that year, W. W. Nunn, who had gone to Brownwood and Fort Worth and Dallas shopping for pews for his church. At that time it wasn't so easy to go out and buy a few pews, and the Rev. Mr. Nunn was an earnest man and frugal: he shopped for a bargain. The pews had to be shipped by freight wagon, of course, but he wrote that they were "as nice as they have in any church in Texas. Just wait till you see them, they are daisies." And then he added that Dallas had "gone wild over phonographs, and motion pictures are everywhere, three to a block, and the people go to them in droves."

But Dallas was a long way off. Ozona waited patiently for the Hollywood culture. Finally Kenneth Cox, son of a leading merchant and owner of one of the first automobiles in town, built the Majestic Theater just off the square, on the corner of the block that contained the Midkiff & Caudle drugstore, the law office of Judge Davidson, the weekly newspaper plant (which had moved), and the W. F. Coates Saddle Shop which also handled coffins. Bunger's Store and a dry goods store also were in this block.

The Majestic, opening with considerable megaphoned and handbilled fanfare, announced there would be three shows a week—on Wednesday, Friday and Saturday nights. The theater was a long, low building, with trapdoor windows that let down inside for ventilation, and a player piano that used perforated music rolls. I was green with envy when I learned that Joe and M. C. Weaver had been given the job of sweeping out and playing the piano. The piano player had not seen the films in advance, and he had carte blanche in his selections from fifteen or twenty music rolls; nobody blamed him if he played "Stars and Stripes Forever" during a tender love scene and then came up with "Beautiful Blue Danube" or "Wedding of the Winds" during a cavalry charge.

I also envied the hitherto undiscovered mechanical genius

of Ernest Dunlap. With no previous experience or training at all, he was suddenly changing the reels and turning the crank of the projector, besides working the light switches. The five-minute intervals between reels found Kenneth Cox, proprietor and entrepreneur, running up and down the aisles in an apoplectic attempt to restrain small fry from throwing all manner of things, or squirting each other with water guns. As Kenneth often pointed out, not even a grown-up spectator was safe.

The Majestic had not been operating a week before someone discovered that it was really not necessary to buy a 25-cent ticket to see the show. Snuggled up against the west wall of the theater building was a one-room, flat-roofed electrical shop, separated from the drugstore by an eight-foot gap, with a board fence below. It was possible to mount to the roofs of the block down at the far corner, by climbing a telephone pole. Then you proceeded, cat-like, over the top of the town, leaped the eight-foot black void, and lay flat on the roof of the electrical shop. The theater's first ventilating window on that side gave a magnificent view of the screen.

This serendipity soon had the roof four deep with impecunious urchins of my age, and if we had had the sense to keep quiet we might have seen an entire serial such as *The Broken Coin,* or *The Purple Mask,* both starring Grace Cunard and Francis Ford. But somebody guffawed at the wrong moment, and we were discovered. Now, when Ernest changed reels, he took additional time to run out in front of the theater, climb another telephone pole that stood handily in the lights of the marquee, and rout the freeloaders.

We were required to post a sentry during every changing of the reels. Ernest had big hands, and when they hove into view on the telephone pole it was a signal for flight over the rooftops—after first jumping the eight-foot abyss. Leonard Armentrout's foot slipped one night and he fell squarely astride the board fence underneath. The rest of us made the end of the block and then came cautiously back up the sidewalk, certain from Leonard's anguished moans that he was dying. Fortunately, no one in the theater could hear him because of the player piano.

Ben Gilbert and Claude Russell and others of us lifted Leonard and carried him across the street to the park, where we put him on the grass and debated calling a doctor.

At this point Leonard sat up. "Doctor couldn't do me no good!" he mourned. "I'm as ruint as a steer!"

Ben let out a great snort of mirth. "Ol' Leonard's cut!" he said. "We might as well take him out and brand him!"

Everybody seemed to be growing up and away from me. Floyd got married and moved to Sweetwater for a while, Bert was working in a store, and Ben got a job driving a stripped-down Ford delivery wagon. All I had in the way of employment was a job sweeping out the Baptist church, building fires in the stove on cold mornings, and ringing the bell for Sunday school and Wednesday night prayer meetings. This paid $2.50 a month, and I saved up enough money to buy a secondhand bicycle. But I also got trapped into attending Sunday school and prayer meeting much more often than I would have done otherwise.

The town was getting so many automobiles that two garages opened for business. On June 30, 1914, the *Stockman* delivered itself of a piece of gee-whiz journalism:

Ed Hall, the Brownwood automobile salesman, came to Ozona Tuesday with Byrd Phillips' new Cadillac car. This car is a dandy, it is a 1914 model, with all the modern appliances like electric self-starter and such things. Automobile experts of Ozona say this is one of the finest cars seen in Ozona in many a day. It cost $2100 laid down in Ozona. Mr. Hall claims this car will make seventy miles per hour any old day. Not only is this car a good one, but it is one of the classiest looking cars made and Mr. Phillips is to be congratulated on his choice.

The shortest distance between two places was no longer a

fast horse, and there would be a time when Crockett County could be called Cadillac Country.

And then, on a hot August day, Ozona heard the news that a war had broken out in Europe.

A Long,

Long Way

13 to Tipperary

"In Mexico there are but two articles: Article Thirty Three (which regulated the conditions of expropriation of foreign-owned property), and article .30-.30."

—A RIO GRANDE MEXICAN, QUOTED BY PAUL HORGAN IN ''GREAT RIVER; THE RIO GRANDE IN NORTH AMERICAN HISTORY''

In 1914, and in years both previous and subsequent to 1914, the Winchester .30-.30 was being used with great frequency along the river that forms the Texas-Mexican border. So much so that the citizens of Ozona might well have been pardoned for not getting too excited, at first, about a war far across the Atlantic. They had one in their own back yard. It was unofficial and undeclared, true, but people were being killed in it and a lot of valuable livestock was being rustled across the river by moonlight.

We have a large history for a nation so young. We are a big country, and in 1914 the residents of, say, Boston, would hardly have understood the problems of the Texas border. Mention the name of Pancho Villa to a Bostonian today, and he might perhaps remember a film somewhat glorifying that cold-eyed, loose-lipped savage, who rode beautifully and killed unmercifully, and still stood for something wonderful among millions of Mexican peons. A little recapitulation may be needed here.

Fighting along the Rio Grande had actually been going on ever since the Alamo, in 1836, but Texas handled it with a few Rangers. In this century—in a time when we were tough and proud and had no buttons to push—the trouble suddenly became national in April, 1914, when bluejackets from the U.S.S. *Dolphin* were arrested while loading supplies in the Mexican port of Tampico.

Admiral Mayo, commanding the Gulf Squadron, demanded a special salute to the American flag. General Huerta, president of Mexico, refused to order the salute. Tensions grew, and on April 21 Admiral Mayo reported to Washington that a German ship was steaming into Veracruz with a large supply of munitions and arms.

President Wilson ordered Mayo: "Take Veracruz at once." This was done, and it was not until nearly three years later that Wilson learned of the fantastic German plot to support Mexico in an invasion of Texas, New Mexico and Arizona, if war broke out between the United States and Germany.

But the border shooting went on unabated.

Crockett County does not abut the Rio Grande—Val Verde lies between. But Crockett County ranchmen have always been interested, and involved, in livestock trading along the border river. In 1914 and 1915 legitimate business deteriorated and shooting increased; in 1914 Carranza and Villa quarreled in their fight against Huerta, and six days after World War I broke out in Europe Carranza took over in Mexico City. But Pancho Villa was still very much on the loose, and the United States began to station cavalry garrisons along the border.

The newspapers received in Ozona—a day late—reported the European war, all right, but they also played up all the atrocities committed along the Rio Grande. By the time 1916 came, the undeclared border war was getting bloody, indeed, and was beginning to affect Ozona in a personal way. Here are some news items, taken over a six-month period, from the Ozona *Stockman:*

January: Avery H. Couch, brother of S. E. Couch, is one of 18 Americans murdered by Mexican brigands after being lured to Mexico on the promise of full protection and guaranteed safety by the Carranza Government.

March: Fear is aroused among populace by roving bands of Mexican transients. Range fires reach ranches of Roy Henderson, Jones Miller, Joe Pierce, J. W. Friend & Sons, Judge Davidson and Beecher Montgomery. J. E. Kay loses eight sections to fire, J. C. Kirby four, Ben Ingham ten.

April: Ranchmen report jackrabbits dying by the thousands from some sort of epidemic. White & Baker lose 2,500 ewes with lambs at their side in cold spell.

May: J. D. Harp, young ranchman, murdered on George Harrell ranch south of Ozona by two Mexican goatherders.

June: United States and Mexico situation is tense. Entire National Guard ordered out by President Wilson.

July: W. F. Coates of Ozona receives word of the murder of his nephew, Will Parker, and Parker's wife, by Mexicans.

II

The *Stockman* apparently did not report the death of my father at the hands of Mexican bandits who raided Boquillas, in the Big Bend of the Rio Grande, early in May of that same troubled year. He was not an Ozonan: he and Mama had been separated for about fourteen years. And the account of losses on the White & Baker ranch due to a sudden and late freeze just after the sheep had been sheared was greatly understated. My brother Dee was the foreman on that ranch, which was eighty miles from town and west of the Pecos. He came home unexpectedly, on horseback.

"Out of a job," he said. "The outfit's busted—plumb wiped out. We lost around ten thousand head of sheep. That's high country over there, and they drifted with the norther and just died in piles!"

There was hardly time for him to find another job before the news came about Papa, and Dee went to Boquillas to find out what he could. This wasn't much. Several people had been killed in the raid itself, and apparently Papa had been taken across the Rio Grande as a prisoner, and then was shot down while trying to escape. Article .30-.30.

Range fires, blizzards, marauding Mexicans, murders along the Rio Grande, and the Pershing Punitive Expedition—all in one year. The war in Europe was a long way from West Texas, indeed.

Wars have always had a lamentable way of making men out of boys before their time, of bringing boom to one community and bust to another, of upping the national debt and lowering the standard of morals. Nobody saw the signs and portents in Ozona in 1914, but those of us who were growing up with the town and the century can look back now and see that the years of World War I put both us and the town out of the adolescent stage and into long pants.

Some of the things that happened during the period were not directly traceable to the war, of course. In 1915 the sheep-ranching business took a great step forward with the introduction of woven-net wire fencing. Ozona ranchers called this "wolfproof fence." It wasn't really wolfproof—few things are—but it did make trapping the pastures a great deal easier for people like Nick Wigzell. It was "sheepproof"—a boon to herders who knew from experience that if one sheep went under a barbed-wire fence and out of the pasture, the whole flock would follow. It cost more than barbed wire, and even a medium-sized ranch might have to put up forty miles of it. But in the long run the ranchman could get along with fewer cowboys or fewer Mexican herders, and this would be an important factor when the war put its drain on the labor pool. And, finally, wolfproof fence was slick wire: livestock did not cut themselves on it and open wounds for blowflies.

At the time the first pastures were being fenced with the new wire, Judge Charles E. Davidson was riding around the county looking at the rock formations. A man who never in all his life stopped learning, the judge had become interested in geology, and was reading every book he could find on the subject. Marine fossils in the ledge rocks showed that the area had once been a vast inland sea, and Judge Davidson became convinced that Crockett County had a great potential of mineral wealth.

There were a few good-natured snickers behind his back, but these came from people who thought "mineral wealth" meant gold or silver. What the judge had in mind, of course, was petroleum, and he persuaded a professional geologist to come to Ozona and make a survey. The expert's report was so enthusiastic that the Ozela Oil Company leased 400,000 acres in Crockett County, and by the spring of 1916 was ready to sink the first test well.

This was on the T. W. Patrick place, across Johnson Draw and near the Sheffield road. Everybody in town could see the raw lumber derrick erected there; everybody could hear the chugging of the gasoline engine and the steady thumping of the bit as it punched its way through the limestone. And everybody said it sure would be wonderful if Mr. Patrick found oil on his place, because, after all, he and his wife had eleven children.

Half the town dropped by to watch the operation, and most of the small boys were there every day. This was far more dramatic than the drilling of a mere water well, although several ranchmen who had sunk dry holes said they would rather have water for their cattle than a stinking oil well any day. The oil rig itself was more impressive, and the hole was a great deal bigger. When they hoisted the bit and prepared to bail out the slush produced by the water that was being poured into the well, boys my size came close and peered down the hole, drawn by a terrible fascination and stimulated to weird speculations.

It was getting down below 400 feet, now, and anybody could see it was just about the right caliber to take a skinny teen-aged kid all the way to the bottom, if he slipped and fell in. I said you'd probably slide down fast and easy, because the sides were as smooth and slick as the rifling in a gun barrel. Then they could lower a rope—if they had one long enough— and haul you out. This would beat exploring Dudley's Cave all to pieces.

Claude Russell said no, you'd suffocate even if you didn't go into the mud over your head, and it would be a lot worse than diving into the Henderson dirt tank and finding the water was too shallow. He said there would be no way of getting you out, so they'd just have to put the bit back in the well and pound you on as far as they were going.

Boyish imagination is both a blessing and a curse, and the thoughts of youth are deep, deep thoughts when they concern a hole in the ground. Just suppose you fell in, feet first, and just before you hit bottom the well blew in with a gusher like they had struck at Spindletop and some other places? Man alive, you'd come sailing up out of the well sitting on top of a fountain of oil, maybe fifty feet in the air!

But the drilling crew may have had thoughts of their own, about damage suits and liability insurance, and having so many kids underfoot. They roped off the hole, and we could no longer look down into its mysteries. Drilling went on until 500 feet had been reached, without even finding water, and then the project was abandoned. Mr. Patrick never did get oil-rich, and his only wealth was in several sons who became solid citizens, and—in particular—a son-in-law named Bob Cooke, who developed a method for barbecuing beef and lamb that is famous in West Texas even today.

It would be several years and a war later before any more oil prospecting was done in Crockett County. But the dry hole on the Patrick place had been a start.

III

Because of distances and the chancy conditions of early automobile performance on uncertain roads, Ozona was growing into an inland empire, a duchy of ranchers, sealed off from most of the outside world. I am sure this was not a harmful thing at all. In the decade from 1910 to 1920 there was nothing at all of value, in any of the neighboring communities, that Ozona could have adopted profitably.

The two biggest sheep ranchers of Crockett County had traveled a bit: J. M. Shannon to New Zealand and to Scotland and S. E. Couch from Canada, where he had been born. Bill West and his wife, Alma, had seen New York City from the lofty towers of the Woolworth Building; a few Ozona residents had been to livestock conventions in Kansas City, and a number of others had seen Fort Worth and Dallas. They felt more at home in Forth Worth, because that was a cattleman's town.

It is safe to assume, however, that at the time of World War I Ozona had never heard of Baedeker—and vice versa. San Angelo was still the metropolis, with two railroads and a hotel building seven stories high, and a standpipe water reservoir that was maybe even higher. They said an awful lot of painters had gotten dizzy and had fallen to their deaths while painting the inside of that standpipe.

Nobody got around very much. Boots McKinney, a member of the younger and more active element, took a little *pasear* to San Antone, went on to Beeville and Cuero, and modestly admitted on his return that he had been "purt' near round the world." And he had helpful observations. "You get hungry down there," Boots drawled authoritatively, "and all you got to do is to step into one of them calfs, and eat." (Boots meant "café," but he was a phonetic speller like a lot of the rest of us. All Ozona had in that line was a "chili parlor.")

It would have been wonderful if the war could have been shut out entirely—if the splendid, peaceful insularity of the little town could have been preserved a few more years. But things began to impinge on Ozona's consciousness. A German agent showed up, and said the Kaiser's government (a very thorough outfit) had long known that the horses born and bred on the Edwards Plateau had great stamina. He bought a few from Crockett County, where nobody yet was taking sides in the European war.

Wool prices went up, especially after Uncle Sam saw a need for thousands of olive-drab Army uniforms. Beef prices soared too. The newsreels, thrice weekly at the Majestic Theater, began running heavily to war scenes. At school we were put on a study period and discussion of the *Literary Digest,* the first —God help them!—of all magazine digests to come.

And gradually it dawned on us that we had a kinship with the people of the British Isles and a stake in the fight across the Atlantic. Now there was a bigger crowd waiting at the post office to get the San Angelo paper when the mail stage came in.

The crowd gave me a great idea. I wrote to the Fort Worth *Star-Telegram* to ask if I might represent that paper in Ozona. As I remember it now, there was never a reply to confirm this association: one of Amon Carter's enterprising minions simply began sending me thirty papers daily. They were only one day old when they fell into my avaricious little hands, and I found I could sell them all to the crowd waiting for the post office to open after the mail had been "put up." It was a dignified business. I never had to yell, "Extra! Read all about it!" I only had to stand there and let customers come to me.

The papers cost me four fifths of a penny apiece, and the page one folio plainly stated that they were to retail for "One Cent a Copy; Two Cents on Trains." I tried, honestly enough, to sell the first batch at the one-cent price, but nobody in Ozona had any use for pennies. So I became one of the first of the war profiteers, with an entirely easy conscience. With the papers selling at a nickel each, I was making more than a dollar every day.

I subscribed to the *American Boy* and *Boy's Life* magazines without knowing anything about them, and—lo and behold!— the latter publication turned out to be the official organ of the Boy Scouts of America, and gave their address: 200 Fifth Avenue, New York City. Off went a naïve, schoolboy scrawl that said "Please register the Owl Patrol, Ozona, Texas."

Peery Holmsley would have frowned at that as not being a proper way to organize anything, but Peery's family had moved to Comanche. Ben Gilbert was now seventeen and had put aside childish things. I had remained in the eighth grade two years in succession because of dropping out of school to work on a spring roundup, and now the people in my class were more of my own age and size. Richard Flowers, Homer Adams, Arthur and Hillery Phillips, Charlie Davidson and Sherman Taylor—all these embraced scouting enthusiastically, and somebody persuaded the young Baptist preacher, Arthur J. Carson, to become our first Scoutmaster. We could hardly wait to pay our 25-cent dues, take the oath that begins, "On my honor, I will do my best . . ." and get into uniform.

The troubles with the Mexicans were getting worse, the war in Europe was somehow getting closer, and by this time there wasn't a pacifist in Crockett County. But it was just as well, perhaps, that national Scout executives such as James E. West and the beloved old Dan Beard, back on Fifth Avenue, were unaware of the trend Scouting was taking in Ozona. The troop met one night a week in the courthouse, every boy bringing a .30-.30 Winchester, a .22 rifle, or a shotgun. We lined up under the stern eye of Bill Odom, a young man who had just finished four years in the Navy, and we sweated through the school of the squad and the manual of arms, even though some evenings there was only one squad. Mama's heart was filled with alarms, and she questioned the need for such military drills. I reminded her that there was a lot of talk about preparedness, and that the Boy Scout motto was "Be Prepared."

Mama didn't say anything after that, but she did worry when the troop went on a two-week camping trip to Devil's River—quite near the Mexican border—in the summer of 1916. She was afraid that the Mexicans might mistake us for soldiers, in our khaki uniforms, and shoot at us.

We were all at the silly and adventurous age that made camp all the more desirable if anything like that might happen, and we went to Devil's River with quite an arsenal of small arms—

including at least one Daisy air rifle that was to become famous. The prospect of camp had suddenly swelled our ranks to nearly twenty boys. I was not only the senior patrol leader, but, because Jay had given me an old cavalry trumpet, I was also the bugler.

Twenty boys overtaxed our available transport. J. B. Smith, the school superintendent—at a distance we called him "Prof" —owned a Ford touring car and was very fond of fishing. He said he would be delighted to go. One of Scoutmaster Carson's colleagues, who shall be known here only as the Other Preacher, also had a Ford touring car. He was far from being the outdoors type, but we needed transportation desperately and invited him. On the morning we left, Scouts piled into his car until it ranneth over.

Devil's River was a beautiful stream, running clear and shining through the rimrocked hills, and bordered for miles below the one-store town of Juno by big, shady live oaks. There were quiet, wide pools, deep and fringed with lily pads, wonderful for swimming and for setting trotlines at night. We found an old boat that would remain afloat if bailed incessantly, and camp began as a boyhood dream and a summer idyll.

All of us had had enough of close association with Prof during the school months just past to last us awhile. I could remember a day around mid-term, when the manual training class was building seesaws in the school yard with a great clatter of hammers and I was at the blackboard by the window, two stories up. Manual training and Latin were elective, and after two days of trying to drive a nail straight I had been advised to take Latin. After conjugating *amo, amas, amat* at the blackboard, I found I could bombard the manual training class with chalk, like an upstairs god. I had just thrown most of a whole box out the window when Prof suddenly walked out into the range of fire and got hit.

He was sharp enough to come upstairs and see who was near

the window. He took me to his office and applied the strap to my backsides. I did not hold this against him at the camp, and only hoped, with the other boys, that he would not try to enforce classroom discipline there. He did not. Prof was far too good a fisherman for that, and he was busy. We had fish nearly every night for supper, and he got sunburned and was pretty well worn out. One morning when I blew the call to colors and the flag was being hoisted, I had the pleasure of reminding him that he was supposed to get up off his bedding roll and stand at attention. Prof never held that against me either, so we were even.

But things were not so with the Other Preacher. One morning we were washing our breakfast dishes in the river, and everybody was joyously contemplating a day of hiking, swimming and boating. Early McBee had rolled up his pants and was standing in the stream to let it wash his tin plate and cup.

Early was about two years younger than I, and nobody could ever have suspected that he had a bent for poetry. But the beauty of the morning suddenly clutched at his throat, and he threw back his head and chanted:

> *Mary went a-fishin'*
> *To catch herself some bass;*
> *She waded in the water,*
> *And got wet up to her knees—*
> *The water wasn't deep enough.*

The little shout of mirth that greeted Early's ode died away as a shadow fell across the stream. We looked up to see the Other Preacher standing on the bank. He had not shaved, and there was a dark shadow on his thin, ascetic, cadaverous face. He puckered his lips sourly and clucked his tongue a few times in reproof.

"No Boy Scout," he intoned piously, "would ever use such vulgar and unworthy language! I seem to remember that the Scout Law says that a Scout is trustworthy, brave, loyal, clean and reverent. I am greatly shocked and disappointed; I am grieved to find that the Boy Scouts of Ozona resort to such speech, and furthermore, and so on."

He delivered a full sermon, and we were trapped, and the morning was wasting. After all, we owed the guy something, because he had provided transportation. But this wasn't a Sunday, and we had not come to Devil's River to hear Sunday-school lectures. Finally, he was done, and we went about the day, but its bright promises had somehow been dulled, and we brooded. We reminded ourselves that Early, after all, hadn't said a single bad word. This was my first encounter with the anticipatory censorship which begins with a built-in expectancy that a book is going to be vulgar, lewd and obscene.

The camp ran its course, and we avoided the Other Preacher after that encounter, although we strove to be helpful, friendly, courteous, cheerful and kind. And at morning colors, I first blew the bugle and then went by the ranks and managed to sneer at the Other Preacher's unmilitary appearance before I reported to the Scoutmaster that the troop was all present and accounted for. We were running that camp on a rather military basis.

We found ourselves out of sugar the first week, and the whole outfit—burning up energy at a fearful rate—was wild for some form of sweetening. Richard Flowers and I, hiking down the Comstock road, found a gallon bucket of molasses that had fallen like manna from heaven off some ranch wagon. We were hailed as heroes.

Going back to Ozona, we had our moment of revenge. Just behind the touring car driven by the Other Preacher was another open vehicle, and one of the boys in it was horsing around with that Daisy air rifle. He kept aiming it over the windshield at the boys in the car ahead.

One of these was Charlie Davidson, son of the county judge. Charlie looked back, and made derogatory signs, and dared the boy to shoot.

This went on for miles. Finally, on a curving, rocky road, the trigger was pulled. Charlie ducked, in the back seat, with beautiful precision. The BB pellet struck the Other Preacher on the back of his neck, and felt like the sting of a bumblebee.

He let go the steering wheel. He clapped both hands to the back of his neck, and yelped "Goddamn! Son-of-a-bitch!" The Ford ran into the ditch, and stalled there.

The kids in the back seat of the Other Preacher's car knew when school was out. They howled, and wrestled, and pounded each other the rest of the way home. The Other Preacher could do nothing with them then, nor later in Sunday school. No divinity any longer clung to him or shaped his end. After a few months more in Ozona, he moved on to other pastures.

I V

On the very first page of *The Adventures of Huckleberry Finn,* Huck says that the money Judge Thatcher put out at interest "fetched us a dollar a day apiece, all the year round—more than a body could tell what to do with."

When I first read the book I accepted this as gospel, and a dollar a day was my ambition in life. Selling the Fort Worth *Star-Telegram* achieved that ambition, but something had happened to the national economy. I didn't realize until later that Mark Twain was writing about the eighteen-forties; all I knew was that a dollar a day wasn't quite enough in 1916. This was my first lesson in the sad American philosophy that, no matter what you earn, it is never quite enough.

A smaller boy had been selling the newspapers for me while I was away at camp, and I still made a profit, and all at once I found I had $50. And then I remembered vaguely that when we first came to Ozona, Meinecke's store had a popcorn and peanut wagon. What had become of it?

I went to see Chris Meinecke. He said yes, the popcorn and peanut machine was gathering dust and cobwebs in his warehouse—it took all of one man's time to operate. And with the special intuition that had made him a leading Ozona merchant, he said, "For fifty dollars, you can roll it away."

I rolled the wagon up to our house and cleaned the windows

and oiled the spring mechanism. Mama had a charge account with the W. L. Watters store—successor, for a while, to G. L. Bunger. I went to Mr. Watters, who was both amused and kind, and he agreed to order 100-pound sacks of popcorn and 50-pound sacks of peanuts for me at wholesale prices.

All the worrisome details that should never be allowed to bother a big executive had to be ironed out: gasoline for the burner, cooking oil for the popcorn, paper bags in two sizes, a big salt shaker—they were endless. But finally the wagon rolled down the hill with the corn beginning to pop and make a minia-ture snowstorm within the glass enclosure, and the peanuts taking on that mouth-watering smell as they roasted in the revolving drum. I parked the machine in front of the post office, where people were waiting for the mail stage. It was a sellout, for both my newspapers and the popcorn and peanuts.

The *Stockman* published a glowing report about the Ozona Consolidated Popcorn & Peanut Company, Unlimited, and said: "Allie is a humdinger and will be one of Ozona's leading businessmen, someday."

Sometimes things just don't work out. But after the first two or three weeks, I found that I was making a profit of about $3 a day, thanks to the tremendous expansion of popcorn when it is popped. Of course, the new enterprise had to face various troubles. Always seeking a crowd, I ran it up in front of the Majestic Theater on movie nights. Kenneth Cox, the theater owner, protested that boys were buying peanuts not to eat, but to throw with skull-cracking accuracy between reels. And then, he said, rats carried the peanuts into his player piano and were ruining it. He wanted the peanut wagon barred.

A zoning ordinance or a city licensing system might have put me out of business, but it was an era of free enterprise, and I moved a few feet farther into the street and continued to op-erate. Finding a place where the machine could be stored at night was a tougher problem. Only the pool hall remained open until eleven o'clock, and minors were not allowed there. But I obtained special dispensation, and was permitted to run the machine there in the evenings, in return for sweeping out. To do this before school every morning except Sunday meant coming down at five or five-thirty.

The town's only barbershop at that time was a railed-off section in the pool hall, and in another small fenced area Bruce Drake operated a livestock commission business. The town had only three Negroes in residence—a woman who cooked at Mammy Kirkpatrick's hotel, a man named Fred Easterling who changed tires at Roger Dudley's garage, and a shoe-shine "boy," in his thirties, who worked at the barbershop and was known only as "Shine."

It had been the custom in Ozona, as in many another small West Texas town, for a delegation of young bloods to call on the colored citizens, individually, after about a year or so. "We figure," they announced, "that you've been here long enough. It's about time you moved on."

This, to be sure, was cruel. But it wasn't as bad as some towns back in Central Texas that had signs at the town limits, saying, "Nigger, Don't Let the Sun Set on Your Head in This Town!" Ozona at least allowed a short-term residence. People liked Fred Easterling, and he stayed for years.

I went down one morning before daylight and began sweeping the pool hall from the front to the rear, after sprinkling the floor with water to keep down the dust. Most of the litter was peanut shells, of my own making. But when I came to the barbershop railing, Shine had swept the area and left a pile of hair cuttings just outside the gate. He was sitting on the steps at the back door, polishing a pair of handsome brass cuspidors, more commonly known as "spittoons."

"Shine," I called, "come and get up this barbershop mess!"

Shine kept polishing. He said, offhandedly, "Well, you has to sweep out anyhow. You just sweep it out with your dirt."

Red flag. I was fourteen, and still in knickerbockers, and I weighed nearly a hundred pounds. At the time I thought nothing about racial discrimination or color, but only a fair division of labor. The barbershop was Shine's responsibility.

"Come on!" I said. "I'm not cleaning up your mess!"

Shine lifted a cuspidor and admired his distorted reflection in its polished surface. He said, "Won't hurt you none. You just sweep it out with the rest—won't hurt you none atall."

This was quite true. No extra muscular effort would have been involved. It was just the principle of the thing.

I went to the back door of the pool hall—it was a long building in the middle of the block, with no side windows or doors. I slammed Shine on the head with the wet broom. A little spray of water and dirt flew into the air.

Shine got up slowly, reaching into his shirt. His hand came out holding a straight-edge razor, and suddenly he had a lot of whites to his eyes. He said, "You hit Shine with the broom, Shine goin' to cut your heart out!"

It was no time to say, "Aw, now, Shine—you're kidding!" because it was pretty obvious that he wasn't kidding at all. And pride would not let me say, "Okay, Shine, I'll sweep it out!" And nobody knows just how much frustration Shine had built up in the town, shining boots for the Saturday night dances, drawing water for the cowboys' baths. The cook at the hotel was Fred Easterling's wife; there was no woman for Shine.

He advanced slowly, purposefully, the razor poised. I moved back, clutching the broom desperately, remembering that the town was still asleep. Shine's eyes had a wild glitter.

I jabbed the business end of the broom into his face. He turned his head slightly, but made no attempt to parry the thrust. He just kept coming.

I backed toward the front door. It was a long way off, and it had a night latch that was locked. If I put the broom down and tried to open the door, that would be when Shine closed in. The advance and retreat took on the quality of a grotesque dance: I backed, and Shine filled, and I poked him again with the broom, but he still kept coming. He said again that he was going to cut my heart out, and if he was only trying to scare me he succeeded admirably. My mouth was drier than dust and my legs were weak. I thought, *Well, this is where they will find me, but Shine can't get away—they'll track him down, and they'll hang him from a high live oak limb.*

Then the knob of the night latch bored into my back, and there could be no more retreat. And at the same instant somebody—I never knew who—went down the wooden sidewalk outside, cowboy bootheels clicking and spurs jingling.

Shine heard this, too. He stopped in his tracks, and put the razor away. He drew a deep, slobbering breath, and said, "Listen—Shine will clean up the mess! You just don't tell nobody about this ruckus, you understand? We be friends—we don't have no more trouble."

Now that the nightmare was all over, I was pretty near to crying. I said, "All right, Shine—all right."

He stayed on at the barbershop for about another year. I never did tell anybody about the razor episode.

v

The war finally came to America, and for such an isolated place as Ozona it arrived with a considerable bang. Floyd was back in the area, and when the news came on April 6 he headed for San Angelo and enlisted in the Navy the next day. That week saw a number of volunteers: Bill Grimmer and Wesley McBee and Condrey Metcalf joined the Navy; a little later, Ben Gilbert and Rex Russell were off to the Marine Corps. Bert Kincaid got caught in a thing he couldn't foresee—he enlisted in something called the Texas Cavalry, and was doomed to nothing more than training at Leon Springs and then a long period of waiting. They were discovering that there was little use for the cavalry in that war.

Hurst Meinecke, turned down by the Navy, registered with the Draft Board, and exactly filled the five percent quota of the first call. He had twenty-three months in the Army and thirteen months overseas. Houston Smith, my high school history teacher, went off to the Army as a second lieutenant, but never got across. Three Crockett County boys did not return. And when it was all over, and the figures were tallied, it was found that 97 men from the county had been in service.

This was no small contribution. The county reached 1,500 population in 1920, but in 1917 the count was no more than 1,400. Only three Meskins, being citizens, were taken from Lima by the Draft Board. There were 29 volunteers and 68 draftees.

Dillard Babb (whose brother had married my niece) was rather typical of the West Texas cowboy who went into uniform. Dillard was standing his first sentry detail when a captain came along, and said, "Let's see your gun." Having been warned to be very respectful of a captain, Dillard handed over the 1909 Springfield.

"Now, you're a hell of a soldier, to give up your rifle like this!" the captain said reproachfully. "Suppose I was a German spy—what would you do?"

Dillard reached into his shirt and pulled out a .45 Colt revolver—his own gun. He shoved this into the captain's belly, and said, "Why, I'd blow hell out of you!"

The officer paled. "My God man!" he said, "Where did you get that gun? Don't you know you're not supposed to carry private, unofficial weapons?"

Ninety-seven men in uniform from Crockett County. If the same percentage had applied all over the nation—by 1910 census figures—America would have had considerably more than 6,000,000 men under arms instead of 4,355,000.

In Ozona, at least one person out of every fifteen men, women and children, went to war.

They came back traveled, sophisticated, broadened; they could talk about the time when Forrest Dudley took a snapshot of Hurst Meinecke on the Rhine, or how Floyd lost the end of his index finger in a submarine battle when he was in an old coal-burning destroyer. They came back restless, and dissatisfied with small-town life as it had been before they went to far places, and saw things, and learned the words to the song about Mademoiselle from Armentières.

It was the old Western story all over again. These people had heard the owl and seen the elephant—only in a much larger way. And Ozona was approaching a new era as a result.

Meanwhile, however, a business enterprise had fallen. War is either kind or harsh to small businesses. After all the young men had gone to follow the drum, and the Saturday night dances were stopped for the duration, my popcorn and peanut business failed. I sold the machine for $50, and bought a Liberty bond. And then, while Mama and I were visiting my sister in Stephenville, I tried to join the Navy. The recruiting people were somewhat hilarious, and threw me out as being both underweight and underage. In the future, if asked about my World War I experience, I had to say "Mama wouldn't let me."

This rankled, and I made up my mind to get even with the United States Navy. But it took a while.

It Was

Once in

14 the Saddle

Come along, boys, and listen to my tale,
And I'll tell you of my troubles on the old Chisholm Trail—
Come-a-ti-yi-yippee, come-a-ti-yi-ya,
Come-a-ti-yi-yippee, yippee-ya!
—"THE OLD CHISHOLM TRAIL"

W ES BERRY WAS RIDING in the rain on the other side of the herd from me, long and lanky and still freckled as ever. I could hear him yipping and yelling and singing snatches of song like the verse above, and I could see him hooking a leg around his saddle horn every now and then while he pulled off his boot and emptied a quart of water out of it.

It was February and cowboys were getting hard to find. Wes qualified, easily enough, while I barely got by. We were taking a herd of about 500 cattle to the railroad shipping pens at Barnhart, perhaps seventy miles from their home ranch, and the drive made us very conscious of how the country was being fenced up everywhere; we had to zigzag down county roads until we came to the next pasture gate, then cross two or three pastures to reach another laned road where the driving was easy for a while. There was the boss—mostly riding ahead and taking side trips to the ranches we passed—and a

Meskin *cocinero* driving the chuck wagon. In all, we were a pretty small outfit, but Wes whistled and yipped and sang:

> *Oh, I jumped in the saddle, and I grabbed holt the horn—*
> *Best damn' cowboy that ever was born . . .*

and every now and then he gave out with:

> *Oh, it's cloudy in the west, and it looks like rain,*
> *And my damned old slicker's in the wagon again . . .*

which was only partly true. It rained every day and night of our weeklong drive—and neither Wes nor I had a slicker. The rain came in a slow, blowing drizzle, dripping from our hat brims and running down our jumper collars, and all our clothes were soaked from morning until night. I developed saddle sores, and the stirrup straps cut into my legs. We dried out each evening beside a campfire that made our clothes steam; we slept warm and dry in bedding rolls on the ground, with our tarps beneath and above the bedding, and the rain whispering softly on the canvas when it was pulled over our heads. We ate like horses every time the chuck wagon stopped, and told each other again and again that this was the life. I think Wes really believed this, because he went on living it for years, but by the time we had put that herd in the Barnhart shipping pens I was beginning to be a little dubious.

Mama and Dee were on one of the Friend ranches, nearly forty miles from Ozona. I joined them there after working for a while in Bunger's store, and Wes Berry was then at another ranch halfway up the road to town, holding down the place alone. He used to call me on the party line every night and hang onto the phone by the hour while I played records for him on the old wind-up graphophone. I got the idea that Wes was pretty lonesome.

We went to town once every month or six weeks—a day there and a day back by wagon—and I became more interested in automobiles because Dee was about to buy a Model T Ford. The pros and cons of the Ford planetary drive as against gearshift cars were being argued at Bunger's store one day when I was there, and just then Hop Hoover gave a very vivid demonstration.

Mr. W. P. Hoover had grown tired of tangling his spurs in the Ford's foot pedals. He took delivery on a shiny black Hupmobile that day, and Hop drove him down into the mesquite flat near the baseball diamond to show him how the gears worked.

They were back a little later, with the right side of the windshield shattered and Mr. Hoover considerably cut and bleeding. While he was being patched up in the doctor's office, Hop shyly and modestly gave an account of the mishap, in his rumbling, bull-calf drawl:

"I never had driven a gearshift car myself, but this here Hupmobile made it plumb easy, because down on the floor under the gearshift lever there is a slot shaped like an 'H,' and everything is marked—'L' for low, and things like that. Well, we started her up at the garage, and I looked down at that slot and seen 'L,' and I knew that stood for low, so I put her in low. Then I looked down and seen 'I,' and I figured that was for intermejut—so I threw her in that. It was the same thing with 'H,' for high.

"Well, we was moving along a pretty good clip—maybe forty miles an hour—and I kind of wanted to see how fast she would go. I looked down at that slot again, and I seen 'R' . . . and I said to myself, 'R stands for ramble!' So, I throwed her in 'R,' and Pa, the dadblamed old son-of-a-gun, he rambled right out through the windshield!"

11

At sixteen I was big enough to lend Dee a hand on the Frank Friend ranch, doctoring wormy sheep and cattle and dipping sheep to prevent scabies, but I was not gainfully employed there. I had dropped out of school at the end of February, after Wes Berry and I made the cattle drive—which meant going back in the same grade the next September. I was still hoping to follow Floyd into the Navy, and Mama was still saying that one boy in the Service was enough, and bless Patty, she'd see that I waited until I was eighteen.

Mr. Friend pointed out a huge live oak tree down in the draw, a half mile from the ranch house, and said it was a buzzards' roost.

"They're picking the eyes out of my lambs!" he said. "I know buzzards are supposed to be scavengers, but they turn predatory—they gang up on a small, weak lamb, and pick its eyes out, and then pull it down and kill it. You've got a twenty-two pump gun. I'll buy you all the cartridges you can use, if you'll kill buzzards."

"It's against the law!" I reminded him. "It's supposed to be a twenty-five dollar fine to kill a buzzard."

He said yes, he knew. He said that law was passed because of two things—the deadly blackleg disease in cattle and the disgusting habit buzzards had of throwing up every time you shoot one. If the buzzard had been eating a cow that had died of blackleg, this final and apparently involuntary act maybe polluted the grass, and other cows eating it could become infected.

"Maybe it was a good law—for cattlemen," he said. "But we're running mostly sheep here, and I can't afford to lose those lambs. I'll lay in a few boxes of cartridges, and you see what you can do. If they're going to roost on this ranch, I reckon they are my buzzards."

Every evening that summer I went down to the draw about sundown. I took cover under a mesquite or a catclaw bush, or a scrub walnut, and waited. The buzzards came in at dusk, always flying the same pattern, and flying low. I told myself that these were German bombing planes returning from a raid, and I was a gunner lying in wait for them, with sixteen shots in my antiaircraft battery.

Their wings made a dry, whispering sound; their very look,

thirty feet above me in the twilight sky, was the look of death and corruption. There were times when I emptied the rifle, opening up with rapid fire as soon as the leaders of the formation were overhead, and I almost always managed to bring down two or three. I learned that a loud slap of the bullet meant only that it had passed harmlessly through the wing feathers, and that the body of a buzzard is a gaunt and skinny thing, hard to hit. It was like Mr. Friend had said: hit one solidly, and it immediately disgorged, even if it fell dead. The crippled dropped with a great flapping of rusty wings that fanned and spread a horrible smell, and they had to be dispatched as something evil. Now and then I found a rattlesnake down in the flat; I learned to respect rattlesnakes, and although I killed them, it was not done with the relentless and bloodthirsty enthusiasm with which I tried to wipe out the buzzards. They were many, and the campaign never succeeded in eliminating them from the ranch. But after a summer's work with the .22, there were many fewer pitifully small carcasses of lambs that had been pulled down and torn apart.

With a war going on, I persuaded Mama that school could wait. We were still on the Friend ranch in November, 1918, and I was a week past my seventeenth birthday. We had no newspapers, of course, and no radio. All we had, aside from an occasional telephone call to Ozona, was Mama's dreams.

She woke Dee and me one morning, in a very jubilant mood. "I just know the war is over!" she said. "I dreamed about a big celebration—guns and firecrackers going off, and people dancing in the street—and I asked somebody what it was for. They said the war was over."

It was the 11th of November. Later that day we got a phone call through to town and asked about the news.

Mama's dream was correct. The Armistice had been signed.

III

That weeklong rain Wes Berry and I rode through just seemed like the last that was ever going to fall on West Texas. Fred

Gipson quotes an old-timer as saying, "It just got drier and drier—and finally it never did rain!" and that is how it was. The area entered upon a drought longer than anybody could remember; the grass sunburned and died, and was very suscep- tible to range fires; the blue northers howled down from the Panhandle with acres of topsoil blowing through the sky. Rich men became temporarily poor, poor men became even more so, and nobody knew how long it was going to last. The ranchmen who could afford to do so began feeding their stock.

Cattle feed at the time was mostly compressed cottonseed cake and cottonseed hulls, with bales of alfalfa hauled in from some place that had irrigation. The dust from the cottonseed cake began giving cows the sore-eye. A lot of livestock died, and the expense of feeding began mounting beyond the market price for the animals.

Still, what else could a man do? The fast transport business had not been developed. F. M. Joslin & Sons had begun oper- ating two or three ungainly Girard trucks from Barnhart to Ozona, hauling freight, carrying the cottonseed cake and the alfalfa, bringing beans and flour and canned goods in one day where the freight wagons had taken three days. But trucks could not yet negotiate the ranch roads, nor were they large enough to carry any appreciable number of cattle or sheep. If you were a rancher and saw your grass running out and your stock losing weight, you faced a difficult decision. You could drive the herd to the railroad while the animals were still capa- ble of walking—and there was a gambler's chance that while you were on the trail and planning to sell them at a loss it might rain. On the other hand, if you waited for a week or two and it *didn't* rain, the livestock might become too weak to put on the trail.

There was no answer, except in the cloudless, blue, burning skies, and in the whirlwinds that twisted across the mesquite flats, and most of all in the rawhide strength and courage of the people who had settled the county. They took up another notch on their belts and went grimly to work to save what they could.

Most of them were in debt past their ears to the stores in Ozona, and the stores in Ozona were running up fantastically large bills with the wholesale houses in San Angelo and Brownwood. During a short period in which I drove the horse-drawn delivery wagon—and later a Model T—for Chris Meinecke & Son, I heard a Brownwood wholesale salesman urge Mr. Meinecke to take a large order. Mr. Meinecke shook his head worriedly, and said, "I already owe your outfit seventeen thousand dollars, and I'm not taking in any cash. I don't see how I can pay."

"Are you still carrying J. W. Henderson on your books?" the salesman asked.

I listened with interest. I had just unloaded three freight wagons and a Joslin truck, all carrying 100-pound sacks of cottonseed cake, bales of alfalfa, and 160-pound sacks of oats. No sooner had all this been stacked in the warehouse than several 7N wagons from the Henderson ranches pulled up by the door, and the whole process had to be repeated in reverse. It seemed to me there ought to be a better way to do this: transfer the freight from wagon to wagon, and eliminate the double handling. But the freight wagons and the wagons from the ranches never arrived simultaneously.

Chris Meinecke said yes, he was still carrying J. W. Henderson, and added sadly that, although Mr. Henderson had been the first president of the Ozona National Bank and was still active in its affairs, he was like the rest of the ranchmen—he was land and cattle poor at the moment. It had been a long time, Mr. Meinecke said, since he had seen a J. W. Henderson check.

The wholesale house representative smiled, and opened his order book. "What do you need, Mr. Meinecke?" he asked. "I have instructions from my company that so long as J. W. Henderson is on your books your credit is unlimited."

O. Henry wrote two classical short stories built around this kind of trust in the Texas cattle country. One was "Friends in

San Rosario," and the other, entitled "A Call Loan," begins
with "In those days the cattlemen were the anointed."

And so they were. Finally the rains came, and the grass
sprang back in that marvelous way it has of doing—a way so
wonderful that anyone who sees it must believe the story of the
Resurrection. Cattle began putting on valuable pounds of good,
marbled beef. The lamb crop was above average, and so was
the wool clip. Money came back into circulation, and now
there were more shiny new automobiles on the ranch roads,
new town houses going up in Ozona, and jobs for everybody.

Ozona has seldom been seriously plagued by unemployment
problems for anybody except the "wetback" Mexicans, who
had waded or swum the Rio Grande to look for work in Texas.
These were beginning to show up on the ranches, hungry,
furtive-eyed and humble men, dodging through the brush. They
were eventually to bring about problems of international im-
port, and we will discuss them later.

But I remembered the previous summer, when a few people
like Rocky Armentrout had been out of work. Rocky was a
cowboy and an all-around ranch hand, young and yellow-
haired, rawboned and sunburned, and not very communica-
tive. He spent most of that summer squatting on his bootheels
in front of Bunger's store, asking about jobs when ranchmen
dropped in, and sighing every time a ranch wagon went by on
the dusty street. One day he broke his long and sorrowful
silence.

"I wisht," Rocky sighed, "that I had a million dollars!"

Ben Gilbert nudged me, suspecting that Rocky had little
conception of such a sum. He said, "Now, Rocky, what would
you do if you had a million dollars?"

Rocky removed his battered Stetson, scratched his head, and
gave his mythical riches some thought.

"Why," he said, "I'd—uh—I'd buy me a *whole carton* of
Bull Durham! And then I'd—well, I'd shore buy me a *whole
carton* of Bull Durham!"

IV

Rocky was not alone in being unable to plan the spending of any riches he might find or the wise use of any talents that might have been bestowed upon him. It was 1919, and the promise of the remarkable next decade was like electricity in the air. Turning eighteen, I felt change and growth not only within myself but everywhere around, and I was filled with a burning restlessness and all the shining dreams of youth. I had to get away.

It wasn't the town. Ozona was never too small to hold me or to call me back to its wide spaces and simple, openhearted friendliness, nor will it ever be. But the horizons were expanding. The boys who came back from World War I that year did much to add to the unrest of the youngsters who had stayed at home. They talked about leave or liberty in New York before sailing, and they had acquired polish and a casual air. Most of them had served in either the 90th or the 36th Division. The 36th went into the Argonne and didn't take off its shoes for three weeks of mud and slaughter, but later its people got back to Paris, and Paris left them bug-eyed. Then there was Rex Russell, who had been sidetracked to Santo Domingo with the Marines and spent the war chasing bandits, playing baseball, and hearing tales of voodoo. Talking to Rex pushed back the horizons in another direction—to the tropics and the banana republics of O. Henry's tales.

I left Ozona twice, the first time for only seven months. In January of 1920, during my second time around in the tenth grade, or junior class at high school, I left the halls of learning permanently. (The graduating class of 1920 consisted of one girl, Lucy Mae Augustine, the sole survivor of twenty students who had entered as freshmen in 1916. Ozona educators had this high dropout problem for years.)

I had been taking a correspondence course in "applied cartooning," without notable evidence of any artistic talent—even though I bought an artist's smock along with other equipment.

But I did illustrate *The Maverick,* which was the high school's first yearbook, before leaving in January. At the moment, my ambitions were crowded enough to cover a long lifetime and rather catholic as to taste. I wanted to join the Navy, be a newspaper cartoonist, become a railroad man, fly an airplane, write fiction, and maybe make a lot of money as a traveling salesman.

It is difficult to see, now, how a business college course would have been of very much help in any of these fields. But Ben Gilbert was going to Houston to study bookkeeping and typing, and that made it good enough for me. We had two suits tailored exactly alike, and amused ourselves on the long train trip by telling people we were brothers. Reaching Houston at night, we went to the only hotel Ben knew about—the Rice—and found ourselves in a room that cost $17.

Ben counted the lights in the chandelier and around the walls, and announced that there were seventeen of them. We turned all of them on, and left them burning the rest of the night. Next day we found a rooming house, and paid for life tuitions at the business college. This left me broke, and I immediately got a job in the check stand at the Union Station, with daytime hours, and enrolled for study at night. Ben had money left, and he signed up for day school.

He went twice to classes. On the second day he had a fist fight with the bookkeeping instructor, who had irked him somehow. He brought his books back to the rooming house, and thereafter devoted his time to other pursuits—principally that of our landlady's redheaded and Junoesque daughter, who was already a divorcee at fifteen.

It annoyed me that I, three years her senior, was nowhere nearly so far advanced. But I was loyal to Ben: I attended only three sessions of night school. I suppose that lifetime tuition certificate is still around somewhere.

Floyd was firing on the Fort Worth & Denver Railroad, out of Amarillo. He wrote me that if I would join him there we could make a lot of money in the fall, when the wheat began to move out of the Panhandle. This was my chance to be a railroad man, and I jumped at it.

The romance of the rails lasted only a few months. I had not seen Floyd since he left for the Navy. When I got off the train, he glanced appraisingly at the several inches I had grown, and said, "Well, I guess you can pass for twenty-one, all right. Have to be twenty-one to get a job firing. You got any money?"

I said no. I said I thought he had money, because he had written that we could earn as much as $80 a week.

"We can—after the wheat begins to move," Floyd said. "I'm on the extra board, now, with about a dozen other firemen, and none of us have regular runs. They call the people on the board in rotation when they have extra runs. But I can always draw pie-books, good for meals in the railroad eating house, so we'll make out all right."

A "pie-book" was a $5 book of coupons, charged against Floyd's future pay, and he didn't realize he was dealing with the appetite of a growing boy.

Next day I told the railroad people that I was twenty-one, took a physical examination, and was hired as a student fireman. This meant three weeks of "scissors" trips as a student, after which I might be put on the extra board. But railroads had a practice of always withholding two weeks' pay, so it would be a month after that before I could draw any money.

Floyd drew another $5 pie-book, and I had to buy overalls and a peaked blue cap. I climbed into a huge, panting steam locomotive early next morning, and the regular fireman pointed to a big scoop, and then mounted the seat and took his ease.

"Better stoke her up a little, Smoke," he said. "You've got an eighteen-foot firebox. You have to bounce the bottom of the scoop on the sill of the fire door, so the coal will spray out all the way. You have to watch the fire to see that there ain't any dull spots, and you have to watch the steam gauge and the water glass."

The engineer opened his throttle and we began to move

slowly out of the yards. I took the scoop handle with my right hand on the grip and the left hand forward, which seemed natural to me. But this stance found me facing the left gangway. After shoveling two scoops of coal into the firebox, I felt the engineer's shoe in the seat of my overalls.

"Get your tail out of my face, Smoke!" he yelled. "Turn around—how do you expect to see my signals?"

Then he put his thumb to his mouth, fingers closed in his palm.

"That means take on water," the fireman said. He scrambled back over the tender with me as we went under the water tower, and showed me what to do. The behemoth panted and groaned. The fireman lowered his voice a little as we pulled down the big water spout and straddled it to hold it against the pressure. "That engineer," he said, "can learn you a lot, and he can break your back, too. Had a dry boiler bust on him once. So he won't leave the water injector to the fireman—he'll come around the boiler head any old time, and crack the injector, and kill your steam. Wants the glass nearly full. They call him High Water Joe Hummel."

I shoveled coal steadily for four hours, scattering piles of it on the lurching gangway through missing the fire door. We got to the top of the Channing Grade, pulling a long string of freight cars, with no great head of steam. Then, sure enough, High Water Joe Hummel got down from his seat to look at the water glass. He cracked cold water into the boiler, and the steam gauge dropped alarmingly, and the regular fireman had to take over for a while. But he did not intend to do any more work than was absolutely necessary, so long as he had a student along, and by the time we were headed for the roundhouse in Amarillo—after a ten hour run—I was tired, sore, blistered, and covered with soot.

"How'd it go?" Floyd asked.

"Well, I popped the safety valve—once."

"With High Water Joe at the throttle? Where?"

"Coming down Channing Grade."

Floyd laughed, and led the way to the railroad eating house. "Look," he said. "We've got to make the pie-books last longer —we've already eaten up as much as I'll have coming. Now, I'll show you a little system. I reckon Mama would say it's like stealing, but I don't figure it's a crime to rob a Big Corporation. Besides, the world owes a man a living."

We went into the place, where at least twenty men in railroad overalls sat at a long counter. We went all the way to the far end of the counter, and each ate a 75-cent meal. The waitress handling that section gave us two 75-cent checks.

Then we went back halfway toward the cashier. Floyd suddenly stopped and slapped a diner on the back.

"Hi, Smoke!" he said. "How's the world treating you?"

"Can't complain," the fireman said, looking mystified.

"Let's have a cup of coffee," Floyd said to me. We slid into seats next to his friend, and they chatted while we drank coffee. That waitress gave us two 10-cent checks.

We went out past the cashier then, and Floyd paid the two dime checks out of his pie-book, keeping the 75-cent checks in his pocket. I could see that a pie-book would last much longer that way.

"Who was your friend?" I asked when we were outside.

"Him?" Floyd said. "Hell, I never saw him before. He just happened to be by two vacant seats."

v

I fired on the railroad, as a student without pay, for almost three weeks, and all the time I became more and more appreciative of Ozona's earlier expressed policy of keeping the railroads away from her door. Then I took a much easier job as a news butcher on the Santa Fe, and began earning $6 or $8 a day, and also I began getting homesick for Ozona.

In September, when it was already turning cool in the Panhandle, I went home. My old high school classmates were now seniors and, what was more, the school had a football team for the first time in its history.

"You've got to come back to school, Allie!" they told me. "We haven't got but eleven men, and two of them only weigh a hundred and five pounds. We need you for the game with Fort Stockton—just two weeks from now."

I said I couldn't afford to go to school. They argued that I could go for just two weeks, anyway, and then play in that game. This was being dishonest, of course; this made me a "ringer." But after the way Floyd and I had robbed the railroad eating house for three weeks, it didn't seem too dishonest.

There was a new English teacher named McNeil—a personable young man who was selling magazine pieces to *Smart Set* and other periodicals, and enjoyed talking to his classes about writing. Only two weeks' association with him was enough to affect my whole life.

We crowded into two Ford touring cars for the 120-mile ride to Fort Stockton, over roads that left us bruised and sore the evening before the game. There were no substitute players at all, and the eleven-man team had to go all the way. Richard Flowers, at quarterback, was then only 105 pounds, but he made up for it in speed and determination. I played right end. In the heat of conflict I forgot all the rules and all the signals I had attempted to learn in several practice sessions; I tackled two Fort Stockton players by the neck, and got the Ozona team penalized for unnecessary roughness. But Sherman Taylor carried the ball for the only touchdown of the game, and Ozona won in spite of the penalties.

Then I took a job for a month on a ranch, building fence with Alvin McBee, and his brother Early—he of the Devil's River deviltry—and their father. Mr. McBee was a perfectionist. His contract called for a fence with posts twenty-five feet apart and the wolfproof wire walking a straight line over the hill. Well more than half the postholes had to be dug in solid rock—Mr. McBee held unswervingly to the line and to his measurements, and would not allow any deviation of a few inches to put them in yielding dirt. The first day of such digging with heavy, jarring crowbars made our arms and shoulders ache and raised huge blisters inside our gloves. The second day broke the blisters, and the gloves stuck to our palms. There were as many ledge rocks the third day, and now the sticky substance was blood, and the gloves were wearing through. Our camp was near a windmill that pumped strongly sulphurous water. It smelled bad, tasted worse, and ruined the coffee and the beans. It probably was very good for the blood.

In the little time I lay awake in my bedroll at night I took stock of my ambitions. The trade of cowboy had really been checked off long before, and now I drew a line through general ranch work because that included fence building and maintenance. Railroading had left me something less than enchanted. But, after all, I *was* an old railroad fireman, and should have developed some muscle swinging that coal scoop, and if the McBee boys could last a month on this job, I could, too.

We finished the fence with the days growing cooler. I drew $40 in pay, kissed Mama good-by again, and went back to Houston. The Navy was still reducing its postwar surplus of manpower, and it was not until July, 1922, that I was enlisted as an apprentice seaman and sent to San Francisco for training.

But I had settled the career question—for at least four years.

Fourteen months later I came back to Ozona on thirty days' leave, after serving in a battleship manned principally by people from New York's East Side and the Bronx. "Kuzn Bill" Easterling, who was publishing the *Stockman* then, listened with growing disgust as I conversed with some friends on the sidewalk in front of his office. Finally he stepped to the curb, spat tobacco juice, and then said, "Son, you talk like a goddam Yankee."

Mama and Dee moved to Sanderson, west of the Pecos, while I was there. I went back to the Navy, and my last real connections with Ozona had been severed for a long time.

Anointed

with

15 Fresh Oil

In 1919 there nestled in the hills of Crockett County a quiet little village of progressive people, all well-to-do or fairly prosperous and content with life, happy that the war was over and rejoicing for the boys would soon be home.

But with these new conditions came complications—first one aeroplane then another. Soon a permanent landing was established, which in turn caused the government to see the possibility for this border country. The benefit to be derived from the aeroplane was the carrying of mail, especially in rainy, muddy weather. Then, one by one, derricks began to spring up like mushrooms over night. Things came to fever heat. One morning a terrible smoke and fire were seen. That was the herald of the first oil well, for the Henderson No. 1 had come in with a 50,000 barrel production, which was followed by many more equally as good.

—''PROPHECY,'' WRITTEN IN 1919 BY ELIZABETH CHILDRESS, SOPHOMORE CLASS, AND PRINTED IN THE HIGH SCHOOL ANNUAL

YOUNG MISS CHILDRESS should have been accorded honor in her own country, a few years later. She called the turn on the establishment of the air mail at a time when Ozona had seen only one or two planes—tandem-seated, open cockpit ex-Army Jennies on barnstorming tours. And the only thing about her oil well forecast was that she picked the wrong ranch, although the general area was correct, and she stepped up the initial production considerably. It wasn't a bad prophecy at all for a pretty little blonde in high school.

A number of things happened in Ozona during that first ten years after I left. Johnson Draw ran wild on April 24, 1922, and put half the town underwater without doing too much damage. L. B. Adams' garage floated across the street and settled on another man's lot, and a five-room house belonging to W. F. Delong—one of the government trappers who was competing with Nick Wigzell for coyote scalps—was lifted from its blocks and carried nearly a mile to the J. W. Patrick pasture. The family was away, and the voyage was smooth: dishes stayed on the dining-room table and two buckets of milk remained on the kitchen floor without spilling a drop.

But it would have been well for Ozona citizens to pay some heed to the old-timers, who said that Johnson Draw did that sort of thing every twenty to twenty-five years. As it was, nobody paid them much attention, and as it was to turn out, they may have been as good in the prophecy line as Elizabeth Childress.

The year of 1922 saw the first real interest in oil leases in Crockett County, and the people of Ozona, while not actually excited, were forced to begin learning a new jargon and place names they had never heard before. Phrases like "the Marathon Fold" and "the Sheffield Terrace," and "structural locations analogous to the locations of the Read anticline" began appearing in the *Stockman*. Kuzn Bill Easterling, the editor, probably didn't understand them himself. He was at his best in a less technical and more folksy field, writing about the wife "of our shirt-front," or reporting that "Tom Smith is nominated for constable, having secured one vote. Tom says local politics are sure rotten, for at least five friends helped chaw his terbacker and promised votes." Or in announcing that the manager of the Mertzon baseball team had written the *Stockman:* "Tell the Ozona Giants that if they want to play ball, come to Mertzon;

if they want to fight, go to Mexico; if they just want to talk, go to ——."

But the oil leases were being signed, and men who were already wealthy in cattle and sheep were suddenly wealthier. In 1925 the first well came in on the L. P. Powell ranch, twenty-eight miles northwest of Ozona. Its initial production was only twenty-five barrels a day, but it was a start.

Crockett County was the fourth county in West Texas to produce oil, and it was not one of the major oil counties. Across the Pecos, to the westward, the Yates field was running wild, and people told all kinds of stories about old man Yates, who had just barely managed to make a living off his ranch until the oil wells came. They said he told his wife that now she could just have anything she wanted, and that she said, "Well, I've been needin' a new ax to cut kindlin' wood with, for a long time." And that the new oil town of Iraan was named for Ira and Ann Yates.

It may have been fortunate that when oil came to Crockett County it came to ranchmen who were already quite well off. There was no stampede to spend the new money. Nobody was averse to getting it, of course, but the general idea was to invest it in something lasting, like purebred Hereford cattle and registered Rambouillet rams.

Apparently the oil boom had nothing to do with the fact that earlier in the year 1925 the town of Ozona embarked upon a large program of landscaping. Until then most of the yards had mulberry shade trees and Bermuda grass lawns. Now it was suddenly discovered that pecan trees—which Ozonans had always associated with watercourses—would thrive in Ozona if well watered. And Bermuda grass became a pest, with its tangled runners. It took a while to eliminate Bermuda grass and get bluegrass growing on the lawns and in the town park, and it took a lot of water. The town had to drill more wells on top of Waterworks Hill; it had to install more modern pumping machinery and build bigger storage tanks.

But in a little while Ozona began to take on the green look of an oasis in the desert.

II

The man who was elected sheriff of Crockett County in 1928 was a most unusual sort. W. S. Willis was a native of Tennessee, which qualified him immediately as being from the state of Davy Crockett; he was a big, easygoing man who carried a gun, of course, but never used it in all the thirteen years he served as a peace officer.

Willis threw rocks instead, and gained considerable fame thereby. In Crockett County, no matter where you may be standing, there is always a rock at hand. Sheriff Willis took advantage of this.

One Christmas while his wife was cooking a turkey dinner for several prisoners who were lodged in the jail to await transportation to the penitentiary, the prisoners were ungracious enough to attempt a jail break. One got out and ran up Waterworks Hill, back of the jail.

Willis was in hot pursuit, and would not have been criticized if he had used his sixshooter. Instead, he threw rocks at the fugitive felon, and dodged rocks in return. The pitched battle lasted for some ten minutes, during which Sheriff Willis saved the county the cost of at least one 45-caliber cartridge. Finally he clobbered his man and brought him back to jail. "I guess," he explained later, "that I won because my rocks went straighter than his."

That way he became a legend. Over in Lima—"Little Mexico"—he was suddenly attacked by a Meskin who was under the influence of marijuana. This time the sheriff did not have his gun. But he found a rock, and knocked the Meskin unconscious with it.

Then he and Warren Clayton, son of the beloved Dr. A. W. Clayton, went deer hunting and ran into a bunch of wild *javelinas*. The *javelina* is a peccary, a wild hog, and some of the boars have tusks that reach from here to here and can cut a dog's throat or amputate a man's leg.

Sheriff Willis shot a *javelina* and thought he had killed him. He left his .30-.30 and ran down the hill to cut the boar's throat, and suddenly the *javelina* was up and on the prod, and up on the hill Warren was yelling, "Run, sheriff, run! He's about to get you!" Willis ran to an uprooted cedar tree with the boar slashing at his legs. He grabbed a rock as he went up the tree, and threw it. It caught the *javelina* between the eyes, and split his skull.

The sheriff's reputation as a rock thrower grew and grew. He was not one of the famous gunmen of the Old West, like Bat Masterson or Billy the Kid, or King Fisher. But he kept law and order in Crockett County, so long as there was a chunking stone within reach.

III

The town that had so successfully not wanted a railroad was standing by to watch Barnhart, thirty-two miles away, become the largest inland livestock shipping center in the United States —"inland," that is, in contrast to places like Fort Worth. And with wolfproof fences going up all over Crockett County, Barnhart became more and more difficult to reach with a herd of livestock. You couldn't drive cattle or sheep along a laned road for three or four days, without access to grass and water, and the huge trailer trucks that haul stock today had not been developed.

In 1924—forty years after the famous Chisholm Trail had been choked to death by fences—Ozona ranchmen evolved a bold and unique plan for getting their herds to the railhead. They organized the Ozona-Barnhart Trap Company, which set about buying holdover traps of grazing land and drilled several wells to provide water for transient herds. It must be remembered that in West Texas a "trap" has always meant a small pasture—perhaps 640 acres or more—where horses or cattle could be turned loose overnight.

The traps acquired by the Ozona-Barnhart Trap Company began south of Ozona and paralleled the stage road to Barnhart, all the way. The company sold 137 shares of stock at $100 per share, and Eloe Baggett, Vic Pierce and Jones Miller were named as a committee empowered to buy the needed land. They purchased or leased sixteen separate tracts, from the McCallum Trap of 489 acres, four miles south of Ozona, on up to Barnhart. There were four McNutt traps eleven miles north of Ozona, including the old McNutt well, two Midway traps on land leased from the University of Texas, two traps on Buckhorn Draw, where there was water most of the time, two dry traps on the old Clint Owens ranch, and several others. Finally, there was a "holding grounds" at Barnhart, consisting of thirty-one acres adjoining the railroad tracks.

The company built corrals and loading chutes here and installed lights for night loading as soon as electricity became available. One herd of a few hundred cattle could graze off that thirty-one acres in a few hours, so it became necessary to expand the Barnhart end of the facilities. The company leased five and a half adjoining sections of range—and the cowboys were back in business. You can't whoop it up very much while driving cattle along a narrow strip between two barbed-wire fences, but you've got room on five and a half sections to hang and rattle, and swing a wide loop.

In its own dry and dusty way, this transportation artery was just as important, and just as dramatic, as the storied Erie Canal had been much earlier. It delivered the goods—bawling and surging, tumultuous and recalcitrant, but watered and well-fed and without loss of precious weight on the hoof. Manager-operators of the system were hired—first Walter Capps, of Ozona, then Ted Adkins, and later a Barnhart man named Fred Kessler. Livestock weighing scales were installed at the loading pens, and the first grazing charges were set at five cents per head of cattle for every night in the traps and one cent per head for sheep.

I know of no similar arrangement anywhere else in the ranch country. The Ozona-Barnhart Trap Company licked the current problem, and held on until the roads were paved and big, fast trailer trucks began roaring along them. Its stockholders still get dividends from the land, through oil and grazing leases.

The twenties were a time of great growth and change. Ranchmen began weeding out scrub stock and breeding toward thoroughbred herds. And none of them would have believed it, but the time was coming when cowboys would be riding pickup trucks more than they rode horses, and nobody would have to sleep out any more with the "dry" cattle.

Ozona had no depression to speak of when the Big Crash hit Wall Street—or even later—because its money was in land and livestock, and not in securities. When President Roosevelt declared the national bank holiday Scott Peters, cashier of the Ozona bank, called a meeting of the town's businessmen and explained the situation to them. A fund of $1,000 was set aside by the bank to be used in making change, and business went on as usual. The Ozona bank reopened on March 15, after having been closed only ten days, and the people of the town promptly expressed their full confidence in its stability by depositing more than $50,000 that day.

In the long run Crockett County may have actually profited from the depression years, because the state launched a tremendous public works program and the county's two principal roads were paved. And all the time there was more of the strange but opulent-sounding oil field language cropping out in the *Stockman*. Such-and-such a company would drill the number so-and-so one location northeast of Shell or Texas or Humble—the discovery was finaled on this or that date for 370 barrels of 41.7 gravity oil, plus 22½ barrels of water, and with a gas-oil ratio of –910-1, through a 14-64 inch choke and perforations at 6,640 to 6,675 feet. It was drilled to 8,513 feet and a failure in the Ellenburger.

I have yet to find an Ozona ranchman who professes to understand all this. But I know of one who opened an envelope at the post office, took out a check for $750,000, and said, "Damn! This puts me in another income tax bracket!"

And as a friend of mine told me, laconically, "Hell . . . you don't *have* to savvy that oil well talk. The main thing to do is to own one!"

Feudalism
Is Not
16 the Word

Of course you know what Ozona is. It's one of the world's last strongholds of feudalism. The land is handed down, and nobody ever sells an inch of it to an outsider . . . and nobody ever runs for public office against an incumbent.

—DR. WALTER PRESCOTT WEBB, TO THE AUTHOR

Dr. WEBB, the late eminent and much-beloved historian, made the observation quoted above without rancor or malice. It was a Saturday night on Friday Mountain, the Webb ranch west of Austin, and he was having a stag party in my honor. Don Pancho (J. Frank) Dobie was there, and so was Fred ("Hound Dog Man") Gipson, and other Texas literary greats. Somebody said they had read a reference to Don Pancho as "the dean of Southwestern letters," and he grinned and said, "Don't call me a goddamned dean!" Fred Gipson sang "Jalisco" in impeccable border Mexican and a horrible baritone, and Dr. Webb told him, "Fred, you'd better stick to writing."

And that way Dr. Webb and I never did get around to a discussion of his remark about Ozona. But he was not the first to say that the way of life in Crockett County was feudalistic, and there was much truth in it. Ranch land in the area does remain in the family, and until the past decade or so many county officers did hold lifetime jobs.

But there is more to it than that.

One can draw an analogy, of course. Feudal lords loved their land, but I doubt that any titled Englishman of feudal days ever loved his sturdy oaks and the green meadows of his sheep-fold with a greater passion than Ozona ranchers love their rocky hills. This affection is early transmitted to sons and daughters. It is a quiet and unassuming love, and modesty goes with it. Some fifteen years ago, a reporter from the San Angelo *Standard-Times* asked Bill West if it was true that he was the biggest landholder in Crockett County.

Bill and his wife, Alma, had long been globe-trotting, leav-ing the ranch business to their sons, Wayne and Massie, their son-in-law, Ira Carson, and their daughters, Wilma and Alice. Bill cleared his throat and said he didn't know about that big-gest landholder stuff.

"Well, Mr. West," the reporter pursued, "they say you have more than a hundred sections. Just how much land do you own or control?"

Bill West studied the reporter for a minute. "To tell you the truth," he drawled, "I ain't never stepped it off."

Mr. West would have snorted loudly at being compared to a feudal baron. He liked grub out of a chuck wagon, and knew how to make son-of-a-bitch stew—which is a highly seasoned dish built around the marrow gut of a beef—and he had ridden some pretty bad horses in his time. But he met the responsibili-ties expected of a ranch owner: he was for a long time president of the bank, while Alma busied herself with church and school work. They helped Ozona march forward.

"Bill West?" said Walter Dunlap. "Listen—there was a dry spell, and I lost all my cows. I was flat busted. Went to the bank and borrowed $20,000 and put it into Angora goats, and Bill West went on my note. Well, you know how goats are—they make a living where a cow would starve, and you shear the mohair. In one year I made enough to pay off $10,000 of that note. Next time I saw Bill West, he said, 'Walter, I tore up that note the other day. You just handle the other $10,000 when it's convenient.' "

O. Henry. "Friends in San Rosario." In Ozona a man's word was as good as his signature on a piece of paper.

The term "feudalistic" has always been applied to large landed estates. The famous King Ranch, on the Texas coastal prairies, where Mexican *vaqueros* and their descendants have worked for more than a century—sure, that's feudalism. The 262,000-acre Parker ranch on the "big island" of Hawaii, where 40,000 cattle graze and cowboys with names like Johnny Kawamoto represent the fourth generation—that is feudalism too. And in these unsettled, unsecure times, one could well wish that there were more of it.

Ozona ranchers learned quickly that land units had to be large. They certainly had to have hire-and-fire control over their cowboys: when a man is out on the range, branding stock for you, you have to trust him and back him up. There was a little social difference with the Meskins—as much their choosing as yours—and you backed them up too. The whole ranch system began to be based on common confidence and regard, loyalty and understanding. It was a good life.

Ozona's labor pool was in the adjoining village of Lima, and the people there were a segment of society that lent itself all too well to the label of serfdom when sociological students first hit on the idea that here was a throwback to feudal days. But the Ozona people did not create Lima. They inherited it. "Meskins" followed the ranching industry, and worked in it, and were not very susceptible to change.

Up through the twenties, thirties and forties, the town stretched out, shrinking the distances of memory, filling up the weed-grown vacant lots with comfortable cottages, and mansions that had interiors done by Neiman-Marcus, and finally adding motels and the "mobile homes" of transient oil workers. Now the houses reached almost all the way south, across Gurley Draw, to Lima.

Lima is where the Meskins have always lived. Recently there has been a commendable tendency to call them "Latin Americans"—especially in print. But this is commensurate with the interest Meskins have shown in citizenship and all its responsibilities. In the old days few Meskins were citizens, and the rest of them couldn't have told you what the word meant. They lived apart because they were a very clannish people, proud with the stoical pride of the Indian. They were poor, and also they were given to the *mañana* philosophy of the border.

It is unfortunate that no artist came along to capture Lima on canvas. Clay Adams was just growing up; he became a wealthy Ozona ranchman who finally had the time to show that he had all the talents of Charlie Russell or Frederic Remington. But he worked on ranch scenes, and by then Lima had been changed.

For a long time the village was mostly a squalid cluster of dirt-floored, *sotol* and mud-walled huts, roofed with *sacaguista*. There were a few unpainted frame houses of two or three rooms, and an occasional more substantial adobe. Signs in the single business block were in Spanish. Blas Vargas kept a store there, and so did the brothers Aguirre—Simon and Firmin— who also owned a shearing machine and supplied crews, and generally prospered. But even these establishments had a south-of-the-border look. Burros and flea-bitten dogs roamed the rocky and dusty roads that served as streets, and gamecocks strutted in tiny back yards, waiting for the next fight. Here and there a gay mantilla or a beaded and embroidered sombrero made a splash of color, and morning-glory vines spilled over a sagging fence.

These people were happy, proud and independent, and if anyone had come along and tried to "organize" them, he would have been lucky to escape with his life. There was guitar music at night, and some tequila drinking, and knives flashed on occasion. If there was any man at all in the Ozona jail, it was a pretty safe bet that he was a Meskin—turned in by his own people when he became *muy borracho*. For its first two decades

Lima went without church or school—but it should be charitably remembered that Ozona wasn't very well provided with such facilities.

A tamale vendor from Lima used to pull a child's red wagon around Ozona, crying his wares. The tamales were delicious, but his sanitation was suspect. There was a rumor that somebody had found a dog's tooth in a tamale, and when a burro was known to have died in Lima, nobody bought tamales for days.

Still, the Meskins had no monopoly on casual culinary practices. Forest Dudley, now a Methodist minister in Dallas, remembers when he went on a hunting trip to Devil's River, and was supposed to stay with a ranch family there. He had just entered the house when a girl called from the kitchen:

"Ma, how can I tell when this skillet is hot enough?"

Ma's answer came succinct and clear from the next room. "Spit in it!" she said.

Forest said he had left something down by the road. He went back for it, and flagged down the mail hack back to Ozona, and hasn't been back to that place in forty-five years.

II

The population of Lima fluctuated with the roundups and the lambing and shearing seasons, but probably there were always a fourth or a third as many Meskins as there were Americans in the county. The men hauled and sold firewood—stolen from the ranches, of course—and their wives took in washing. The men who worked on the ranches were born *vaqueros,* and were content to spend months at a time *vaya con borregos,* or "gone with the sheep."

The changes were gradual. The Ozona conscience is a conservative sort, generous indeed in the long run but perhaps not impulsive. It began working back in 1912, when Ozona asked itself what it was doing for the Meskin children who had been born to citizenship.

They moved a one-room schoolhouse to Lima that year,

when the new Ozona consolidated school was built. Mary Burchett was the first teacher, and a good one. Several years later she was succeeded by Lela Johnigan, a pretty high school graduate who captivated her Latin charges so much that before long everybody wanted to go to *la escuela*. The school became crowded. There are many kids in Lima, señor.

It was a revolution of sorts. Some of the old-timers viewed it with alarm, although they still wrote checks to pay for what was happening. They said if you improved a man's mind you might make him discontented with his lot.

The one-room school finally had to be replaced by a four-room building, and instead of one teacher there were four. But now the enrollment had increased to some three hundred pupils —and also the Ozona school buildings had become palatial by comparison.

The conscience nagged. In 1937 the Woman's Missionary Society of the Methodist Church opened a Community Center in Lima, and patterned it after the famous Hull House in Chicago. It began as a summer project, then became full time with the employment of Miss Mary Riddle. She was so fascinated with the work that she stayed ten years. Citizens then established the Mary Riddle Scholarship Fund and kept the program going.

The women were in the driver's seat again, just as they had been when they persuaded the menfolk to vote out the saloons. They saw to it that Lima had a very modern school plant— with a swimming pool—by the 1950's. This was South Elementary, and for the first time its graduates were being accepted in Ozona High School. Most of the boys, to the whole town's delight, proved to be stars at baseball, basketball and football.

But Ozona's problems were not over. The small Negro population had grown enough to have about thirty children of school age. The Meskins were every bit as segregationist-minded as the Anglo-Saxon citizens; they would not send their children to school with the Negroes. The town paid again through the pocketbook and set up a third school system, with equal facilities, two teachers, and an arrangement for the pupils to get high school credits.

To attract good instructors to such an isolated locality, the town bought lots, built a number of comfortable ranch-style houses, and made them available to teachers at rent of about $30 a month. This has resulted in top-grade teaching staffs for all the schools.

The Community Center, under the leadership of Mrs. R. A. Harrell and other civic-minded women, has continued to expand. In 1962 it had 150 children a day from Lima and had begun desegregation with kids of all three races at the kindergarten level. There were lessons in swimming, music and drawing. The piano class had forty-eight students, 153 children were in Scouting programs, and Lima boasted proudly of having seven Eagle Scouts. Adults were taking courses in English and citizenship, and a class in driver's education was well attended. There was a beautiful Catholic church in Lima now, built in traditional Spanish Mission style. The village had a Protestant church too, and the city fathers of Ozona had paved the streets and installed a sewer system. Sam Martinez ran an excellent Mexican restaurant, sent two sons to college, and was an active and respected member of Ozona service clubs. He was typical of the new, grown-up, modernized Lima.

There was finally nothing much on Ozona's conscience. Her people had done good works, quietly and modestly, and Lima was far superior to the "Meskin towns" of other Texas communities.

Still, there was an uneasy air about the place. It was no longer easy to find shearing crews, sheepherders, or all-around ranch hands in Lima. Two years ago the Ozona ranchmen financed and staffed a "shearing school" in an effort to teach young men the fast-vanishing skills required to handle a shearing machine "drop" and strip off the fleece. Not many were interested. The pay was good, but shearing was seasonal work and took a man away from town; the youth of Lima had found that if they wanted to leave home they could get jobs in chemical or aircraft plants, or oil refineries, and some were making careers in the armed forces. Married men wanted work in town, where they could be with their families.

One seldom heard the old *vaya con borregos*. Nobody was gone, any more, with the sheep.

And citizenship has more advantages than just the right to vote. *Que parada, señor!* Do you know this thing what they call the unemployment compensation? For a few months, you work. Then *ser gallo*—you take the siesta under the pecan trees in the park, and maybe drink a little tequila. When the *rancheros* come and ask you if you want the job, you laugh and say you are still drawing the money.

III

"Feudalism" is not quite the word. The feudal system did not admit the existence of a middle class nor allow room for it. Ozona has always had its land barons, but it has always had a pretty solid middle class. Despite any sociological critics, the way of life there has proved its worth: it nurtures good citizens, conservative and constructive thinkers, and stalwart patriots.

I wrote to the Rev. J. Troy Hickman, now associated with the First Methodist Church of Corpus Christi, to ask his views on Ozona's "feudalism." He was active in the town for a number of years, is an accomplished observer and journalist, and wrote features for a number of publications. Here is his reply:

"In perspective it seems to me that my little wisdom about Ozona can be summed up by saying that, like other things human, Ozona is what it is by necessity; and could not possibly have been any other way, given the same conditions. The first families who set the early community tones, the isolated location, and the relation between large blocks of land and human lives and livings, combined to make this unique little community what it was and is. The incidents of changing national patterns of communication, the oil industry and other things beyond their control will, in time, make them something else. The process is already under way."

I note that the Rev. Mr. Hickman does not attempt to elaborate on "what the community was and is." Nor can I attempt to do this. There is something indefinable about Ozona, and for one I shall be sorry to see it become anything else.

And if I could have had the pleasure of talking with Walter Prescott Webb a little longer, perhaps I could have come up with a descriptive phrase for Ozona. Maybe one should say that it is run on the *"hidalgo* system." *Hidalgo* is a Spanish contraction of *hijo de algo,* meaning a son (of a man) of property. This would cover Dr. Webb's comment about the land being handed down, since virtually all of today's Crockett County ranchmen are the sons of the original property owners.

The Life

and Hard Times

17 of Juan Garcia

Bill Jordan is a Border Patrolman stationed down at Port Isabel, and maybe you've seen him on TV. Bill is six feet, six inches. He can hold a Coca Cola bottle at arm's length, drop it, draw his gun, and shoot it to splinters before it hits the ground.
—J. W. HOLLAND, SAN ANTONIO DISTRICT DIRECTOR
OF THE U. S. BORDER PATROL

BILL JORDAN'S PRESENCE at Port Isabel, and that of scores of other border patrolmen along the wild 889-mile Texas bank of the Rio Grande from Port Isabel to El Paso, is largely made necessary by the pitiable plight of a ragged little man we shall call Juan Garcia.

Juan is a Mexican "wetback"—an alien who wades or swims the border river to look for a job that will earn him solid *Yanqui* dollars. Sometimes he is barefoot and has a piece of rope holding up his faded *pantalones;* always he is hungry. Despite his lowly status, however, Juan has played a considerable role in the economic and sociological development of Crockett County, and has been one of the most controversial figures to appear in Texas since the days of the Governors Ferguson—Jim and "Ma." He and thousands of his brothers

[186]

have come more and more into the editorial pages of newspapers and have sparked acrimonious debate in the legislative
halls of two nations.

Ozona ranchers time and again have proved themselves
among the most generous of all people. They wish all men well.
But of latter years, some of them insist that the civic better-
ment of the village of Lima has really backfired—in a manner
that helps Juan Garcia. "You educate a man beyond his raisin',"
one of them said, "and the next time you need a ranch hand,
there ain't any. I reckon you can't blame the local Meskins
—they've got cars, now, and we've got highways. They can
take off for the Lower Rio Grande Valley and pick grapefruit,
or they can work laying a pipeline. They don't want ranch
work. Then your lambs start droppin', and you're damn well
goin' to hire any man who comes along and really wants to
work! That's American, ain't it?"

The right to work is, indeed, an American ideal. But the
Immigration Department considers it un-American to hire
Juan Garcia. There is a tacit understanding between the ranchman and Juan, to the effect that Juan had better take to the
tules if he sees the *chota*—the Border Patrol—snooping around.
But maybe Juan gets in a couple of months' work before he is
caught. He goes back to Mexico with the *Yanqui* dollars jingling his pocket, and cannot resist boasting about how rich he
has become.

And then all of Juan's friends strike out to cross the river
and get rich, too. Not all the officers in the entire force of the
Border Patrol could stop this infiltration.

Of course what has happened and is still happening here is
not really the result of improved educational facilities such as
Ozona established in the village of Lima. It is a part of a much
larger picture that takes in the shrinking of the frontier, the
advancement of science, and the development of communications. Nobody needs blame himself, or anyone else. But an
imbalance has been created. The West Texas ranchman is still

pretty much dependent—at least in season—on Meskin help. But the Meskins are no longer dependent upon him.

There have been wetbacks from the earliest days, but the term seems not to have been coined until the 1930's. West Texans still tend to differentiate between "Meskin" and "white man," although there is not always a derogatory inference. Indians are not offended by being called Indians . . . and the Meskins run strongly to Indian blood. It is not as bad as it was in the nineteenth century, when a youngster asked the notorious King Fisher how many men he had killed, and Fisher countered with, "Counting Meskins?"

By the 1940's there was a general tightening of immigration rules and security measures along the border—a desirable wartime precaution, because Texas was loaded with training camps and defense plants. By the 1950's the problem was rising full force. Ozona ranchmen had begun to turn their land into game preserves, to keep out hordes of hunters from Dallas and Houston and other places, and they began padlocking their pasture gates—which it would seem they had the right to do if a man has the right to lock his front door.

But the Border Patrol, looking for wetbacks, insisted that no agent of the federal government is required to have a search warrant and was not averse to shooting off the locks. Things had come pretty far along the road to rebellion against federal law.

By now every American taxpayer was paying the costs of an increased Border Patrol, as well as the expense of hauling whole busloads of wetbacks back to Mexico after they had been rounded up on the Texas side. The Rev. J. Troy Hickman, then in Ozona, deplored this expense in an article published in the *Stockman,* pointing out that the wetbacks could and did return almost immediately.

"For one thing," he went on, "the wets are doing us no special harm. They are helping themselves and their families.

And they are helping us by furnishing workmen where workmen are wanted. This mutually profitable state of affairs is not bad at all, even if it is illegally irregular. Perhaps it is the law, rather than the fact, that needs to be mended."

The law was not mended, and likely never will be. Organized labor has gotten into the act. It was easy to find a local Meskin who would say he had been done out of a job by a wetback. What he did not say was that his employment was conditioned on the ranchman's driving him back to town—perhaps forty miles—at the end of every working day and picking him up again in the morning. Organized labor lumped the wetbacks into the same category as the thousands of "commuters" who live in Windsor, Ontario, but work in Detroit—and both groups were tagged as a menace to the American bread earner.

This is simple reasoning, and in the case of the wetbacks in West Texas it is about as absurd as the answer an Idaho sheepman reportedly got out of the War Production Board in 1943. Winter was hanging on toward the lambing season, and he sought permission to buy extra tarps for shelters. He received the following reply:

Dear Sir:
It is impossible to allow you such a large amount of canvas for the purpose of making lambing sheds. As an alternative, we suggest that you postpone your lambing season until more favorable weather.

King Canute and the tide had nothing on this. When the ewes begin to feel labor pains, lambs will drop in spite of hell and high blue northers—and a large number of ewes will need assistance.

II

When Juan Garcia crosses the Rio Grande just after dark he is motivated by very simple reasons. In Mexico, if he is lucky enough to have a job at all, he earns the equivalent of $15 U.S. a month and lives in a hovel. North of the Rio Bravo he can get $75, $100, or even $125 a month—plus his keep—working on the ranches. Six months of such fantastic pay (provided he has not been caught by the Border Patrol) and he can go back to Mexico and buy a bunch of goats, a few cows, or even a small farm. In six months he has been lifted from the status of *pelado* to that of *haciendado.*

Farther down the river, where the days are hotter and therefore lazier, Juan can apply—legally—for seasonal work on the Texas side, in the grapefruits and the lettuces and other farm products. He then becomes a *bracero,* or contract laborer, and the Border Patrol cannot touch him, because he has a pass good for perhaps 210 days. But that is in the Lower Rio Grande Valley—a very long way off. Four or five hundred miles upstream, where they are building the Amistad Dam, there is no farming. But Juan Garcia understands the ways of sheep and goats.

"It's not a question of doing a white man out of a job," an Ozona ranchman told me last summer. "I just can't hardly get a white man to work on my ranch. You remember when every cowboy had his own working rig, and nobody ever sold his saddle? There was a teacher who asked 'Who was Benedict Arnold?' and a kid said, 'He was an American general, but he sold his saddle.' Well . . . today, if I found a cowboy with his own saddle and bedding roll, I'd just drop dead with surprise. And when I do hire a white man, he expects me to drive him back to town, forty miles, every night."

Perhaps the labor unions, very sensitive about overtime pay, do not realize that ranch work actually goes on twenty-four hours a day. At lambing time, somebody has to go out with a lantern and do a little stint as a midwife, washing his hands and arms with disinfectant and then anointing them with petroleum jelly or vaseline, because every so often there is a "breech presentation," or what in a hospital would be a forceps case. Somebody also needs to be handy with a mild tincture of iodine to swab the blessed little raw navel of every single blankety blank newborn lamb, and it is smart to carry a small baby syringe to feed some of the little cusses until their mothers' milk comes down. And—oh, yes—you need a pair of hand clippers to "crutch" the ewes before lambing. This means shearing off the wool around the udder, so that baby won't have a dirty, wet "tag" in his mouth instead of a life-giving teat.

And maybe the labor union bosses don't understand that a flash flood in the night can wash the water gaps out of a half dozen fences, and unless they are fixed by an hour after sunup, your livestock and mine can be very expensively mixed up. Or if a divide windmill breaks down, cattle and sheep can lose very valuable pounds going farther for water, or can even die of thirst.

"You take the local Meskins," the Ozona rancher went on. "Now, I've seen the time when they were mighty good hands, but I reckon we spoiled them. They'll work, now, when they feel like it, and they'll lay off when they want to. Ranch work ain't like that. I'll take the wetbacks when I can get them, because they shore-enough appreciate a job, and they don't know when to quit."

In some seasons Juan Garcia can walk across the Rio Grande dry-shod, because irrigation dams far up the river steal its flow and demean it as a frontier still boldly shown on the map. But once on Texas soil and searching for his individual *Gran Quivira*, he has to trudge a hundred miles or so to be at all safe. He sleeps on the ground, daytime, or keeps into the chaparral well off the roads, and watches for windmills spinning in the sun, because these mark ranches.

All the time he can feel the hot breath of the *chota* on his neck.

With fences in Crockett County, and windmills supplying water day and night, there is considerable absentee ownership on smaller ranches where it does not pay to have a resident foreman. It is not very far from any ranch to a paved road, these days, and a ranchman can drive to his town house in Ozona in an hour or two. Most of the larger predators have been trapped out; his flocks or herds are reasonably secure overnight or for even a longer period.

But when he goes to Ozona, or takes longer trips to San Angelo or Forth Worth, he never locks the ranch house. There is always food on hand, and the stove is ready.

In the old days this was for the neighbor who happened by, on horseback or in a wagon, and ranch owners were downright offended if a man did not " 'light and sun his saddle, and fix some grub." Today it is for the wetbacks. "Some hungry Meskin," the ranchers say, "may come by and need to fix himself a meal, so I always leave some bacon and beans and canned goods. Hate to see any man go hungry, but it's more than that. I got some pretty high-priced Hereford calves and Rambouillet lambs out in my pasture, and I shore don't want any barbecues down in the mesquite flat!"

Cases of theft are so rare as to be almost negligible. Either Juan Garcia is basically honest or he's smart enough to know that if he is caught with stolen goods it will go much harder with him.

"And they are mighty light eaters," Ernest Dunlap told me. "Beans and coffee—that's about all they want. I figure they just ain't had much to eat, and their stomachs have shrunk. I appreciated the good ones I had working for me, and tried to give them a little more fancy grub. And they just wouldn't eat it."

Coming up from the border river, Juan has to cross a highway or two, along with the sandy "bar ditches" at the sides of the pavement. In dry weather the Border Patrol drags the bar ditches, and then scout cars cruise slowly along the road and officers watch for footprints headed north. In one case they found footprints going south, but they didn't look quite natural. Further investigation revealed that a wetback had crossed the highway at that point—walking backwards.

Damned clever, those Border Patrol men—and they need to
be. Up toward El Paso a pair ran across a most unusual trail,
and one told the other that he had followed a few cow tracks
in his time but this was his first experience in trailing a two-
legged cow. A few miles out in the mesquite they overtook
Juan Garcia. He was plodding along valiantly—with cow
hooves strapped to his feet.

Most ranchmen are open-minded and gracious enough to
admit that the Border Patrol has been ordered to do a job,
and is doing it. Most of the Border Patrol officers say they can
understand the plight of the wetbacks and the needs of the
ranchmen. They add, however, that the law is the law.

And of course there have been exceptions to this mutual
understanding, on both sides.

III

As late as December, 1962, the wetback dispute was fanned
to glowing heat by a letter purportedly written in defense of
the Border Patrol, and published in the San Angelo *Standard-
Times*. This letter, and some of the quick rejoinders from both
sides, are worth presentation here:

Editor, Standard-Times:

I want to appeal through your paper to the common sense folks
of West Texas on behalf of the United States Immigration Service.
The function of these federal officers is misunderstood and downgraded in this area, especially in Crockett, Sutton, Val Verde and
Terrell Counties.

Their task is made unreasonably difficult due to the utter lack
of cooperation by the ranch people.

Border Patrolmen have told me of numerous cases where ranchmen have failed to be helpful and courteous.

When the call of duty finds these officers far from town at noon
time or in the early dawn, they are seldom invited in for coffee or
a meal.

Their families are not accepted by many of the ranch people in
the towns where they live.

Their children are shunned on the school grounds.

These grevious (sic) discourtesies can only be attributed to arrogance and a lack of respect for federal authority. Some of the more illiterate and radical ranchmen in one county actually believe they have the right to work these wetbacks, and the Border Patrol should be required to produce a warrant before being allowed to roam about their premises and out into the pastures. This and other equally unreasonable demands are being rightfully ignored. The patrolmen assume that authority.

In most cases this land has come into the hands of the present owners due to the fact that their fathers and grandfathers came out to this area at the turn of the century and bought the land at a shamefully cheap price, pushing the peace-loving and less aggressive folks over to the Ft. Stockton country. They feel now that they have the right to keep and control this land that came to them by forfeit.

If these people are ever to come of age as citizens of this great country, they must be brought to heel, not only by the Border Patrol, but also by the working people who have with considerable sacrifice left their homes in the North to make notable contribution to a backward area.

We would all take keen interest and pleasure in striking out into the country on week-ends for picnics and fishing. These ranch people would like to deny ingress to the patrol, allowing dangerous aliens to press deeply into this country of ours.

We all admit that the patrol has resorted to Gestapo methods to apprehend wetbacks. They are forced to send informers through the ranches, posing as mexicans searching employment, and to stage midnight raids. They prowl the open pastures at night, search all the outbuildings, and even peer in windows of ranch homes, in an all-out effort to find the aliens who would replace good and honest laborers who try desperately to make ends meet.

We also admit that wetbacks have been shot and killed as they attempted to swim the Rio Grande to the safety of their own side. We should all applaud the dedication of these federal officers as they endure the hardships for a pittance.

For some unknown reason the ranchers actually seem to like and respect the mexicans. Those of us who were raised in Chicago and other centers of culture and learning realize the ever-present danger of Communist infiltration from our enemy to the south. The Border Patrol recognizes this danger, and is stoically enduring the slights and indignities hurled at them from three sides in order to render the supreme service to the country they love.

> Respectfully submitted,
> Eddie Koslov
> Del Rio, Texas.

This letter could have been any of several things: a piece of not-so-clever satire, a backhand slap at the Border Patrol, or a deliberate attempt to stir up trouble. The use of upper-case for "Communist" and lower case for "mexicans" and the reference to "our enemy to the south" are indicative of something; the inclusion of Chicago among "centers of culture" caused uplifted eyebrows in Ozona. And were the terms "apprehended" and "Respectfully submitted" written from force of habit? How about the name, "Koslov"?

Two of the Border Patrol's most senior and most respected officers—J. W. Holland, District Director at San Antonio, and Bruce L. Long, Chief Patrol Inspector of the Del Rio Sector —promptly pinned "Koslov" to the wall. They wrote a letter of their own to the *Standard-Times*, reporting that they could find no one named Koslov in Del Rio, and then took apart his allegations, one by one.

We . . . did not quite understand just what the writer was trying to prove by his reference to the culture and general conduct of the residents in the area covered by his letter. We believe that with very little effort he could have found that the percentage of college graduates in the area . . . is higher than in any other section of Texas, if not the entire nation. We also most certainly resented the implication that anyone should be applauded for, as he so grossly misrepresented, shooting people "as they were attempting to swim the Rio Grande to the safety of their own side."

Ozona ranchmen were angry for a few days after the Koslov letter, and then shrugged and said, "What the hell." A rancher in the hill country at Mason far outdid "Koslov" in clever letter writing, and then got down to serious business: He told the *Standard-Times:*

> Eddie says the wetback comes to "replace good honest laborers" —like himself. The truth is, the good and honest have jobs; they don't complain. The gripe comes from the culture boys who detest work and seek only a check. The check they like best of all is the government check.
>
> The reason the Mexican is hired is because he does hard work. The hole in solid rock cannot be dug with the culture of the North. Well, maybe it could be with one of Al's (Capone's) guns. It would help the southwest, if before the post were placed in the ground, a portion of this culture went into each deep hole with concrete on top.
>
> In his last paragraph Koslov says he can't understand why the rancher would like and respect a Mexican (Eddie again used the small m). This is because the cultured man quite often doesn't think like a normal human being. Koslov, we like him for the following reasons: (1) when he comes on the ranch he is a lot hungrier than you have ever been living in a rich nation. In his land there are no government checks. So we pity the hungry man who wants to do hard labor to eat and feed his family back home. (2) He does not complain about a common task and does the job with a smile. (3) He does not steal. (4) He doesn't always keep his eye glued on the clock and on some days when overtime is involved, he is the first to finish the job. (5) He respects the right of all men and can have his feelings hurt easily. (6) He is always grateful for the things you give him. (7) Since he is not arrogant, we respect him.
>
> Homer Martin.

IV

District Director Holland pointed out that there had been rare occasions when "overzealous border patrolmen were not too tactful or diplomatic," but that, "Conversely, border patrolmen have often rendered assistance to individuals and communities in time of need or after a disaster."

All of which is true. And the controversy over Juan Garcia

goes on. I have before me a letter written by a West Texas lady, a one-time classmate of mine. She says relatives of hers in the Sonora country east of Ozona "saw with their own eyes some of the Gestapo methods. Another Sonora woman was on the ranch alone. The Patrol drove up, piled out of the cars, guns drawn, and processed Mexicans (i.e., legally hired *braceros*) began to scatter at the sight of the guns. The Patrol men fired at the Mexicans as they scurried up a hillside. [The woman's] children were playing on that hillside. She took the matter to the Headquarters of the Patrol in Del Rio, forcing the officer in charge of the 'foray' at her place to describe just what had occurred. Till today, she does not know whether or not that officer was discharged."

Rocky times—rocky times in Texas, where once the only law was packed in a Ranger's holster. It may take some time, down by the Pecos, for the people to get used to any enforcement of federal authority.

But there is another side to the coin, and an Ozona ranchman told me of an incident which indicated that the Border Patrol is not all that quick on the trigger. Two patrolmen swooped down on a ranch on the Pecos in wintertime, and flushed a wetback who dived from a steep bank and swam the stream. As he climbed out on the farther side, the officers pulled their guns, and one shouted, "Halt, or we'll shoot!"

The dripping Mexican turned and faced them. With full border bravado, he pulled open his shirt and yelled, "Shoot!"

"Aw, go on!" the officer laughed, holstering his gun. "We'll get you the next time!"

Chances are good that they did, and chances are that Koslov's report of Mexicans being killed swimming the Rio Grande are what West Texans call "windies." But it should be remembered that the Border Patrol guards against the smuggling of things more evil than hungry men seeking work. In 1953 J. W. Holland pried the doors off an automobile, opened the trunk, and seized a fortune in refined marihuana.

Holland went into the service in 1930, and drove a 1929 Ford that had bloodstains above the steering wheel to remind him that his predecessor had been shot there. "We had some shooting down around Laredo in the old days," he says. "Sometimes we'd shoot it out at night, and then maybe meet next day on the International bridge, and ask who got hurt."

One of Holland's patrols picked up three wetbacks on a ranch and took them into a restaurant for breakfast. The Mexicans chose hotcakes, and the three orders were brought with individual bottles of syrup. The wetbacks eyed each other covertly, not knowing just what to do. Finally, the leader drank the syrup from his bottle, then rolled the hotcakes as one does tortillas, and ate them. *Ole!* The others followed suit.

And San Antonio policemen observed two Mexicans who were very politely trying to eat potato chips with their forks. They turned out to be wets.

Whether attended by any violence or not, the war goes on between the ranchmen, who are trying to get cheap and dependable laborers, and the authorities, who are trying to keep them out. For the most part, there is at least a surface politeness. "If a hungry Mexican shows up at your place, go ahead and give him a few days' work," patrolmen have reportedly told ranchers. "We'll be dropping around before long—we'll pick him up. But in the meantime, he might as well have something to eat."

It is a fact that in recent years the Border Patrol has stepped up its activities considerably, taking advantage of improved roads and an increased personnel force. The U.S. Immigration service has done the same. The latter branch has adopted a policy aimed at discouraging the use of wetbacks: it refuses to allow a ranchman to hire *braceros* for the 210-day legal contract period, if it has been proved that he employed wetbacks.

Back when the restrictions were not so tight, Ernest Dunlap worked a wetback named Augustin Zamorra for more than five years, and Augustin was not picked up once—although he made periodic trips to visit his family in Mexico. The Border

Patrol just didn't come around. But in the summer of 1962, by contrast, Ernest said that officers visited his ranch west of Ozona on an average of twice a month.

"That old Meskin sure was a good hand," he recalled. "If he was out on the ranch tonight, and there came a heavy rain and he didn't have a horse caught up, that wouldn't stop him. He'd be out at daylight with an ax and some wire in a wheelbarrow. He'd push that wheelbarrow two or three miles to the first water gap in the pasture fence. If it had been washed out, he'd have it fixed by the time I got out there from town."

v

There was one time, a few years ago, when Ernest Dunlap went to considerable trouble and expense to acquire Augustin's services legally. He drove to Eagle Pass, about 150 miles from Ozona, and across the Rio Grande to the Mexican town of Piedras Negras. At the far end of the International Bridge, an enterprising young Mexican opened the door of his car, jumped in, and said, "You want tequila, no?"

Ernest said, "I want tequila, no."

"Oh, then, you want pretty girl. I got one sure too pretty. She don't sleep for nobody!"

Like all the rest of the Dunlap clan, Ernest has a magnificent sense of humor. "Well, if she don't sleep for nobody, what do I want with her?" he laughed.

"Oh, she sleep for you!"

"Well, I'll tell you," Ernest said. "All I want is one wet Meskin that I'm looking for, named—"

"Oh, you want *braceros!* Why you no tell me? I get you three thous'!"

"I don't want three thous'. All I want is one Augustin Zamorra."

The Mexican youth was a real entrepreneur. He could get a cab to bring Augustin from his home fifty miles in the interior. The road was sure too bad and the fare would be $28. Ernest said he had learned he could get a cab for $14. *Bueno,* the boy would go for fourteen. Then Ernest parked and managed to get Augustin on the telephone.

"Don't pay a cab, señor," Augustin told him. "I can come on the bus for one dollar. Fine road, all the way."

But the processing office at the border had already closed for the day, so Mr. Dunlap had to stay overnight in Eagle Pass. Next day, after he challenged the usual procedure of giving Augustin $10 to facilitate the processing on the Mexican side, he waited six hours for his man. Finally, with some bad grace on the part of the unrewarded officials, Augustin was allowed to come through.

"But that wasn't all," Ernest said. "Before you go down to the border to get a man processed, you have to go to the employment office in San Angelo. The man there has to certify that he doesn't have a citizen seeking work who can fill the job. Then he gives you a list of some hundred and twenty items that you have to supply the processed Meskin—things you wouldn't furnish the average cowboy here, if you could find a cowboy any more."

"Such as what?" I asked.

"Well," he chuckled, "I think the last list they gave me specified Delsey toilet paper, whereas the one before that let you provide Great Northern. And things like soup spoons. Then you've got to keep a time clock. A processed man can't go to work until eight o'clock. He works until twelve, and then from one to five. You've got to keep a record, and pay overtime.

"Now, of course, this old Meskin was up and drinking coffee before daylight. And I don't have to tell you about ranch work —you can't do it by the clock. If you've got something to round up, you're out and getting started by daylight."

"I know," I said, and mentally hummed a verse from my own brief and rain-soaked days as a cowboy:

> Oh, I'm in the saddle before daylight,
> And when I quit the moon shines bright,
> Come-a-ti-yi-yippee, come-a-ti-yi-ya,
> Come a ti-yi-yippee-i-ya!

"Well," Ernest drawled, "I told Augustin about the rules. I said, 'Augustin, no more drinking coffee until eight o'clock, you know!' And he looked at me, and said, '*Yo no sabe el reloj, señor.*' [I do not understand the clock.] And that was that."

Augustin worked on the Dunlap ranch, as a *bracero,* for some three years. It was necessary to renew the arrangements every six months on the American side of the border and annually on the Mexican side. He was a good hand, indeed, and Ernest was paying him as much as he would have had to pay a man from Lima—if he could have found such a man.

But then Augustin went home to Mexico because of a curious misunderstanding with his wife—a misunderstanding which points up the difficulty of communication. She had somebody write him that she would like to get a *pasaporte* and come up for a visit. Augustin interpreted the word as *soporte,* meaning "support," and thought she was about to sue for divorce. He hurried south of the border, although later he did work, for a time, on the Walter Dunlap ranch west of the Pecos.

"You can't hardly get a Meskin any more," Ernest said after a moment of silence. "But my ranch house is down under a hill, and every couple of weeks the Border Patrol drives up on the divide. I can see them looking the place over with their *anteojos* [binoculars]."

The Koslov letter's charge that Border Patrol men are seldom invited into the ranch houses for coffee is not true, if one can believe a story that may possibly be apocryphal, although I like to think it did happen somewhere.

It seems that two wetbacks were in the kitchen one morning early when the *chotas* drove up. There was no way to get out of the house without being seen, so they took refuge in the attic. The ranchman asked the Border Patrol men to come in and have coffee.

While they were sitting at the table, chatting about the dry spell, the ceiling suddenly gave way, and the wetbacks fell into their midst, literally tail over teacup.

Ozona

and the World

18 Outside

In the West Texas sheep, goat and oil-well country they will tell you solemnly that when a citizen of the city of Ozona dies and goes to heaven, it is necessary to clip his wings, hobble him and corral him snugly behind a high wire fence to keep him from fleeing the Golden City and stampeding back to his native Crockett County with the speed of a startled steer.
—HAROLD H. MARTIN, ''MILLIONAIRES' TOWN,''
SATURDAY EVENING POST, FEBRUARY 18, 1950

LOOKING BACK over the years when I lived there, and going through the files of the Ozona *Stockman* for the years when I was gone, it seems to me that my home town has marched along with the weather. Progress has been steady enough, actually, but you can distinguish between the dry periods and the money-making rains, and some years were more significant than others.

The outside world was not always really aware of what was going on in Crockett County. Oil discoveries were reported, of course, because they had to do with the almighty dollar. But nobody wrote up old Nick Wigzell when he finally retired from active trapping because it no longer paid. There were government trappers around, on salary. And Nick, smelling of his wolf bait and the polecats he had skinned, could have told you that most of the predatory animals had been exterminated. You seldom saw a lobo wolf any more.

The most dangerous livestock predator was just rising to prominence. It wasn't a panther or lobo wolf or coyote, but an insect known as the "screwworm fly." It was twice the size of a housefly, with a bluish-green body, three dark stripes along the back, and an orange-colored head, and they said it had come up from Venezuela. It was to cost West Texas ranchmen millions of dollars before it was through.

But larger predators occasionally made news of a sort. Paul Perner and Joe Pierce surprised an eagle that was trying to catch fish out of a header tank, and had its wings so wet that it couldn't fly. It attacked Paul, instead, and sank one set of claws in his shirt front, and lacerated his head with the other. Joe Pierce grabbed a *sotol* stalk and managed to club the bird to death with it. The wingspread was 10 feet 3¼ inches; the claws were eight inches long.

And then W. Tom Brown, operating a filling station and a small truck farm that grew cantaloupes on the Sheffield road, at Liveoak Creek, got into the news—fatally. He had tamed a black bear. The bear got under the bridge, or in a culvert, and Mr. Brown went after him. The bear clawed and bit Mr. Brown to death.

This was reported in the San Angelo *Standard-Times,* but nobody got the real point of the story—the kicker. That week the Sunday-School theme in one of Ozona's churches happened to be that God is omnipresent. He is everywhere, at all times.

Young Buddy Russell raised his hand. "Where was God," he asked, "when the bear et Mr. Brown?"

Next question, please.

World War II broke down the last of Ozona's delightful seclusion, and for all time. Crockett County put 457 men into uniform. A few of these may have been transient oil workers, but even so, it was a very creditable figure, again representing all walks of life. This time many of the boys from Lima—citizens by birth—fought for their country. A number of Ozonans were attending Texas Agricultural & Mechanical College, or had been graduated from that institution, and they were commissioned: Texas A. & M. had more commissioned officers in the Army than did West Point.

And when it was over, and the boys came home, all of them were traveled and sophisticated, and physically tough. Ranch problems? They had operated bulldozers in the steaming jungles of the South Pacific, where a man's sweat never dried; "pushing cedar" on the windy West Texas divides, in the new drive to clear land for grass, was easy. They had flown combat aircraft. Going up in a Piper Cub with an automatic shotgun to bag golden eagles that had been killing lambs—this was pure sport.

The Meskins from Lima came back walking tall and feeling self-assured. For the first time, really, they had a stake in this country.

This was Ozona's third generation, young and capable and full of beans. For the most part the old-timers were proud to step aside and let them take over the reins.

II

Ozona made the cover of the *Saturday Evening Post* in 1950, and accepted its new fame with equanimity, aside from a general resentment of the stress placed on the town's riches. Ozona had never advertised itself, beyond the sign placed at the corner of the square not long before. Now, it read in the *Post:*

The big sign on the square which proclaims Ozona the "Biggest Little Town in the World" annoys the neighboring metropolises. They are offended by the smug satisfaction with which Ozona refers to its richest residential thoroughfare as Silk Stocking Street, and even the well-heeled ladies of San Angelo—population 55,000—are sometimes miffed at their department stores for holding out their most elegant gowns until the wealthier ladies of Ozona—population 3500—can have first pick.

This minor carping Ozona endures with serenity, holding, no doubt with justification, that it stems from envy, and only rarely does a resident take the trouble to rebuke his city's critics.

A large number of Ozona citizens were named in the *Post* article. Most, if not all of them, received mail as a result— letters ranging from offers to sell gilt-edged mining stock to downright and shameless pleas that "you have money, and I am trying to support a family on $30 a week. How about sending me a few hundred dollars?"

Many of them were sorry that the *Post* article was printed. It cheered them a great deal a short time later when the San Angelo *Standard-Times* came editorially to their support. Referring to the "brash capers of Glenn McCarthy" (who had just built the plush Shamrock Hotel in Houston, and was tossing his oil millions about) the newspaper said this was "in striking contrast to a community of wealth, of innate courtesy, and of genuine freedom and friendship, without any loss of dignity, in West Texas." The editorial went on:

We refer, of course, to that inland empire of grass and goats and sheep that sprawls all over the map around the village of Ozona. There may be some little exaggeration in the Saturday Evening Post article about this town, but it rings true to the spirit of the people and the place. . . . Here are comfortable homes presided over by gracious women of charm and contentment. When not dressed in the flimsy feminine garb that has always enhanced the attractive features of the sex, these women can, with equal effectiveness, lay aside their dinner gowns, put on their ranch gear, and drive trucks loaded with cake for feed, or doctor calves infested with worms when their country estates are short of hands.

Here are people who need no plush-seated importation of glamour from Hollywood to make life tolerable, and no gaudy display to make life attractive. All they need is a good rain at the right season and the chance to ride their own ranges, watch their young'uns rope and ride, and keep sufficient balances to meet the levies of the income tax collector. If anybody doubts the proper pride of the people of Ozona in the land they live upon, he can quickly disabuse himself by trying to buy just any portion of Crockett County. . . .

The people there may not have built a Shamrock Hotel, or bogged down with high society in plush surroundings, but they know how to care for themselves and their horses out on the ranges of Texas. Yes, wealth does something to people, but more important still, real people do something with wealth.

III

The year 1954 was a busy one for Ozona. There was increased oil activity, and more rain, and more money in the bank. And in March two misguided young men from Junction decided to rob that establishment.

Ozona National, housed in a colonial style building on the main street, has always been a wealthy institution. At its first opening, in 1905, nineteen original deposits totaled $12,-847.85. In October, 1962, when the Texas State Historical Survey Committee gave the bank a medallion, it was noted that the deposits were $7,690,000.

No Ranger happened to be around that afternoon in 1954. The two twenty-one-year-old boys parked their car nearby, and entered the bank at eight minutes before the three-o'clock closing time. There was an appalling lack of planning in all their effort: they apparently thought the bank closed at 2:30, which is customary in Texas.

Their names were Billy Bruce and Henry L. Smith. They were armed with a single rusty .22 pistol—a very unimpressive weapon in a town that had cut its teeth on .38's, .45's, and .30-.30 Winchesters.

Bruce and Smith locked the door behind them, and went through the usual routine. It was a holdup, they said, and they didn't want to kill anybody, but they would shoot if necessary. They said they didn't like the attitude of Charles E. Davidson, Jr., a rancher who was talking to Lowell Littleton, the active vice-president in charge.

"I didn't like their attitude either," Charlie said later. "But I didn't say so at the time."

Besides Littleton, there were seven other employees in the bank. The robbers ordered them all to the back, and one held them at gunpoint while the other went through the tellers' cages, scooping paper money into a suitcase.

Then Mrs. Royce Ballinger, bookkeeper for the West Texas Utilities Company, came to deposit company funds. It wasn't three o'clock, but the door was closed. She peered inside and saw no employees at all, but only a man in a brown hat going through the tellers' cages. She went into Ratliff's store, and announced that the bank was being robbed.

Nobody believed her at first. But when the alarm did spread, there was a reaction the young men from Junction could never have foreseen.

Every rancher in the Ozona country drives a pickup truck, and so do a lot of townspeople. In the old days, when a man rode a horse, he had a .30-.30 in a scabbard on his saddle, which was a lawful way of carrying a gun. In later days, the guns—various kinds—were transferred to the pickup trucks. There wasn't a truck around the town square that day that didn't have some kind of armament.

Before anyone could summon V. O. Earnest, the sheriff, and Billy Mills, the deputy, armed men were at the bank. Byron Williams, an oil broker, and Dick Henderson, a rancher, were yelling for the robbers to come out. Neither knew how many men were inside or how well they were armed. They were both reluctant to shatter the glass of the front door.

Things began taking on a comic opera twist. Ernie Boyd started across the street at this time to go into Smith's drugstore. He was principal of South Elementary School and a seasoned veteran of the Italian campaign. But what he saw stopped him.

"It looked like an army," Ernie said. "Men were running to their pickups and their cars, and coming back with weapons. I didn't know what was going on, but I was the only man without a gun, and the street didn't seem like a safe place to be. I went all the way back to the cash register, to be out of the line of fire, and watched from there."

Deputy Billy Mills arrived. He ran to the bank, and then sprinted back to his car and got a submachine gun.

"When I saw Billy with that," said Ernie Boyd, "I knew the bank was being robbed."

Up the street to the northward Lottie Lee Baker, former president of the Woman's Club and bookstore proprietor, came out into the street when she heard the shouting, and saw at least thirty armed men converging on the bank. She and others gathered on the street to watch, and this was when the whole affair began to deteriorate into a comic opera.

Nobody wanted to break the glass on the front doors. The robbers, by now, saw they had picked the wrong town, because there were too many guns against them. They panicked suddenly. They had failed to case the joint earlier for avenues of escape, and all they could do was run out the back door—and into the walls of a dead end.

The only way out was up. They left the suitcase there and used an electric light meter for a handhold, and scrambled to the roof of the adjoining store building. They ran a block over other roofs, and jumped down at the back. Smith broke a bone in his foot, but still made creditable speed in a dash for Johnson Draw.

All this was futile, with so many armed men in town. Pickup trucks had already been driven to the draw crossing on the Sheffield road—one of the four ways to get out of town, and a road block had been set up there. Bruce and Smith wheeled and tried to scurry back toward town, but here came Dick Henderson and Byron Williams, with guns much larger than the rusty .22. Here, also, came B. B. Ingham, Jr., a large and powerful man who inflicted the final humiliation. He called for the pair to throw up their hands, and one was slow. Mr. Ingham lifted him off the ground with a kick in the seat of his pants—and with a sharp-toed cowboy boot too.

Sheriff Earnest arrived and took the men to jail. They were tried in District Court at Rankin on the 15th of the following June, and each got five years in prison. Ozona, still laughing, remembered when a horse thief got more than that.

A Night

of Hell

19 and High Water

It was said (during a drought in Texas) that water was so scarce that even the churches were affected: the Baptists were forced to sprinkle, the Methodists to use a damp cloth, and the Presbyterians to pass out rain checks.

—W. EUGENE HOLLON,
''THE SOUTHWEST, OLD AND NEW''

THERE ARE NO WINDMILLS any more atop Waterworks Hill in Ozona, which means that Progress has sawed off the skyline as oldsters remember it. Kids with nigger-shooters can no longer kill bullfrogs around the open tank at the ice plant, and eat frog's legs broiled (without salt) over a campfire. As I recall this delicacy, it was horrible. The frogs were undersized. The kids were underprivileged—and had to do *something*.

They swam when they could in Johnson Draw. This dusty watercourse still runs through the western third of town, and Gurley Draw comes in from the east to join it near the village of Lima. Wags who were not above such things used to snicker that Ozona nearly always had a pair of dry draws.

And yet there were times and seasons when summer rains washed the grasses flat and filled Johnson with a brown turbulence and the joyous chortling of toads that came out of some secret hibernation to ride tandem on the tide. North of town in

Floyd Henderson's pasture was a swimming hole that was ten feet deep when the draw was up. (One of the vagaries of our language is that the draw was "up" only after it had "come down.") Older brothers threw the younger kids into this pool regularly and systematically; it was, they said, the only way to learn to swim.

The water shrank daily: by tomorrow it might cease to flow. You swam in it while you could—you swam from morning until sundown, and between dips you blistered your legs and backsides at a campfire on the bank. Going back to town from the swimming hole when the shadows of the mesquites were lengthening, Ozona kids enjoyed a sport now sadly gone with so many other things of the older West. More cows were around in the era before the Rambouillet sheep became king, and consequently there were more cowchips. Boys fought their way through a mile or two of pastures by throwing cowchips as a New England lad threw snowballs. The hard and dry ones could knock you off your feet if they struck just right, but the real triumph of arms was to hurl a cowchip that was at its prime. At that time it had a hard crust that would withstand launching and the trajectory of ballistic flight, but at the instant of impact in the target area it became one with the custard pies Mack Sennett was just beginning to make famous.

I suppose there are few old swimming holes anywhere. Kids can swim any time now in Ozona's four sanitized and supervised pools—and there went half the fun. Their fathers and grandfathers had the swimming hole north of town, and one on the old Broome ranch south of Mexico Point, and one at Baggett's Grove, nearly four miles away. German Waterhole, west of town on the S. E. Couch ranch, was less frequented.

Water doesn't stand in any of these places now, like it used to. Johnson Draw looks flat and tame and bears an unfortunate resemblance to the Los Angeles River. On one of my last trips to Ozona, Mr. Will Baggett, a pioneer ranchman and leader in soil and water conservation, drove me to the Baggett ranch to show me some of the new flood-control dams. I asked him if flash floods had ruined the old waterholes.

"It wasn't the flash floods," Mr. Baggett said. "Just not enough cattle using them any more. Most of the waterholes in this country were originally made by the buffalo. Herds of buffalo trampled loblollies in the mud—they loved to wallow —and they packed the earth so that it would hold water. Cattle did the same thing later—while there were enough of them. But now you have sheep, and the cattle drink out of stone troughs."

Today's white-faced Herefords, Black Angus and Santa Gertrudis breeds may enjoy drinking from stone troughs, not having known any other way of watering. But the old range cow wanted to *feel* the water, teat-deep, around her, as if to assure herself that there was plenty of it. She wanted to wade in until her more sensitive parts were submerged in a cooling protection against flies and gnats, and she liked to stand there awhile, drinking and slobbering and blowing, perhaps absorbing moisture by the process of osmosis. Then she would drip on the bank and pack the mud there, and help make that loblolly into a waterhole.

In 1960 Crockett County ranchmen were running more than 300,000 sheep as against less than 12,000 head of cattle, and the wool clip was more than two million pounds. No accounting was given for goats, which do not like to get wet any more than sheep do, but ranchers had turned more and more to Angora flocks during the dry years. Now West Texas annually crowns two pretty girls as Miss Wool and Miss Mohair—with the participation of other sheep and goat areas through the Southwest.

II

At the time of the 1922 flood—when the old-timers said it happened about every twenty-five years—nobody had built houses very near Johnson Draw. But ranch pastures pressed in to the town limits on all sides, and when the influx of oil workers came there were not many other places left to put up a dwelling or park their trailer homes. All was well for a number of years, but then the cycle ran out.

In June, 1954, a hurricane named Alice attracted the anxious attention of Florida and other East Coast points. It formed 500 miles out in the Gulf of Mexico and, after some indecisive horsing around, moved to the mouth of the Rio Grande near Brownsville, to lash the river valley with high winds and heavy rains. Then it broke up, and people in the coastal areas breathed more freely. West Texans were disappointed: they desperately needed rain.

They got it. On Saturday, June 26, Hurricane Alice somehow regrouped her scattered forces over the Pecos and Howard's Draw, at the western edge of Crockett County, and moved toward the northeast. It began raining hard.

It rained all day Saturday, and all Saturday night—a gully washer, fence-post lifter, cowchip floater of a rain. Cattle and sheep, as well as wild animals, obeyed an instinct stronger than that of human beings and moved to higher ground. Bridges went out and highways were closed.

Rain fell all day Sunday, and most of Sunday night.

Tourists on Highway 90, which is near the U.S.-Mexico border, were diverted when the thirty-year-old Pecos River bridge collapsed. They came up through Ozona, hoping to get across the Pecos on Highway 290. The motels in Ozona were jammed Sunday evening, and with traditional hospitality citizens opened their homes to the travelers.

By six o'clock Sunday evening, Johnson Draw was up to the level of the Ozona bridge. Down the line Vic Pierce had thrown up an earthen embankment around his ranch house, after measuring 11 inches of rain. South of the Pierce place, a gauge at Bud Kincaid's ranch showed 14 inches. Wayne West had measured 8½ inches at his ranch earlier in the afternoon, and a draw was running wild between the ranch house and the hangar where Mr. West kept his private plane, just a hundred yards away. L. B. Cox, Jr., ranching at historic Howard's Well, had counted 7 inches of rain at noon, and it was still coming down.

All of this, and the fact that the downpour was just as heavy on the high divides that form the watersheds for both Johnson and Gurley Draws, set the stage for tragedy—and the only disaster the town has ever known. Before it was over fifteen people would be dead.

III

Not many Ozona residents went to bed that Sunday night. Around twelve o'clock local peace officers went from house to house in the lower eastern part of town, warning residents that Gurley was rising.

"The water had stolen up on us like a snake," the Rev. J. Troy Hickman reported. "We got the dog from the back yard storehouse, and left the house. The car pushed water ahead of us as we left, but the water was quiet and had no current. We drove downtown and parked near the Highway 290 crossing on Johnson Draw. It was running, but hardly high enough to be interesting. Townspeople we knew drove by or stopped and chatted."

The town square was crowded. Truck drivers had been re-routed, along with the tourists, because of the bridge mishaps. One car, with a large red motorboat in tow, was parked at the side of the square, and the driver, unable to find a motel room, was asleep in the automobile.

There was no warning except the steady lash of the rain. At 4 A.M., Johnson Draw came down like a tidal wave. The water came well up toward the square, which is on high ground, and in the murky dawn the all-night observers began to see houses spinning down the current and crashing into each other to shatter windows and rip off porches. The flood was now filled with tragic debris: trailer houses, trees, drowned live-stock, automobiles, and buoyantly bobbing empty oil drums.

It was still raining.

Growing daylight painted an awesome picture of gray skies and yellow, foam-lashed waters that ran from hill to hill and left a few housetops sticking up. People were calling for help from porch roofs, telegraph poles, and even from the insecurity of the higher fence posts. Mrs. Ben Lemmons, living at the eastern edge of the San Angelo highway with a high, rocky hill just behind, would not abandon her home: she spent the night perched on top of her refrigerator. The water came to her door, but did not enter.

Two oil field workers borrowed the red motor boat from the man who was just passing through—nobody ever got his name —and cruised up and down residential streets, carrying refugees to safety. Many an Ozona resident believes there was something more providential than coincidental about this, because the town can go a whole year without ever seeing a power cruiser of any kind.

The people who lived in automobile trailer homes suffered the worst. They were in the low part of town. They had no foundations, literally or figuratively, to speak of. They were transients.

"We didn't know anything about it, until the trailer next to ours bumped into us," said one trailer owner. Part of his family had died in the flood.

Johnson Draw took its toll principally from the unknowl-edgeable, the outsiders who did not realize what a flash flood can do in the sharply tilted Southwest. It also struck at the underprivileged, because the small Negro settlement, in 1954, was near its banks. At the time there was no other place where these people could live.

From the early days of those community Christmas trees that held a present for every child in town, Ozona has always taken care of its own. By eight o'clock that Monday morning, with Johnson Draw still roaring sullenly between the rimrocked hills, a town meeting had been called. It took only thirty min-utes to set up committees to handle food, clothing, medical care, housing, transportation and information. Forty families were sheltered in the Junior High School and the Davidson Memorial Gymnasium. The Red Cross went to work. Mrs. R. A. Harrell was chairman for disaster measures, and in a short time she had obtained Red Cross commitments for $180,-000. The Churches of Christ sent more than $6,000 through Hubert Baker, their Ozona chairman. The Negro population was resettled on higher ground made available by Mrs. B. B. Ingham, Sr., and Ranchman Early Chandler at once began development of a new residential area on the hill west of town. Some very fine homes stand there today.

A small contingent of troops was sent from Fort Hood early during the disaster period to help maintain order and to assist in the search for the bodies of the flood victims. Several local Meskins and two wetbacks were first seized as looters, and then released to work in the cleanup. Three suspected looters, all Americans, were later arrested in Eldorado.

Surrounding towns—particularly San Angelo—sent money and gave generously of bedding, clothing and other supplies. There was an immediate demand for flood-control measures that would prevent any recurrence of the catastrophe, and after several years and considerable correspondence with Senator Lyndon Johnson, the series of dams shown to me by Mr. Will Baggett had been completed. They are a formidable work of engineering, and it would seem unlikely that Johnson Draw can ever go on the rampage again.

But it is also hard for me to believe that there will never be another old swimming hole, leaf-shaded by hackberry and live oak trees and bordered with rank-smelling broomweeds and still more pungent wild gourd vines, with quiet brown water waiting to caress the naked skin of boyhood.

IV

The famous Ozona Flood obtained national notice for a day or two, and then lost the news spotlight to a much bigger flood sweeping down the Rio Grande and drowning many more people. Ozona citizens would have been glad to miss the publicity entirely, and if they had not been too happy with Harold Martin's *Saturday Evening Post* article four years earlier, they were even less pleased with a column he now did for a Georgia newspaper.

News of the flood, Mr. Martin said, "was as surprising as would have been a dispatch from the nether regions reporting that the Styx had overflowed its banks and quenched the fires of Hades." He went on:

Ozona, a metropolis of 3000 souls, 2000 of them of Mexican descent, is famed for two things—the dryness of its climate and the opulence of its 100-odd millionaires.

It lies to the south of San-Angelo, the mohair or goat fur capital of the world, in the midst of a dusty plain, flat as your palm, that stretches for miles on either side.

The drive there, in times of normal rainfall, which means burning drought, is like the southern approach to torment. The asphalt highways bubble under the sun. A dry wind, full of dust, burns on the skin with a blow torch heat. The tumble weed drifts, and the lizard pants in the shade of the mesquite. . . .

They (the ranchers) have made enough money to move wherever they wish, but out of a stubborn love of this dry and bitter land, they have chosen to stay to make a tiny oasis of green in the midst of the sun-baked desert. Their ranch homes are shabby, old adobe houses, thick-walled against the sun, sitting beneath lean cottonwoods. Their "town houses" are palaces, decorated by folk of artistic bent brought in from Dallas, New Orleans and New York. . . .

To an Ozonan water is as precious as liquid gold, and pickle juice is worth even more, for flowers won't grow unless the alkaline soil is neutralized by pickle juice, or vinegar.

Now the flood waters have rolled over Ozona, roaring in the arroyos, chasing the goats and sheep to high ground, flooding the little shacks of the Mexicans, flowing through the deep carpeted drawing rooms of the rich.

And I'll bet I know what the San Angelenos are saying—those

sedate folk who always looked upon wealthy Ozona as an upstart town, full of brag and bluster:

"Just like those rich so-and-sos down there—showing off again. Trying to prove anything that's theirs—even a flood—is bigger and better than anybody else's."

It should be charitably assumed, from the standpoint of good taste, that Mr. Martin wrote this clever little piece as well-meant satire—before reports of the fifteen deaths in the flood had been received. Even so, he did not enhance his reputation for accuracy. His "2000 Mexicans" were a very considerable increase over the actual Latin-American population, and in using that figure—which would have left 1,000 Americans —he made his "100-odd millionaires" statement absurd. The Mexicans are not millionaires. Neither is one person out of every ten men, women and children in Ozona.

The *Stockman* struck back at Mr. Martin in a heated editorial which pointed out, among other things, that "Mr. Martin didn't get too well acquainted with Ozona people in his two or three weeks' stay here." The editorial was revealing as an indication of the hurt and rage with which Ozona responds to criticism or misstatement of the facts. It's a town where the business houses all close their doors for a funeral—no matter whose. It's a town that tries desperately to do the good and wise thing—and do it magnanimously—and it has had a high measure of success in that. It's a town that need not take a back seat for anyone, but it is only two generations removed from its Algerian days of "Struggling Upward," and can be sensitive.

Most of all, Ozona (as Mr. Martin said) loves its "dry and bitter land." Therefore, it wants everybody else to love it, too.

But in most cases it does take longer than an acquaintance-ship of two or three weeks.

Ozona

20 Revisited

This is King Fisher's Road. Take the Other One.
—OLD SIGN ON A TEXAS RANCH GATE

OZONA PEOPLE still leave their ranch houses open, but they close their gates with care. Leaving a pasture gate open is a cardinal sin. Years ago, when the automobiles were first beginning to multiply like a herd of sheep with a hundred percent lamb crop, some unsung genius invented the "bump" gate—and it is still popular. This is a heavily timbered affair, two lanes wide, suspended by cables from a central upright iron pipe. Approached in low gear, it can be bumped open long enough for a car to go through, and then it shuts automatically. Before the highways were laned, there was a bump gate for every pasture fence. There were several on the road to Arthur Hoover's ranch—and Maggie Deland Crawford still remembers when her first husband, a garage man, had to go out to the ranch and fix Mr. Hoover's car.

The car was new, and so was Mr. Hoover, as a driver. Mr. Deland got the motor running, all right, but deemed it wise to follow Mr. Hoover to town. As they approached the first bump gate, Mr. Deland was alarmed to see that the car ahead was not slowing down at all.

Arthur Hoover hit the bump gate at more than thirty miles an hour. The gate retaliated by swinging 180 degrees and smacking the rear of the car with enough force to knock it out

[219]

into the mesquites. This happened repeatedly, until Mr. Deland was finally able to catch up.

It is probable that Arthur Hoover developed a sort of immunity to being smacked from behind while driving his car. Not very long ago, they say, he was struck in the rear by a tourist's machine just as he was turning off U.S. Highway 290 to get on his own ranch road via a bump gate. Nobody was hurt, but a highway patrol officer investigated.

"Mr. Hoover," he asked politely, "did you signal that you were about to make a turn here?"

"Signal?" Arthur exploded. "Why, I've been making this turn for more than forty years! *Everybody* knows that I turn off here!"

Everybody knows, too, that pasture gates must be closed behind you. Except, perhaps, a few of the outsiders—the oil field workers and the crew laying the pipelines. Ranchmen probably have had more trouble with the oil men in that regard than in anything else.

A rancher may have a dozen oil wells on his ranch without— unfortunately—getting a dime from them. This is because the University of Texas still owns large tracts of land in Crockett County, and leases the grazing rights to the ranchman whose pastures surround the tract—and then leases the oil rights to an oil company. It is because of this that the University of Texas is one of the world's wealthier institutions of learning.

The oil company has the right to bring in its drilling rigs. The ranchman has the right to expect that the workmen will not set his grass afire in a dry spell or leave his gates open. It doesn't always work out, and a few years ago there was a rather famous lawsuit brought by John Dublin, Jr., against the Continental Oil Company, in the District Court of Crockett County.

Came now John Dublin, Jr., to complain that on or about the 10th day of October, 1953, the defendant company's trucks

pulled down the plaintiff's fences in order to enter the said lease
. . . and so on. There was nothing new in the legal preamble; it
was an old story. But then attorneys for Mr. Dublin suddenly
"exploded," in the way football teams *"explode"* for sports
writers:

In a verdant pasture adjoining the premises wherein Defendant's
exploration activities were carried out dwelled a young, stalwart,
handsome bull, a prized blue-blood of Taurus' aristocracy, whose
master, the Plaintiff herein, had planned a destiny so blissful and
replete with joy as seldom befalls either man or beast outside of
celestial realms. Playfully romping with all the innocence of young
maidenhood in the green pasture beyond, a herd of forty seven
heifers lived in the carefree abandon of maids in their teens. Separated from them by the machinations of man, taking the tangible
form of a cruel and relentless barbed wire fence, our young hero
oftentimes gazed longingly across the way at their playful antics,
with a disconcerting yearning filling his bully young chest, and the
blood coursed hotly through his veins, the stimulus of emotions
which stemmed solely from the instincts with which his Heavenly
Father had endowed him, and were—due to his lack of any of
those delightful experiences as a young bull of the world—as completely unknown to him as the experiences themselves. Though our
young principal in this tragic drama had looked longingly with no
more than curious wonderment at the pristine beauty of the bu-
colic pastures beyond and the lovely creatures who grazed therein,
Fate, in as capricious a whim as could be most cruelly dealt, and
as indeed was, did entice him with a gesture of short lived blissful
joy, a joy which was but a brief interlude in a bovine Garden of
Eden leading unsuspectingly to the Stygian blackness of an igno-
minious fate too cruel to relate, but must perforce be detailed
below.
   Meanwhile, during this embryonic awakening of our young hero's
bullhood, the maidenly heifers in the full ripe bloom of youth
cavorted rapturously and munched contentedly in these crisp days
of October, 1953, unaware of the gathering storm clouds that were
to rain disaster and degradations upon them and the amorous
young creature in the neighboring abode, turning these plains of

their foresires into a vale of blood and tears. Alas, no vigorous promptings were requisite to the downfall of the young principal, here to be so sadly related.

> *"In tragic life, God wot,*
> *No villain need be;*
> *Passion spins the plot,*
> *We are betrayed by that within."*

For it came to pass that on, or about, the 10th day of October, the Defendant by his agents, employees or representatives, did enter upon this bovine land of contented enchantment, and on this day and subsequent days thereto, to-wit, the 10th, 28th and 29th days of October, did upon the completion of their activities thereon, negligently and carelessly tear down and did leave down the fences of Plaintiff's pasture, and did thereby leave an enticingly open door to which our stalwart young bull soon took advantage.

In maidenly shyness did these young heifers gaze upon the handsome creature now advancing haltingly over ground before untraversed by hooves such as his. His nostrils flared, his heart beating tremulously in anticipation of he knew not what, yet crescendoing within him under the sure direction of the baton of instinct. No thought of flight disturbed their fresh young hearts.

> *"(Nay, love, look up and wonder!) Who is this*
> *Who cometh in dyed garments from the South?*
> *It is thy new-found Lord, and he shall kiss*
> *The yet unravished roses of thy mouth."*

Led erringly by the instinct of generations before him, our young principal accomplished his mission. A dozen brown eyes watched his departure, not with the wide-eyed wonder of morning passed, but with the dewy-eyed softness of young cowhood untimely and prematurely brought upon them. But, alas, the dark clouds had gathered.

> *"On the high hill*
> *No ivory dryads play,*
> *Silver and still*
> *Sinks the sad autumn day."*

Ere another day dawned, Plaintiff's foreman had discovered the torn down fence and repaired it. Frustrated by this barrier to a new life he now knew, fretted by these new ardors and demands that youth be served, he lunged, tore and jumped at the fence until it no longer stood before him. Torn and bleeding, he trotted off to his newly acquired domain of pleasure. This ill-fated day took place Sunday, November 1, 1953. Monday, November 2, 1953, dawned with the accursed barrier again before him. Again his charging removed the evil thing, but the damage was done. Torn, bleeding, and gravely injured, he was deprived of his usefulness for the glorious work which had been planned for him. Purchased at a cost of $550 as a calf, pastured and fed to young bullhood, he was sold for a lowly $330 to adorn ignominiously the festive board of mankind.

Of our young heifers, two died, seven had calves prematurely before their normal calving time, ranging from July 20 to August 30, 1954, becoming afflicted with worms, all of this to the damage of the Plaintiff, including the forced sale of the bull, to the amount of $1500.

So ended a sorrowful saga that belies the often-heard observation that the best ranch breed is a mixture of Hereford and oil well. According to Miss Leta Powell, the clerk of Crockett County, the record shows that the case was settled out of court.

II

At this writing, it is likely that a lot of fences are being torn down and many pasture gates left open on the Ozona ranches. Because now it has been discovered that natural gas is anywhere you find it under those rimrocked hills and mesquite flats.

Before 1963 was half over, six completed "strikes" caused oil men to describe the Ozona area as "the hottest spot on the North American Continent." Young Elizabeth Childress's 1919 "prophecy" finally came full circle—there is a "No. 1 Henderson." This well is near one known as "the Strawn," which was flowing 3,400,000 cubic feet of gas per day. Another was producing 1,220,000 cubic feet per day—and the Ozona *Stock-*

man again is filled with the oil-slick talk about "calculated, absolute open flow through perforations between 9,371 and 9,555 feet, which had been acidized with 2,000 gallons and fractured with 60,000 gallons and 85,000 pounds of sand," and so on. And if the *Stockman* is filled with this, it is certain that the Ozona National Bank is filled with the lovely smell of new money.

Only now it may be spreading out more, and spilling into the pockets of people who are not millionaires at all. The "hottest spot" includes the town of Ozona itself, and even the owner of a city lot can lease it for drilling.

Crockett County greened up in 1963, one of the fattest years on record, so there is a boom in livestock too. It has always been this way down in that part of Texas. Next year may see no clouds in the sky, and ranchmen may have to truck their livestock off to market before it gets unprofitable to feed it. But it will be comforting then to have oil and gas dividends coming in, to tide them over until a good rain.

The Oil and Gas Division of the Railroad Commission has just named two new fields in Crockett County. This contributed to my education: I had no idea how oil fields were named. I like to think that it was done at least with a little proper ceremony, and not just by any office in Austin. They might shatter a bottle of high octane gasoline on the rear wheel of an old Studebaker chuck wagon, or anyway on a fence post, as the Railroad Commission man intones: "I christen thee 'Ozona Northwest (Canyon)', or 'Ozona East (Spraberry).' "

I like to think, too, that in 1916 when they were drilling that wildcat well on the old T. W. Patrick place, if they had only had the equipment and the daring to go down 8,000 feet, instead of a measly 500—whoosh! The lid would have been blown off, in more ways than several.

Still, I am thankful that it didn't happen then. In 1916 Ozona wasn't grown up. The towns of Ranger and Burkburnett and Borger had oil booms in those early days, and they weren't grown up either. In each of them oil set off a wild stampede of dust and mud and scramble, and attracted the rough and slovenly and criminal from all over.

III

A headline in the Ozona *Stockman,* July 10, 1962, read:

> Allan Bosworth, Navy Captain, Author,
> Former Ozona Student, Is Awarded His
> High School Diploma After Forty Years

Ozona, as I have said before, does things in a magnanimous fashion. Where else would they have called a special meeting of the School Board, in the middle of the summer vacation, to make such a kind and sentimental gesture?

Nowhere on my diploma, in its handsome and expensive blue leather binder, with the ribbon across it, does it say anything about its being purely honorary. With this, I could go on to college. In fact, some of my Ozona friends have urged me to enroll in Sweet Briar, Bryn Mawr, or Hollins.

I drove in through the Hill Country on the east, so that I could see the lovely Llano River and then come by way of Schleicher County and Eldorado, where the Bosworth family wagon rolled so long ago. Everything was familiar: A plowed field outside Eldorado, and probably the last one for more than a hundred miles, until you got across the Pecos and went up northward to the Billie Sol Estes country. The long, level, dun-colored divides—they had been "pushing" cedar and scrub mesquite with bulldozers, to clear the way for grass, and some of the pastures looked wrecked forever. The break in the rim-rock, where the road descends to the curving and widening and friendly mesquite flats, greener, now, and with a windmill or two showing on the skyline. And then everything was both familiar and changed, the way it is when you come back after a long time. Even when I throttled down to twenty miles an hour I was still going nearly ten times what the wagons used to travel.

The hills, of course, were eternal, but probably the paved highway had been relocated. I could not be sure when I was passing the townsite of Emerald, where the road used to go, showing you a skeletal rock foundation or two, and the twisted, rusting remains of a torn-down windmill. Nor did I ever see the old Friend Horse Ranch, where I lived for a time as a small boy.

I cruised back, taking the Sonora road. There was a liquor store, aptly named "The Oasis," just a few yards over the Crockett line, in wet Sutton County. And there were radar towers on the high divide to mark an Air Force radar base, which was new to me, and which unfortunately, at this writing, has been ordered disestablished.

Then, before I knew it, I was rolling into Silk Stocking Street at the east end of Ozona, past an unbelievable number of green, pecan-shaded lawns and beautiful "town houses." Quite suddenly, I was home.

I went by the office of the *Stockman,* to ask about a place to live for a couple of months. Evart White, the editor and publisher, greeted me, introduced me to his assistant, Ernie Boyd, and immediately asked me to go home with him for dinner, which—in West Texas—is lunch.

I commented that the country looked a little dry. Evart said it was. "Yesterday," he said, "there was a big black cloud in the north, up about Barnhart. I stepped out on the sidewalk and drew a few deep breaths, trying to suck it down this way. But it didn't rain."

I went around the square, and people were calling me "Allie" again. This is my real given name, and is on Navy records. But when you publish magazine stories under such a by-line, you get fan letters from readers (if you get letters at all) beginning "Dear Sir, or Madam." I began to use "Allan."

But people in Ozona were calling me "Allie" again, and I dropped forty years, and listened. They said, "Listen—you remember when ol' Nate Baker went along as camp guide and cook for a bunch of preachers that was dove huntin'? One eve-

ning they asked Nate if he ever shot doves, or quail. Nate said,
'Hell, yes, shot a lot of 'em in my time.' 'On the wing?' asked the
preacher. And Nate said, 'On the wing, on the head, in the ass
—I shoot 'em anywhere!' "

They kept saying, "You remember the time . . ." and if I
didn't remember it I could always whip out a notebook and take
notes. And some of them said, with kindness and generosity,
"We wouldn't tell just anybody this, Allie. But you are one
of us."

IV

Oscar Kost's Boot and Saddle Shop, on the south side of the
square, brings out all the nostalgia for the old days. It has the
good smells of leather being worked, and of harness and neet's-
foot oil; it shines with the glitter of silver-mounted buckles and
conchos on cowboy leggins, and the yellow and red stars, but-
terflies, and what-have-you on ornate, stitch-pattern cowboy
boots. Oscar doesn't sell many of the old high-heeled boots any
more: today's style has a medium heel that is better for walking,
and for driving pickup trucks. He deals in hackamores, bridle
reins, bits, belts, slickers and roping ropes, as well as in cattlemen's hats and spurs. The Ozona Junior Rodeo was at hand,
and he was busily outfitting small fry contestants.

He sold me a pair of modified boots, and I felt better watching the parade and seeing the Junior Rodeo. A surprising number of beautiful horses showed up, utterly unaware that they
were almost obsolete. Besides the large number of adults who
rode splendidly—despite an all too prevalent spill of midriffs
over their silver-buckled belts—there were more than 150 kids
in the saddle, some of them no more than four years old.

For two days the kids jingled their spurs around the town
square with an understandable pride and a pardonable swag-
ger; on two nights they competed in rodeo events that showed
that the skills of the Old West have not been lost. Future ranchmen, barely in their teens, rode bulls of fearsome size, wrestled

steers, roped calves, and worked with the girls in the spectacular team business of "ribbon roping," in which the boy ropes and throws the steer, and the girl runs out and ties a ribbon to its tail.

Nowadays—and this seems only fair—the horses ride, too. The highways and some of the ranch roads are paved, and pavement is hard on a horse's hoofs. Virtually all the mounts for the rodeo had been brought in from the ranches in horse trailers, usually drawn by pickup trucks. This is poetic justice: the pickup and the jeep have been supplanting horses on the range.

Crockett County grew up bowlegged and saddlesore, and saw the horse reach his peak in Texas. In 1890, two years before the trial run of the first American automobile, Texas had 1,350,000 horses. Twenty years later, despite the advent of the gasoline buggy, they had increased to 1,369,000. But from that time they were on the decline. In 1920 there were still 5½ horses to every motor vehicle, but the automobile was coming up fast.

In 1940 Crockett County had 2,303 horses. A year later it registered 982 motor vehicles.

In 1960 the entire state of Texas owned only 218,000 horses, including mules, and the automobiles outnumbered them 18 to 1. Good-by, Old Paint!

"Talking about horses," they said, "do you remember—no, you wouldn't, because it was after you'd gone. Hasn't been too long ago, really. Arthur Hoover must have had nearly a thousand head of horses on his ranch, just because he loved horses. He couldn't ride 'em all, but he didn't aim to sell none, either.

"Well, one summer day a man came out to Arthur's place, wanting to buy horses. He found Arthur out in the pasture, moving sheep, wearing a floppy old Stetson and a ducking jumper and a pair of work pants. He told Arthur he wanted to buy some horses.

"Arthur told him, right off, that he didn't want to sell any horses. The man hung around, trying to stay out of the dust and still get a word in edgewise. It came time to noon the sheep. He approached Arthur again, and Arthur said, 'I won't even talk about it!'

"The sheep stuck their heads under the cedar bushes to get a little shade, and Arthur lay down and stuck his head under a cedar bush too, with a rock for a pillow. He pulled his hat brim down over his eyes, and clasped his hands across the chest. The man asked him again, and Arthur didn't answer.

"The man wrote a note so Arthur could read it when he woke up from his nap. It said, 'I will give you $1000 for ten head of horses.' He rolled up the note and stuck it into Arthur's hands.

"Arthur pushed back the brim of his Stetson, and got out his glasses. He read the note, but never said a word. He took out a pencil and wrote on the bottom of the paper, and handed it to the man. Then he put his pencil and glasses away, pulled down the hat brim, and folded his arms again. The interview was over.

"The man read what Arthur had written. It said, 'I won't take it.' "

v

Ozona is really not isolated at all now. When I inquired for one of my old friends, they said, "Oh, he drove up to Fort Worth today—probably be back tomorrow." And another couple said, "We're going up to Angelo this evening to have dinner and see a show—better come along."

Fort Worth is halfway across the broad state of Texas. San Angelo is more than eighty miles . . . but that's nothing but just rock-chunking distance to Ozona people. Herman Knox, the personable and outgoing Cadillac dealer, counted up and said there were thirty-six Cadillacs in town, or one for about every ninety men, women and children. The average Crockett County ranchman, he said, drives about 50,000 miles in a year. As the champion he would pick George Montgomery, who consistently puts 80,000 miles on his odometer in twelve months, and then buys a new car.

Mr. Knox can count on selling twelve or more new Cadillacs annually—provided it rains—along with a comfortable number of Oldsmobiles, Buicks and Chevrolets, and he says that Woody Mason and other dealers do right well with Fords, Chryslers, Dodges and Pontiacs. All the dealers are especially happy around High School Commencement, because by tradition a number of seniors will receive brand-new automobiles as graduation presents, and will drive them off to college in the fall. The Ozona High School grounds already look like a parking lot at some busy supermarket, but the school trustees have stubbornly preserved a motte of small and scrawny live oaks north of the original stone school building. They tied their horses there when they were students, and went to classes booted and spurred.

Knox's operation is characteristic of the town today. Virtually every house in Ozona is air-conditioned, and so are practically all the automobiles Knox sells. But there is still the matter of rain.

"If it rains, and ranchers don't have to buy feed for their stock, I can sell new cars," Knox said. "If there's a long dry spell, they have the old ones overhauled. In this town you spend ninety percent of your time just looking for a cloud."

Then he told me about Mrs. J. W. Owens, who qualifies as a pioneer. She trades in her Cadillacs every other year, although they show only about 12,000 miles of use. She likes any Cadillac at all, so long as it is pink, and after she gets a new model there is one extra, not made at the factory, that has to be installed. This is a coffee can mounted in the driver's compartment. In Mrs. Owens' day, no respectable woman ever smoked, but about half of them dipped snuff. She still dips.

"Be careful," she tells anyone riding with her in the Cadillac. "Don't step in the cuspidor."

For all of its spanking-new automobiles and a number of private planes—despite its scores of beautiful and expensive homes, and all other aspects of modernity, wealth and good taste—Ozona looks back with a tender nostalgia to its frontier past. This shows in many ways. The Junior Rodeo is a part of it, because riding horseback now is more of a social grace than an occupational skill. The town's small but well-stocked museum houses relics of Indian and cowboy days. B. B. Ingham, Jr., has preserved the outward appearance of a real "old-time" ranch house, on the Pecos—and inside the house, side by side with his big freezer and his television set, were the showcases of his own private museum. Old Fort Lancaster's ruins are only a few miles away, and B. B. Ingham is probably the leading authority on the history of that frontier post. He has collected and catalogued hundreds of Indian arrowheads; he has Library of Congress bulletins and University of Texas papers to authenticate his display of coins, bullets, harness buckles, and many other relics sifted from the alkali soil around the old fort and in the Pecos caves. He has published a number of articles on this collection, and then set out to learn for himself the secret of chipping flint for arrowheads. No archaeologist could tell B. B.'s products from the original.

When I went to high school with him, around 1916, the late Clay Adams used to spend much of his time sketching racy-looking automobiles that he could never have seen. They bore a resemblance to the famous Stutz Bearcat. Having finished a sketch, Clay would write the opening of a short story—or maybe it was a novel—in which the hero, always driving a powerful, sleek roadster, found himself on a lonely road just as a storm broke. He ran to the nearest house, found nobody home, and went in. As he groped in the darkness, something warm and sticky fell on his hand. It was blood. . . .

At this point Clay always pushed his composition book over to me, and I was supposed to finish the chapter, if not, indeed, the entire story.

He looked forward in those days. There is every evidence that he had many talents and could have been both writer and artist. He became a wealthy ranchman, instead, and then finally got around to the hobby of painting and wood carving. By now he was looking backward.

Emma Adams received me in the beautiful Spanish Mission style town house Clay had fortunately enjoyed for a number of years before his death. In his book-lined study there was the same evidence of a longing for the old days. Clay had painted "Four Old Timers"—three longhorns, with an ancient Eclipse windmill in the background. He had carved, among other things, an exquisitely faithful figure of a lean and bowlegged cowboy, squatting on his bootheels and rolling a Bull Durham cigarette—even the little sack of tobacco with its round tag was there, and the cowboy had the drawstring in his teeth.

The culture and taste in Ozona today does not suggest any *nouveau riche* at all. It might always have been there. Very probably this is due to the ingrained and inbred conservatism that has always ruled the county, in its politics and in its progress. It was the old "Be sure you are right, and then go ahead" philosophy. And there was much truth in the San Angelo *Standard-Times'* observation that "wealth does something to people, but more important, still, real people do something with wealth."

VI

"Went out on Rowdy Hoover's ranch, one time, way back," Ernest Dunlap said. "Seems like they had just been to town, and their boy—he was about four years old—had a sack of candy. He stuck the sack out at me and said, 'Have some candy!' I took a piece, and was eating it when he stuck the sack out again, and said, 'Have another piece of candy!' So I did. And then he stuck the sack out, and said, 'Just take damn near all of it!' I have always figured this was a good example of Ozona hospitality."

The just-take-damn-near-all-of-it brand of hospitality was about to get me down. I sang for my supper, yes—I spoke before the County Historical Society. I spoke before the Lions Club and the Rotary, and the next time I went in the El Sombrero restaurant for some good Mexican food, Sam Martinez didn't want to take my money. "I heard you at the Lions Club," he said.

There was a public barbecue in the park, and any number of private ones. It was impossible to visit all the ranches. One afternoon I went to the R. A. Harrell ranch for a barbecue, and then by driving about forty miles got to T. A. Kincaid's ranch in time for a Kincaid family reunion.

It was sundown when I arrived, and up on a hill behind the ranch house was a tremendously tall television tower, silhouetted against the sky. When I asked T.A. about this, he grinned.

"Couldn't get anything on TV, down here in the hills, without it," he said. "So I had it put up. Next time my pilot was bringing me to the ranch—we've got a landing strip down there in the mesquites—he said, 'Why, you son-of-a-bitch, that thing is right in the line of approach!' Now he has to go around it."

There are several reasons why T. A. Kincaid needs a private airplane and a pilot. He was recently president of the Texas Sheep & Goat Raisers Association. He won the Hoblitzelle Award for service to agriculture a few years ago. He has been on a number of national committees in the promotion of agriculture. Last year *Progressive Farmer* magazine selected him as a Man of the Year for providing "farsighted, extraordinary leadership in behalf of the livestock industry." "Kincaid moved," the magazine said, "that we adopt plan for action and development of Southwestern Screwworm Eradication Program."

In my boyhood T. A. Kincaid, Sr., used to run as many as 10,000 head of sheep on his ranch, and it was a natural thing that T.A., Jr., should grow up knowing the sheep business. The big ranch had to be divided—there were several exceptionally pretty Kincaid girls—but T.A., Jr., carried on. He went to Texas A. & M., and of course had a commission in the Army Reserve.

He was beyond the draft age, but he left the ranch and went off as a captain in the Army, and fought a few administrative battles before finally getting home to his sheep.

The barbecue at the Kincaid ranch was something, with at least fifty relatives and friends attending. No liquor was served, and T.A. asked a blessing. Later I finally got him aside to ask about the Screwworm Eradication Program.

The ranchers of Crockett County voluntarily contributed more than $50,000 to this program in 1962. In return, they received untold benefits. By the end of June there had been only two cases of screwworm infestation of livestock reported in the entire county.

What is happening here, something that T. A. Kincaid helped get moving, is an extremely remarkable thing. Science has turned the sex habits of the screwworm flies against them in such a way that they are apparently doomed to racial suicide.

This is not a Crockett County story, by any means, but Crockett is one of the counties most involved. A number of years ago an entomologist named Dr. Raymond C. Bushland and one named Edward F. Knipling hit on a fantastic idea. They observed that female screwworm flies mated only once, and died some three weeks afterward. They figured that if they could sterilize the male flies they could bring the species to eventual extinction.

It was years before they had a chance to experiment. Meanwhile, the screwworm fly was taking a terrible toll on the Texas ranges. It is so called because its larvae are shaped like a screw; it infests only fresh cuts—and it kills livestock.

West Texas ranchmen, eager for any help, guffawed about Bushland's idea and asked how he was going to catch flies and sterilize them. But Bushland was working on his own, to *produce* irradiated and sterilized male flies, then turn them loose to compete with native flies.

It turned out he was right. There is a plant in Mission, Texas, which now produces millions of flies every week. They are sterilized by radiation, and then air-dropped over a huge area—

part of it even includes northern Mexico. Some four billion flies a year are to be dropped over this area, and West Texas.

It seems a downright unfair thing, to trap and make any species extinct by taking advantage of its sex habits. But there is a lot of blood and beef being expended at Mission—6,000 gallons of blood and 100,000 pounds of beef, every week, to keep the plant going. And two dozen planes are flying seven days a week to drop the sterile flies.

With luck, the screwworm fly can be eradicated in a couple of years. Much will be owed to people like T. A. Kincaid, who sponsored the program. And many an old cowpuncher like myself, who had to doctor wormy steers, will give thanks.

VII

Ozona has grown up. She has made her fortune in cattle and sheep, and oil and gas will only put her in that higher income tax bracket for which other ranchmen will say "Damn!" Being ultraconservative, they will continue to cuss the federal government for handing out money; being human, they will continue to collect incentive money on lambs and wool, which netted them some $600,000 in 1962.

But, actually, Ozona already has just about everything the heart desires. Her citizens are pretty well-traveled now. It's not every small town that has been written up in the *Saturday Evening Post*, or had the fashion editor of the Dallas *Times-Herald* and an editor of the *Ladies' Home Journal* agree that Ozona women are the best-dressed in the world. (It turned out that the two came through Ozona on an Easter Sunday, when all the lilies were not arrayed like the Ozona girls—but then that's beside the point.)

And there is evidence of an increasing impact upon the outside world. World War II began it. Now a younger generation from Ozona has spread its wings.

There is no end to the Ozona story. As a matter of fact, the story may only be at its beginning, now, when I look back over the long years since 1907 when I saw the place for the first time as our wagon came down off the divide.

But the town has been fortunate in having wise counsel, and adopting Davy Crockett's motto. It has been nearly always right when it went ahead.

Essentially, nothing has changed. Tourists who stop long enough to photograph their kids beside the Davy Crockett monument or take a snapshot of the sign that says "The Biggest Little Town in the World"—these people should stick around a little longer. To them it probably seems that Ozona is dreaming under the sun.

She isn't dreaming at all. She is wide awake, and doing, and doing incredible things. And still taking the time to step out on the sidewalk and look for a cloud in the sky or wake in the night and give reverent thanks for the drowsy music of rain on the roof.

Bibliography

PRIMARY SOURCES:

Boyhood recollections.
Old family letters.
Interviews and tape-recorded talks with Ozona's "old-timers."

SECONDARY SOURCES:

Files of *The Ozona Kicker, The Ozona Optimist,* and the *Ozona Stockman.*

Anniversary Edition of *The San Angelo Standard Times.*

Records of the Clerk of Crockett County.

Sheep and Goat Raisers' Magazine.

American Guide Series, *Texas, a Guide to the Lone Star State.* N. Y., Hastings House, 1940.

DAY, Donald, *Big Country, Texas.* N. Y., Duell, Sloan & Pearce, 1947.

DENHAM, Claude, *History of Crockett County* (thesis).

GARD, Wayne, *The Chisholm Trail.* Norman, University of Oklahoma Press, 1954.

GIPSON, Fred, *Cowhand: the Story of a Working Cowboy.* N. Y., Harper, 1953.

HOLLON, W. Eugene, *The Southwest Old and New.* N. Y., Knopf, 1961.

HORGAN, Paul, *Great River: the Rio Grande in North American History*. N. Y., Rinehart & Co., Inc., 1954.

KUPPER, Winifred, *The Golden Hoof*. N. Y., Knopf, 1945.

NORDYKE, Lewis, *Great Roundup*. N. Y., Morrow, 1955.

PHARES, Ross, *Texas Tradition*. N. Y., Holt, 1954.

MADISON, Virginia, *The Big Bend Country*. Albuquerque, The University of New Mexico Press, 1955.

TOWNE, Charles Wayland, and WENTWORTH, Edward Norris, *Shepherd's Empire*. Norman, University of Oklahoma Press, 1945.

Texas Almanac, *Dallas. Dallas News,* 1961-1962.

STOKER, W. M., Thesis on Crockett County.

WEBB, Walter Prescott, *The Great Plains*. N. Y., Ginn & Co., 1931.